Retreating the Political

This collection of essays presents, for the first time in English, some of the key issues at the heart of Philippe Lacoue-Labarthe and Jean-Luc Nancy's work. Including several unpublished essays, *Retreating the Political* offers some highly original perspectives on the relationship between philosophy and the political.

The authors ask if we can talk of an *a priori* link between the philosophical and the political; they investigate the significance of the 'figure' – the human being as political subject – in the history of metaphysics; and they inquire how we can 're-treat' the political today in the face of those who argue that philosophy is at an end.

Retreating the Political brings together some of their responses to these investigations. We see as a result some of the key motifs that have characterised their work: their debt to a Heideggerian pre-understanding of philosophy, the centrality of the 'figure' in Western philosophy and the totalitarianism of both politics and the political. Through contemporary readings of the political in Freud, Heidegger and Marx they reveal how philosophy relies on the political for its reinvention and representation and how its has done so since Socrates' meditation on the *polis*.

Philippe Lacoue-Labarthe and **Jean-Luc Nancy** are both Professors of the Faculté de Philosophie, Université des Sciences Humaines de Strasbourg and Visiting Professors at the University of California, Berkeley. Their most recent books include *Musica Ficta*, *The Experience of Freedom* and *The Birth of Presence* and have all been translated into English. **Simon Sparks** is a Leverhulme Trust post-doctoral research student, also at Strasbourg.

Warwick Studies in European Philosophy

Edited by Andrew Benjamin
Professor in Philosophy, University of Warwick

This series presents the best and most original work being done within the European philosophical tradition. The books included in the series seek not merely to reflect what is taking place within European philosophy, rather they will contribute to the growth and development of that plural tradition. Work written in the English language as well as translations into English are to be included, engaging the tradition at all levels – whether by introductions that show the contemporary philosophical force of certain works, or in collections that explore an important thinker or topic, as well as in significant contributions that call for their own critical evaluation.

Retreating the Political

Philippe Lacoue-Labarthe and
Jean-Luc Nancy
Edited by Simon Sparks

London and New York

First published 1997
by Routledge
11 New Fetter Lane, London EC4P 4EE

Simultaneously published in the USA and Canada
by Routledge
29 West 35th Street, New York, NY 10001

© 1996 Philippe Lacoue-Labarthe and Jean-Luc Nancy, edited by Simon Sparks
English translation Routledge 1997
Originally published in French by Editions Galilée; 1981, 1983
and Flammarion; 1979

Typeset in Perpetua by J&L Composition Ltd, Filey, North Yorkshire

Printed and bound in Great Britain by Clays Ltd, St Ives plc

British Library Cataloging in Publication Data
A catalogue record for this book is available from the British Library

Library of Congress Cataloguing in Publication Data
A catalogue record for this book has been requested

ISBN 0–415–15162–7 (hbk)
ISBN 0–415–15163–5 (pbk)

1. retraiter *v. a.* Terme d'administration. Mettre à la retraite . . .

2. retraiter *v. a.* Traiter une seconde fois une matière. Matière retraitée par le même auteur. — H. XIIe s. «Fait li buens reis de France: se tut ert retraité E de çà e de là, n'i aureit amistié», *Th. le Mart.* 111. — E. Lat. *retractare*, de *re*, et *tractare* . . .

Littré.

Retrace, v. 1697. [- Fr. *retracer*; see RE-, TRACE v.] 1. *trans.* To trace back to an origin or source; to track through preceding stages. 2. To trace again with the eyes; to look over again with care or close attention 1726. b. To trace again in memory; to recall 1748. 3. To go back upon (one's steps, way, etc.) 1794.

Retreat, v. late ME. [In XV f. as prec., or − (O)Fr. *retraiter*, with accommodation to the sb.] 1. *intr.* To withdraw, retire, draw back. b. Of an army or a combatant: To retire before a superior force or after a defeat 1596. c. In *pa. pple.* with *is*, *was*, etc. 1648. d. To recede 1863. 2. *trans.* To draw or lead back; to remove, take away. Now chiefly in *Chess*, to move (a piece) back from a forward or threatened position. 1523. †b. to diminish, reduce.

Oxford English Dictionary

Contents

Contents

Editor's Preface

The manner of philosophical exposition is of paramount importance to both Lacoue-Labarthe and Nancy. Derrida has rightly spoken of the singular 'experience' of reading their work, and anyone who has already been fortunate enough to encounter their writing will attest to the *unheimlich* nature of their way of working. But if one cannot in truth, be at home with Lacoue-Labarthe and Nancy's work, then this is part of their overall strategy and constitutes a signature of sorts.

In editing these texts, and whilst also respecting the individual strategies of each translator, I have tried to maintain a fidelity both between the texts at hand and to Lacoue-Labarthe and Nancy's French (and to the enormous differences in the manner of their individual philosophical expositions). Many of the syntactical and rhetorical gestures which Lacoue-Labarthe and Nancy draw upon in their work are not strictly reproducible in English. As an English reader, even an English reader of French texts, one listens with different ears, and a signature, *de jure* and *de facto*, inhabits that strange *Abgrund* between translation and its impossibility. Thus, the necessary force which has dictated the lexical and syntactic choices made below often denotes simply the irreproducibility of what Derrida has identified as the 'rhythm' of their text, a rhythm 'which is not interrupted even when it multiplies caesuras, asides, parenthetical clauses, precautions, cautions, warnings, signs of circumspection, parentheses, quotation marks, italics – dashes above all – or all of these simultaneously'.[1] If this makes their texts difficult to read, and difficult to read in any language, then this is the sign of an attention to language itself, to the manner of philosophical thought, above all to *style*, and the mark of the precision which is their own.

Certain terms crop up time and time again in these texts. A word on their ambiguities:

1 *retrait*.[2] The centrality of the term *retrait* to this volume demands that some notification be given as to its problematic. (The reader is also referred to the entry from Littré which opens this book.) Although its double sense is well captured by the English *re(-)treat* − to withdraw, to treat again − the unfamiliar gerund form employed in the title of this book will, almost necessarily, give rise to certain misunderstandings. Lacoue-Labarthe and Nancy first inflect the term *retrait* in 1979 in 'La panique politique' where it is a matter of a retreat of (political) panic in order that an other politics can take place.[3] In 'The Jewish People do not Dream', a paper which forms a supplement to 'La panique politique', and apropos the 'retreat of identity', Lacoue-Labarthe and Nancy provide a working definition of this term (I have left the word *retrait* in the French):

> A *retrait* does not mean an absence, that is to say a presence simply removed. No prior identity can here be removed. To draw back [*se retirer*] is not to disappear, and *is* not, strictly speaking, any mode of being. Let us say, dispensing with all other analyses, that the *retrait* is the action of disappearing appearing. Not only to appear *in* disappearing, but to appear *as* disappearance, in disappearance itself. The more general question, as is well known, is here that of an inscription which traces itself only in drawing back [*retirant*] (into the unfigurable density of matter) the very incision which inscribes it.[4]

One might say that, for Lacoue-Labarthe and Nancy, the double sense of the re-treat would allow them to think how things stand today with respect to the political. What would delimit the present is the retreat or withdrawal of the political as that which is most obvious, as that which, in the face of actually existing totalitarianism(s) and the 'everything is political', goes without saying and is consequently never said. It is on the basis of this retreat that Lacoue-Labarthe and Nancy propose their re-treatment of the question of the political. And it is only in the face of such a retreat, in the *closure*, precisely, of the signification of the political, that it *can* be re-traced or re-treated by raising it in a new way. Moreover, one can, following

Heidegger, also make a philosophical claim for the political on the basis of the *retrait*: the political – which in its essence is nothing political – *is* only on the basis of its own retreat: 'the contours of the political trace themselves or retrace themselves only on the basis of the retreat, in and of the political, of its essence.'[5]

Retrait has here been translated as either 'withdrawal' or as 'retreat' depending on the context, and, except in one or two noted instances, these English terms have been reserved for this alone.

2 *la politique/le politique*. This distinction has been rendered throughout as 'politics/the political'. This has proved wholly unproblematic except for those rare instances where Lacoue-Labarthe and Nancy qualify the noun *le politique* with an adjective: for example, *le politique nazi*, *le politique moderne*, etc. Accepting a certain violence, this has been translated as 'the Nazi political', 'the modern political', etc. The capitalisation of 'Politics' or 'the Political' which occasionally arises (in, most notably, 'La panique politique') is carried over from Lacoue-Labarthe and Nancy's French.

3 *l'autre/autrui*. Following usual translations of Levinas these terms have throughout been translated as 'the other' and 'the Other' respectively. *L'autre* should generally be taken as signifying alterity in general, the logical category of irreducible other-ness which confronts the same (*le même*). *Autrui*, on the other hand, is to be understood as the personal other, the you, in whom the general alterity of *l'autre* becomes concretised. Where Lacoue-Labarthe and Nancy capitalise these terms then this has been carried over into the English and the French noted in brackets.

4 *achèvement/accomplissement*. Insofar as both these terms can be used in French to translate the Heideggerian concept of *Vollendung*, they have been rendered throughout as 'completion' and its cognates. The reader should bear in mind, however, that while both *achèvement* and *accomplissement* 'mean' completion, the French terms differentiate between the completion *as such*, and the *movement* of completing, respectively. On *Vollendung*, one recalls Heidegger's remarks in 'The End of Philosophy and the Task of Thinking':

The old meaning of the word 'end' [*Ende*] means the same as place: 'from one end to the other' means from one place to the other. The end of philosophy is the place, that place in which the whole of philosophy's history is gathered in its uttermost possibility. End as completion means this gathering.[6]

All references to published texts have been included in footnotes, even in those numerous places where they are absent from Lacoue-Labarthe and Nancy's text. Of course, this cannot be reprimanded and should surprise no one. As Nancy himself once wrote somewhere:

> Maybe some French have a certain lack of philological seriousness. But without trying to make excuses, one should also take into account a Nietzschean heritage of rebellion against a certain philology. Therefore, the omission was sometimes done deliberately from the outset. . . . You sometimes have to take books out of libraries, and sentences out of books; that is a way of giving them another chance or letting them run another risk.

Still one more chance and yet another risk denied, then. This notwithstanding, full bibliographical data has been supplied for all references in this book (the above citation has been exempted from this: I leave it, for Jean-Luc, *hors de contexte*). All translations from Lacoue-Labarthe and Nancy's works cited in the text or in the footnotes are the work of the respective translators. Translations from other cited works have often been modified, and this has usually been noted accordingly. The addition of all other material – translator's notes (TN), editorial comment (EN), etc. – is denoted by the use of square brackets. Where gothic brackets have been used ({. . .}), this is to indicate the author's own additional comments.

Acknowledgements

There are several people who must be thanked for their work on this book. Firstly the other translators, Richard Stamp (who also proofread, checked/ found references, and so forth), Céline Suprenant, and Leslie Hill (for a last-minute rendition of 'What is to be Done?'), both for providing immaculate texts, and for approving my editorial additions and changes to their faultless efforts. The responsibility for all errors, omissions, etc., lies squarely with the editor.

I would also like to thank Andrew Benjamin for commissioning the volume and supporting my efforts throughout, and Miguel de Beistegui and Leslie Hill for their continual linguistic and philosophical assistance. Emma Davis at Routledge deserves special credit for maintaining her cool in the face of unforeseen delays and my naïveté vis-à-vis the workings of publication. This volume could not have been achieved without the additional help of Ian Lyne, Ann-Marie Scanlon, Sean Scanlon and Colin Thomas.

Finally – but, as is always the case with these 'finally's, most importantly – I want to thank Philippe Lacoue-Labarthe and Jean-Luc Nancy for their advice, encouragement and assistance throughout this volume's preparation, and for returning to their earlier work in order to prepare the short texts which conclude it. I hope they like it.

Editor's introduction: *Politica ficta*[1]

Nous ne vivons plus dans l'origine. Nous existons dans le tardif, dans l'après-coup historique. Ce qui n'exclut pas que l'extrémité du tardif soit aussi la pointe du nouveau. C'est le même exactement cela qu'il nous est demandé de penser.
> Philippe Lacoue-Labarthe and Jean-Luc Nancy, *Le mythe nazi*

Philippe Lacoue-Labarthe and Jean-Luc Nancy's work has, over the last twenty years, taken the form of a careful and extensive study of the philosophical tradition, an often painstakingly detailed account of its texts, from Plato and Aristotle, through Descartes and Kant, to Nietzsche and Heidegger.[2] It is a work which, recognising philosophy's closure or delimitation, follows rigorously the Heideggerian project of the *Destruktion* of the history of metaphysics, repeating the gestures through which this history exhausts itself. And yet it would be wrong to think that this means we can, in some way, know what to expect; that, in some way, we will always know what will happen next. For, as Lacoue-Labarthe and Nancy recognise, it is precisely in this gesture of repetition, in the unending – and, essentially, endless – repetition of the philosophy's movement toward its own exhaustion, that the possibility of 'something else' emerges. As they more then anyone else have reminded us, mimesis always involves rupture and a differentiation from itself, repetition always invokes a disconcerting reinvention or mobility. Should one be surprised, then, at the debt – more or less acknowledged, more or less thematised – to Heidegger? Need one recall what Heidegger says regarding that essential thinking which follows the way back (*Rückgang*) into the ground of metaphysics, viz., that it takes place as the experience of something other than metaphysics? Indeed, is this not what is meant by *Wiederholung* (repetition) in the following lines from *Being and Time*:

> *Repetition is handing down explicitly* [*Die Wiederholung ist die ausdrückliche Überlieferung*]. . . . The repeating of that which is possible does not bring back again [*wiederbringen*] something that is 'past', nor does it bind the 'present' back to that which has already been outstripped. . . . Repetition [*Wiederholung*] does not abandon itself to that which is past, nor does it aim at progress. In the instant, authentic existence is indifferent to both these alternatives.[3]

What better illustration of what is meant here by repetition do we have than Heidegger's own de-structive relation to the history of philosophy? What better illustration than what is outlined in §6 of *Being and Time* as the essentially destructive task for philosophy, and that is to say the repetition of the 'positive possibilities' of its history? The repetition of the gestures through which philosophy reaches the point of its own exhaustion is the gesture, itself preeminently philosophical, by which philosophy can be made to release its unthought. Which, in effect, amounts to saying the following: repetition itself as the very possibility of philosophy. In this way, the repetition of philosophy's exhaustive movement at its end comes to be seen both as the proper of philosophy and as the installation of the displacement of this propriety.

For Lacoue-Labarthe and Nancy as for Heidegger, it is this repetition of 'that which is [and, perhaps, which has been] possible' which will generate the possibility of something different happening. This would be, then, the exigency for thinking at the end of philosophy – an end which in no way signals the renunciation of thought but, instead, the need to think that end, its tensions, its demand, its very history. Accordingly, as both Lacoue-Labarthe and Nancy are well aware, the repetition implied in the gesture of *Destruktion* will necessitate its own repetition – hence their particular attention to a certain Nietzsche and to Heidegger's own *destruktiv* gesture. This necessity is surely what Lacoue-Labarthe is referring to when, in the remarkable opening pages of *La fiction du politique*, he writes:

> Philosophy is *finie* – finished, finite; its limit is uncrossable. Which means: we can no longer – and we can only – do philosophy, possessing no other language and having not the slightest notion of what it might mean to 'think' outside of 'philosophising'.[4]

Lacoue-Labarthe and Nancy's thinking is, then, a thinking of philosophy's exhaustion, and that is also to say of a thinking of the essential finitude of philosophy. (As should become apparent, the genitive which links finitude to philosophy is necessarily double.) As such, Lacoue-Labarthe and Nancy's is a thinking, a *philosophising*, which maintains itself in the tension between the 'no longer' and the 'only' of philosophising to which Lacoue-Labarthe refers in these lines. Moreover, it is this tension, generated, as one sees, by a recognition of the finitude of philosophy, which will sustain the labour of repetition. Put differently: this limit of philosophy is also its condition of possibility. If, within the horizon of philosophy's closure or completion, we can 'no longer' and 'only' do philosophy, then we are forced, as Lacoue-Labarthe avers, to 'open ourselves to . . . that exhaustion of philosophy today'.[5] And this opening, itself exhausted or a figure of this exhaustion, would be the most basic formulation of what, for Lacoue-Labarthe and Nancy, it means to do philosophy.

Politics (and) philosophy

A vast and complex trajectory, then. An equivocal and troubling repetition, as Derrida has noted.[6] But why do the texts translated here demand that one retrace — however schematically — the trajectory of this repetition? Answer: because these texts cannot be said to form a 'political' supplement or appendage to the careful and extensive philosophical work that Lacoue-Labarthe and Nancy have not ceased to pursue. The political, and that is also to say its philosophical examination, is not extrinsic to philosophy. The political is, essentially, philosophical. And yet it cannot be said simply to be inside philosophy. The political is not the philosophical, nor a moment within it. The one is not another name for or another manifestation of the other, even if the political will remain unthinkable except in terms of philosophy as onto-theology, except, that is, in terms of the contemporary *après coup* of the inaugural (but nonetheless abyssal) Platonic moment:

> . . . in the mimetic or memorial *après coup* of the Greek 'sending' which defines the modern age, the effectuation or installation of the philosophical *as* the political, the generalisation (the globalisation) of the philosophical *as* the political.[7]

It would be fruitless to identify the philosophical and the political. And to mark an *a priori* commonality (of origin, of project, of *form*), and that means to mark their co-belonging or 'reciprocal involvement',[8] is not the same thing as to identify them. Indeed, what one could perhaps say is that, for Lacoue-Labarthe and Nancy, the political marks the place where the distinction between philosophy and non-philosophy, between philosophy and its unthought, becomes blurred. This place, the place of the political, would always have the character of a limit. But this limit, as should by now be apparent, is not simply restrictive: it marks both an inside and an outside. Lacoue-Labarthe and Nancy ceaselessly remind us of this fact. In marking out the limit of philosophy it therefore traces an identity. The political is both at the limit of philosophy and forms its limit. If this is indeed the case, moreover, then its correlate – that the philosophical describes the limit and identity of the political – will also hold true. This is precisely what Lacoue-Labarthe and Nancy will identify below as the 'essential (and not accidental or simply historical) co-belonging of the philosophical and the political.'[9] Indeed, as far as they are concerned, the political is always understood as resolutely philosophical. And that is *also* to say that the philosophical will itself always be political. If these texts are, essentially, 'political', then this is first of all only insofar as they are philosophical. Thus the tension between the 'no longer' and the 'only' of philosophising would also be apparent in the matter of the political. Let us say, then: 'We' are no longer and can only be political. We have lost any sense of what being political might mean, and yet we are constrained (by the 'age', by an imperative, an *il faut*, they will say, by history) to be political, whatever that might mean. Which amounts to saying that, for Lacoue-Labarthe and Nancy, the political itself is *finie* – both finite or subject to a certain finitude but also, and more crucially, *finished. The closure or completion of the political*, then: this is, albeit brutally phrased, the thesis advanced in the texts of *Retreating the Political*. The goal of these introductory remarks will simply be, then, a less brutal phrasing of, and more nuanced approach to their thesis.

But where do these texts come from? How can one begin to characterise their point of departure: personal? political? philosophical? And, specifically, how to characterise the point of departure for the term under which they are collected – the 'retreat of the political' – behind whose ambiguity stands the semantic field of *le retrait du politique*, and from whose various significations they take their determining preoccupation?

Of course, one will always be able to answer these questions in terms of the simply anecdotal or merely personal. And one would not be wrong to do so.

More important, however, is the attempt to explain the place from which these texts originate in a manner which is attentive to the specifically philosophical locus which is their own. However, both the anecdotal and the philosophical, albeit in sharply differing ways, open onto the space peculiar to these texts, onto what must properly be called the political. This space is not simply one political space amongst many others. It is not, even if this will always be indissociable and, to an extent, *necessary*, the space of a political position held – jointly or individually – in accordance with a political ideal or even in adherence to a particular programme or ideology.[10] It is, broadly speaking, the place of the political *as such*. Thus, if it is a matter of the political circumstances of the composition of these texts and of the clearly defined political and philosophical determination from which they take their mark, it will also and always be a matter of the circumstance of the political itself.

On 23 July 1980, Lacoue-Labarthe and Nancy delivered the opening address of a colloquium devoted to the work of Jacques Derrida.[11] Not a simple *Festschrift*, the colloquium sought to 'take off' or 'depart' from (*à partir de*) Derrida's work. Initially at least, the colloquium took its name and impetus from Derrida's essay 'Les fins de l'homme', the ends of man. Although published in 1972 in the collection *Marges – de la philosophie*, Derrida had delivered this text some years earlier, in October 1968, at a conference on 'Philosophy and Anthropology' in New York. And, as he himself notes in the body of the text, its composition dates from even earlier, from April of that same year. This is dated 'very precisely'.[12] And still more precise is the date he gives to the actual completion of the manuscript, to its final typing and polishing, and to the writing of its prefatory remarks: at the close of the text, one finds the date '12 May 1968'.

Given the singularly and properly political concerns of the essay (and, in particular, its opening remarks) – the question of the subject, of the human (of the *anthrōpos logikos*), of the institution of philosophy, of philosophical nationality, of the essential and not simply accidental relation between 'the possibility of an international philosophical colloquium' and 'the form of democracy' – should one have to point out that this was, in all respects, a timely meditation? May 1968 was, as everyone knows, the time when 'the universities of Paris were invaded by the forces of the social order, then reoccupied by the students in the upheaval'.[13] Let us call it a political text, then. And one which, in its opening lines, would announce the entire problematic for *Retracing the Political*:

Every philosophical colloquium necessarily has a political meaning. And not only due to *that which has always linked the essence of the philosophical to the essence of the political*.[14]

Let us leave to one side the matter of this 'not only' in these lines from Derrida: let us leave aside, that is, the political – and undoubtedly politicised, in the most banal sense of the term – essence of colloquia in general. And let us leave to one side, also, the political significance or meaning (*signification*) of every philosophical colloquium, including, undoubtedly, the colloquium with which we are concerned here. Leaving these matters aside, then, the question that remains: what of this *a priori*, and that is also to say essential link between the philosophical and the political? What is it that from the very beginning – but from the very beginning of what, precisely: of philosophy? politics? – has bound the essence of the political to the essence of the philosophical? What needs to be said regarding this originary co-belonging of the philosophical and the political?

These questions form the matrix of the project with which Lacoue-Labarthe and Nancy are concerned in *Retreating the Political*. And it is precisely in relation to Derrida's text that they first come to be raised. As they write in their initial description of the proposed discourse *à partir de* Derrida:

> The colloquium *The Ends of Man* cannot be described as simply 'philosophical'. It should be devoted to the possibility of traversing and displacing, in every sense, the philosophical, literary, critical, poetic, signifying, symbolic, etc. regimes; and, consequently, of traversing and displacing the 'political' and its 'meaning' as well. The stake of the colloquium would be, in every respect, to breach the inscription of a *wholly other* politics.[15]

It is a question, then, of a general displacement of meaning. In terms of what has already been said, moreover, this displacement can already be understood in terms of the *destruktiv* repetition which confronts thinking at the closure of philosophy. However, one immediately sees that, amongst the various displacements which Lacoue-Labarthe and Nancy propose to effect, the displacement of the political stands out. Alone amongst the philosophical, the literary, the critical, etc., it is the only term placed within the security of quotation marks. Which would indicate what, precisely? An uncertainty on Lacoue-Labarthe and Nancy's part? An obedience to the Heidegger of 1927 for whom 'politics' is what fundamental ontology is not?[16] Probably not. Almost certainly not. That 'consequently' must not be seen as the mark of a derivation, but as the indication of a specific privilege. But why this privilege of the political? And, since these things would seem to be related here, what of this wholly other politics? Wholly other to what? To politics, perhaps? But, then: What would such a politics look like? Would it be recognisable as a politics? Indeed, could a wholly other politics be said to *be* a politics? Could a wholly other politics have a political – and that is to say, within 'the political institution of so-called Western thought',[17] a particularly *praxical* – application? This seems unlikely. Or, to put this more exactly: any such move from the political to politics or to a politics of the political will always remain unthinkable within the historical lexicon of politics and political action. Why? Because it is precisely this lexicon and its topology that the breaching of the problematic of the political places in question. Indeed, a wholly other politics might be nothing other than precisely this putting into question.

This becomes clearer when one considers the following question: if, as we have seen, the gesture of Lacoue-Labarthe and Nancy's work involves a recognition and a working through of the exhaustion of philosophy, then is it not also necessary to take account of the exhaustion of the inherited relation between theory and practice? Of metaphysics as the speculative thematisation of some *principium* for action? Which is not to say that in this recognition, the Greek unity or procession – teleology, even – between *thēoria* and *praxis*, a unity which 'defines' politics as political action, comes to be displaced. On the contrary. But if, for Heidegger, the gesture of this recognition will have consisted in an understanding of *thēoria* such that the question of *praxis* is always already answered,[18] a gesture which, of necessity, will have lead him to an anarchic reformulation of action's ground (God, substance, *cogito*, knowledge) away from the, respectively, theological, ousiological, transcendental, metaphysical formulation of its question; if this, in all essentials, is Heidegger's response, then for Lacoue-Labarthe and Nancy, quite another – political (and this means philosophical) – sort of gesture will be involved.[19]

Figure

If it is here that Lacoue-Labarthe and Nancy's indebtedness to a certain (Heideggerian) pre-understanding of the matter at hand becomes manifest, then it is also here that the originality of their formulations is most striking. For if they follow Heidegger in understanding the unity of the onto-theological epoch in terms of a derivation of practice from first philosophy, they inflect this understanding in quite another direction. Their originality lies in an attempt to formulate this unity of onto-theology in terms of the concept – if indeed it is one – of the figure. Or, to put this in another way, a formulation of onto-theology as the will-to-figure. As regards the political as the matter at hand, their originality lies, then, in an attempt to isolate the poetic or figural (figurative, even) essence of politics, of political praxis, or, what amounts to the same thing, of 'the political institution of so-called Western thought'. Which is to say what, precisely? What is to be said about this fundamentally figurative nature of politics – and that is also to say of the political? In order to return better equipped to this question, I want to examine the general question of the figure as it is articulated by Lacoue-Labarthe and Nancy.

It seems to me that the emphasis upon the figure and the figural impulse of onto-theology can be said to be what sustains the entirety of Lacoue-Labarthe and Nancy's work. Their engagement with and repetition of the history of philosophy and its exhaustion will always have taken place in terms of a generalised and implicit consideration of the figure. *Cogito, figuratur*, as Descartes might have written in the *Meditationes* – and as Nancy does perhaps write in *Ego sum*.[20] But what is it that Lacoue-Labarthe and Nancy call *la figure*? How are we to understand it? What gives itself to be thought by the figure? Rather than piloting a course through the whole of Lacoue-Labarthe and Nancy's work, I will, with a certain schematic economy, draw here on a single article, an 'exchange of letters' between the authors of this book entitled 'Scène'.[21] The focus of this epistolary exchange is the word *opsis* in Aristotle's *Poetics*. As is well known, *opsis* ('η 'οψισ: appearance/appearing, apparition, spectacle – *scène*, precisely) is one of the six components which, for Aristotle, 'gives tragedy its qualities'.[22] By taking different sides (respectively that of *opsis* and that of the 'reader' who alone can take in the entirety of the tragic effect), Nancy and Lacoue-Labarthe tease out the philosophical force of the terms generated from within the tragic *opsis*: mimesis, *poiesis*, *technē* – a whole theatrics of thinking, in other words, which falls within the essential lexicon of the figure. I cite this passage (from Nancy's opening letter to Lacoue-Labarthe) in its entirety:

The question of the *opsis* or of the 'scene' seems to me to communicate in a very precise and decisive way with a more general question of the 'figure' which has preoccupied us both. In your work this preoccupation comes from a suspicion concerning what you have called 'onto-typology', and that is to say concerning a figural and fictional assignation of the presentation of being and/or truth. Essentially, it is in the extension of this problematic that I have spoken of the 'interruption of myth' as an element or as a decisive event for a thinking of being-in-common today. Now, it seems to me that our divergence on the matter of the *opsis* is played out around this: you tend always, to speak very quickly, toward an effacement of the 'figure' (you speak freely of 'de-figuration', and again in 'Il faut',[23] where you also invoke a 'breakdown' [*défaillance*] of the figure as a sort of beyond-figure), whereas I feel myself continually led back to the exigency of a certain figuration, because the 'interruption' of myth does not appear to me to be a simple cessation, but a cutting movement which, in thus cutting, traces another place of articulation.[24]

Putting to one side the specificity of this divergence (the figure, on the one hand, as a locus of representation and the work of identity and, on the other, as the opening onto an ipseity), the question that still needs to be addressed is this: Why do Lacoue-Labarthe and Nancy accord such a centrality to the figure? Answer: Because, for them, metaphysics, in the process of completing itself, is historically and *essentially* committed to the mobilising figures in order to represent itself. Responding to the constraint of an originary programmation – *in fine*, the Platonic determination of being as *eidos/idea*, and therefore of being as the fundamental *tupos* of a transcendental production – the epoch of onto-theology, what Lacoue-Labarthe and Nancy call the epoch of philosophy 'actualising' itself as the political (and vice versa), is nothing other than the epoch of the bestowal of (the) meaning (of being, of existing) through figures. And this means, most decisively, through the figure of man, the figure of a human *tupos* determined as the *subjectum* or as the Subject of meaning. Or again: the human Subject itself as the absolute figure or exemplar of meaning. It is in this sense that, following Derrida's analyses in 'The Ends of Man', they will speak below of 'the almost undivided domination of anthropology' as bearing today witness to 'the qualification of the political by the subject (and of the subject by the political)'. Once again, as they write in their Opening Address: 'what completes itself (and does not cease to complete itself) . . . is the discourse of the re-appropriation of man in his humanity, the discourse of the actualisation of the genre of the human.'[25] It is this actualisation, and hence exhaustion, of the human as the absolute figure of meaning that Lacoue-Labarthe and Nancy identify as the figural completion of metaphysics.

xxii

Distinguishing themselves from Heidegger, Lacoue-Labarthe and Nancy will insist upon the figure not as the metaphysical echo of a more originary experience of being, but (and this, in its refusal of Plato's depreciation of mimesis, is, for Lacoue-Labarthe, the departure from the scene of Heidegger's 'unacknowledged mimetology'[26]) as the mark of an originary figuration at the heart of being itself: being itself as an original *mimeme*; as the mark of an originary fiction at the heart of metaphysics. But what remains to be said regarding the notion of the figure if, as seems likely, we can say, alongside Nancy but also misquoting him, that the epoch of figuration is as old as the West?[27] Answering this question demands a certain amount of care insofar as it cannot be a matter of mapping the figure of the figure onto that of philosophy. But answering this question will also have to take account of a historically necessary inscription of the figure at the heart of philosophy. For it is certainly true, moreover, that matters can never be so simple and, as Lacoue-Labarthe and Nancy's divergence over the figure attests, the weapon here is double-edged, and the figure, like the repressed, always makes its return.

In this rapid presentation of Lacoue-Labarthe and Nancy's development of the figure as itself the central figure of metaphysics, and in trying to point to a radical difference from Heidegger's equally forceful delimitation, I have tried to suggest a way in which one can begin to understand what it means for Lacoue-Labarthe and Nancy to 'take stock of the political presupposition of philosophy' which is itself 'the very position of the political, from the Greek *polis* to what is deployed in the modern age as the qualification of the political by the subject'.[28] Indeed, one sees that this presupposition can be nothing other than the presupposition of the figure, and this all the more so once the political presupposition of the figure itself become clear. What would the 'political determination of essence' be if not the figural (i.e. fictioning) essence of the philosophical? With this formulation in mind, I would like now to turn directly, once again, to the matter of the political where, our suspicions aroused, the presence of the figure becomes much clearer.

Lacoue-Labarthe and Nancy's emphasis upon the figurative essence of politics and of the political is fundamental to each moment of *Retreating the Political* (and beyond). This essence will take many names: identification, poetry, mimesis, *poiesis*, mimetology, *oeuvre*, immanentism, fiction, myth, sacrifice, *scène*. One might say that this series is, for Lacoue-Labarthe and Nancy, the very lexicon of the political itself. And it is not by chance that it can also be seen, for them, as the lexicon of onto-theology itself, now rethought as onto-typo-logy or, what

amounts to the same thing, onto-politi-ology. What remains constant throughout this mutation of terms (which, in truth, is nothing of the sort) is the
following: an understanding of the political as the will — and that is also to say
the *imperative* — to realise an essence-in-common (a community, even) on the
basis of a figure of that in-common. It is this realisation that *identifies* a
community as and with itself, in which case the figure would be seen as the
identity principle of community. And this whether it be a matter of a 'we', 'the
people', 'spiritual or religious type', 'the nation', 'humanity', 'project',
'destiny', etc. Indeed, for Lacoue-Labarthe and Nancy, it is precisely this
imperative force of the figure — an imperative which is never received as
such (no injunction will ever be pronounced: for example, of the type 'always
use figures'), and which is more of the order of a historical *de jure* and *de facto*
necessity — for the political which, from the very beginning, delimits its *a priori*
relationship to the philosophical. One sees this very clearly in the Socratic
meditation on the *polis*, for example, where good, i.e. specifically philosophical
governance, is described in terms of an essential *poiesis*, a 'natural' or demiurgic
mimesis — what Kant will call *eine bildende Kraft*, a 'forming force' — of the idea
of the just in order to forge the *polis* as a unity. And again in Heidegger where
the force of Hölderlin's *Dichtung* — and of the poetic saying *as such* — will reside
in the fact that 'he is — or ought to be — the "poet of the Germans"' and hence
the only one capable of fashioning Germany anew in the face of '*die deutsche
Not*, which has a single content: the fact that Germany does not exist'.[29] (This
fashioning is, in passing, what Heidegger will, in 1935, call '"politics" in the
highest and most proper sense (*im eigentlichen Sinne*)'.[30])

Figuration, then, as the onto-theo-(typo)logical essence of the political. And
it is in this sense that one needs to understand statements such as the following
from Lacoue-Labarthe:

> Why would the problem of identification not be, in general, the very
> problem of the political?[31]

Or this from Nancy:

> Mythic thought, in effect — operating in a certain way through the dialectic
> sublation of the two meanings of myth — is nothing other than the *thought of
> a founding fiction, or of a foundation by fiction*.[32]

Or again from Nancy:

This question forms today the contour, if not the aporia, of the actual paradox of the meaning of the political/political meaning: is there still meaning without figuration or configuration?[33]

As Lacoue-Labarthe and Nancy will suggest in *Retreating the Political*, it is precisely a figurative impulse which effaces transcendence and generates the essentially totalitarian impulse of the, specifically Western, political – as Nancy writes elsewhere: 'does meaning not become "totalitarian" truth as soon as it takes figure [*prend figure*]?'[34] Such statements, if they are true, and that is to say if the political is, essentially, a matter of the figure and of the figuration of an essence, would lead us to insist upon the following questions: Is there something which would allow the political to be thought outside of the will-to-figure? Can the political be thought in a way which does not stem from the will to realise its essence as figure? Can the political be thought, finally, in a way which would disrupt what Lacoue-Labarthe and Nancy have called 'the destiny of metaphysical politics'?[35]

To rethink the political beyond the identity principle of the figure; to rethink the political as the non-figure of the 'Narcissus' which does not panic and shares (perforce the French *partage*) its lack of identity: such would be, then, Lacoue-Labarthe and Nancy's aim in *Retreating the Political*.

The retreat of the political

I have stressed the centrality of the figure in Lacoue-Labarthe and Nancy's work, and particularly that part of their work presented here, in order to suggest a means of understanding the relation between what they delimit as 'the closure of the political' and what they call 'the retreat of the political'. Neither of these formulations is straightforward. For just as the concept of closure or end can be understood all too readily in terms of the time of a teleological termination, so the retreat lends itself to be thought as a simple withdrawal or a pure receding. As one might suspect, however, things are rather more complicated here. Thus, on the one hand, and as Nancy writes in *Le sens du monde*:

> The adversaries of the thought of the 'end' are wrong insofar as they do not see that the words by which one designates that which arrives at its end (history, philosophy, politics, art, world) are not the names of subsistent realities in themselves, but the names of concepts or ideas entirely deter-

mined in a regime of *meaning* which finishes itself off and which completes itself before our very eyes. . . . If there is an illusion which it is necessary to guard against today more than ever, it is the illusion which consists in hanging onto these words (history, philosophy, art) as if they were immediately things. . . . Which does not mean that 'end' is only the end of a certain 'conception' of something. It means that there is no longer any assignable meaning there.[36]

The end is not the end. Nor is it the end of an epochal conception. In this time of end or exhaustion (and a certain Heideggerian eschatology is *almost* inevitable here), what is involved is a drawing back of any specificity which could be ascribed to the political. In terms of that thinking of finitude remarked earlier, one might say that what is involved in the withdrawal of meaning is the recognition of the essential finitude of the political. Whether this withdrawal takes place as the actualisation of the political 'in the sense of the "well-known" and in the sense of the obviousness (the blinding obviousness) of politics',[37] or in terms of the metaphysical completion of the political 'to the point of excluding every other area of reference',[38] Lacoue-Labarthe and Nancy's writing allows this to be formulated in terms of the totalitarian figure of the political: namely (a) the totalitarian *form* of the political; and (b) the political *itself*, in its completed and completing figure, *as* totalitarian in its domination. Indeed, is this anything other than what has already been located as the 'destiny of metaphysical politics' – and that means the absolute figure (here the correlate of the philosophical subject of modernity) of the political in its closure? In the epoch of the end, the political completes itself in the figure of totalitarianism. And this 'end', as Nancy avers, means that the political no longer has any assignable determination: *in fine*, it no longer 'means'.

But where, on the other hand, does all of this leave us? Must we make the political mean something? Do we need to smuggle the figure back in by the back door, this time as the figure of the political or perhaps even of the *polis*? Do we need now to re-ground the political by allowing it, precisely, to 'take figure'? to offer a 'new' institution (a new figure) of and to politics or the political?[39] to 'replay' the political anew by wresting it from its 'inappropriable limit',[40] by allowing it, for the first time as it were, to 'take place'? to re-appropriate for ourselves the decisive means of identification?[41] to 'wrest myths from the hands of the fascists' in whatever form of totalitarianism we find them?[42] Each of these gestures could only be a possible response to what

Lacoue-Labarthe and Nancy identify as the retreat of the political on condition that 'one could, quite simply, take the political out of its retreat', that 'the retreat of the political is only a simple pulling back'.[43] Assuredly, and as we have seen, this is not the case. In each of these gestures, then, the retreat would make its return. And, clearly enough, it is for precisely this reason that Lacoue-Labarthe and Nancy will resist all such challenges. But, as I mentioned, the weapon is double-edged, and such resistance is not easy. Lacoue-Labarthe and Nancy skirt dangerously close to these temptations. They are not immune to figures, and 'it is not certain', they write, 'that one can ever avoid a grounding gesture.'[44] Indeed, such a gesture is only avoided – but, in truth, it can never be totally avoided – by proposing another response: a response which goes hand in hand with this initial meaning of the retreat, accompanying it in the moment of its effectuation in order the better to retrace its paths anew. And it is here, as interruption, as de-figuration, that the second and most important sense of the retreat – the retreat now as the re-*tracing* – of the political emerges.

As we have see, the retreat of the political and its closure is a matter of the effacement of any assignable and specific meaning. In the light of these for-mulations, one recalls Lacoue-Labarthe and Nancy's remarks from the address to *Les fins de l'homme* cited earlier: that what is at stake is the 'traversing and displacing of the "political" and its "meaning"'. And it is precisely this traversal and displacement that, following Derrida, they call the retreat (here in its second sense): a movement which, accompanying and operating on the basis of the first sense of the retreat as the withdrawal of meaning, 'would thus retrace the contours of this specificity, whose actual conditions would need to be reinvented.'[45] One should, I think, take note of this formulation of the retreat as *re*invention. For Lacoue-Labarthe and Nancy it cannot be a matter of invention as such. Invention would, in the terms already advanced, presuppose a grounding gesture, the invention, precisely, of a new figure from out of the latent figure of invention; and that means that, insofar as it would presuppose an originarity in itself, invention would always be the invention of a figure itself oblivious to the founding figurality of any such response. And so the *re*inven-tion, then, of a non-figure (the re-treat): a term which we would have to add to Lacoue-Labarthe's 'de-figuration' and Nancy's 'interruption'.[46] And it is this gesture of reinvention, and the retracing to which it would give rise, which would correspond to Lacoue-Labarthe and Nancy's counter-gesture to those listed above, the counter-gesture by which, however 'slightly', they 'free [themselves] from the blinding obviousness of the political'.[47] The question that then holds would be the following: does the confluence of these terms amount to anything other than what was identified at the outset as the central problematic of repetition?

Perhaps, in this sense, the retreat of the political means nothing other than the retreat of every projection or instance of a figure of community. For sure, Lacoue-Labarthe and Nancy do not, as such, propose a possible form that might correspond to a politics of the retreat. This, perhaps, goes without saying. But they do, willingly, engage with the political as a question – and that means with the injunction to protect it *as* a question, to protect its receptivity 'to what is at stake in community'.[48] It would be, then, a matter of a resistance and of a holding open, of a work 'which is neither that of a disengagement, nor that of a military action', a work 'consonant with the retreat'.[49] A matter of what not so long ago would have been called an 'engagement' – which is something quite different from a pledge given to one politics or another[50] or, indeed, one might add, to one *figure* of politics or another. A matter of recognising that, today, to be political is to already run the risk of a certain complicity with the totalitarian logic at the heart of the political, but recognising that, today, nothing less than our being political is called for. It would be, finally and very simply, 'à donner forme à une question'.[51]

1

La panique politique[1]
Philippe Lacoue-Labarthe and Jean-Luc Nancy

Anyone who describes a panic as one of the plainest functions of the 'group mind' arrives at the paradoxical position that this group mind does away with itself in one of its most striking manifestations.

Freud, *Group Psychology and the Analysis of the Ego*[2]

If he lives among others of his own species, man is *an animal who needs a master* . . . But this master will also be an animal who needs a master.

Kant, 'Idea for a Universal History with a Cosmopolitan Purpose'[3]

1 The notes which follow are indeed, discounting the usual formalities, *notes*. They were taken down in a summary and discontinuous fashion during a teaching project in progress over the last three years, a project which it is out of the question to expound in an article. At the same time, they constitute the first point of reference for a future exploration. If we are provisionally risking them here in this somewhat off-putting form, it is for a political reason: it is today necessary, indeed urgent, to demand a rigorous problematisation of the 'relation' between psychoanalysis and politics. The minimum of rigour henceforth consists in the refusal of a double impasse: that over which psycho-analytic instrumentations stumble when put more or less deliberately at the service of a received political thought (which may range from one communism or another to social democracy), for in this way one merely succeeds in reinforcing the initial problems which had to be explored; and the impasse of the proclamations (oscillating from the anarchist left to the libertarian right) according to which, once the libidinal trap of the political is unveiled, one ought to abandon it to the declining history of its Western delirium, and

1

substitute for it an aesthetic or a moral doctrine. (We will not here go back over the political interests – and on the political interests of psychoanalysis – brought into play in each case.)

In other words, we are refusing the attitudes of theoretical (and practical) panic where, through a narcissistic discourse, everyone protects himself or herself from the feeling of the dissolution of the ties which guaranteed the cohesion of the Western mass.

This double refusal is not naïve. It does not come from an angelical desire to surmount the confrontations and deadlocks of politics. If confrontation is necessary, we know where to put ourselves; and, since it seems unavoidable today to be as specific as possible, let us say: on the left, as for example, Freud himself. But if it is a question of analysing, we also know where we ought not to put ourselves: namely, in submission to the political, to psychoanalysis, or to both. From now on, a demand 'from the left' and a demand for rigour move together through the deconstitution of this double submission. And here again, here especially, we have something to learn from Freud, no doubt one of the least submitted thinkers, including to his own doctrine.

2   We are constrained to exclude from these notes the examination of most references other than Freudian ones. This does not mean that we are proposing another and purer 'return to Freud'. It is a question, rather, of something of Freud which henceforth makes its return because it has not yet really taken place, neither with him nor after him. Nor does this mean that we should have come or come back to Freud without the help or without the examination of what allows one today to *read* him. In this respect moreover we may recall, despite the lapse of time, what our reading of Lacan, *The Title of the Letter*, recorded as regards the debt and everything else. But with respect to the solicitations of the political problematic in or from psychoanalysis (Girard, Deleuze, Lyotard, Goux, Legendre, Castoriadis, Kaufmann), we cannot in these notes initiate the numerous discussions which would be necessary.

3   And in any case, we are choosing a quite different perspective as a point of departure. It is less a question of asking oneself what Freud says or does not say, or allows one to say about the political, than of wondering what the question of the political does in and to psychoanalysis. That is to say, first of all, it is a question of wondering about the place and the function of the analysis of culture (*Kultur*, civilisation, culture, the institution and the operation of

humanity as such). One has already been able to pick out, here and there,[4] the determining role of the motifs provided by the analysis of culture for psycho-analysis itself (if one understands by this the analysis of the individual *psyche*). But there is more. The analysis of culture might constitute, from the very inside of psychoanalysis, a displacement of such importance that it would seem to imply an *overflowing* of psychoanalysis.

Freud himself was unable to get the measure of this displacement, and we are still only able to pick out the basic facts of the problem. These at least are clearly found in Freud, and, for example, in the 1935 postface to *An Auto-biographical Study*. In this text Freud designates the group of works written from 1920 to 1923 as his *last* important works in psychoanalysis proper (let us recall that in this group, concerning which Freud previously said that, in them, he was giving free rein to speculation, *Beyond the Pleasure Principle* and *The Ego and the Id* frame *Group Psychology and the Analysis of the Ego*: the two great texts which determine late psychoanalysis frame the text marking a transition in the analysis of culture). After which Freud declares that he has not written any-thing of importance for psychoanalysis. And he continues:

> This circumstance is connected with an alteration in myself, with what might be described as a phase of regressive development. My interest, after making a lifelong *detour* through the natural sciences, medicine and psy-chotherapy, returned to the cultural problems which had fascinated me long before, when I was a youth scarcely old enough for thinking. At the very climax of my psycho-analytic work, in 1912, I had already attempted in *Totem and Taboo* to make use of the newly discovered findings of analysis in order to investigate the origins of religion and morality. I now carried this work a stage further in two later essays, *The Future of an Illusion* and *Civilisation and its Discontents*. I perceived ever more clearly that the events of human history, the interactions between human nature, cultural devel-opment and the precipitates of primeval experiences (the most prominent example of which is religion) are no more than a reflection of the dynamic conflicts between the ego, the id and the super-ego, which psycho-analysis studies in the individual – are the very same processes repeated upon a wider stage.[5]

At the end of a life of psychoanalysis – at the end of the life of psychoanalytic inauguration – a 'regression' thus leads an almost already posthumous Freud towards the 'wider stage' of culture. Would the *wider stage* not be a stage still other than the 'other stage'?[6] A stage *more other*, which would certainly not mean 'wholly Other' but, in a much simpler and much more complex way, the stage (if it is still a stage) of the *Other*. As for the 'regression' towards the 'fascinations' of the young Freud, would its function not be to go back, at the end, towards something like a more primitive stage of psychoanalysis itself? And a still more primitive stage than any primitive stage, and perhaps off-stage [*hors-scène*] or ob-scene [*ob-scène*],[7] would it not be a matter of the stage of the *Other*? The problem of culture is never anything else for Freud than the problem of the Other or, to put it in a very banal way (on the register of the, apparently, constant banality in *Civilisation*), it is the problem of coexistence, and of pacific coexistence with the Other. It is therefore not a political problem, and not exactly *the* political problem because it is not certain that this problem arises for politics or that it arises on its own. But it is surely the problem of *the* political, which is to say, that concerning which the political begins to pose problems. . . .

Why would such a problem – the Other – refer to the other of psycho-analysis, or else to an altered psychoanalysis? Why and how would it lead psychoanalysis towards something like an origin obscure to itself? This is basically what one would need to begin locating.

4   These questions have neither the form nor the intent of a psychoanalysis of psychoanalysis; they aim neither at confirming nor at disinstalling its identity by means of an abyssal operation which could throw light (but which light?) on the (social, political, philosophical) unconscious of Freud and of his science. The analysis of culture is *precisely not* an analysis of psychoanalysis, a model to which all recent attempts at interpreting and at interpellating the social, institutional, economic and political position of psychoanalysis have remained subject.[8] It does not consist in a remainder unanalysed by Freud (in the perfectly legitimate sense in which Lacan has ceaselessly analysed the remainder left by Freud, or by Freud's biologism, energetism and psychologism, as regards language). That the analysis of culture might, however, eventually have repercussions for the self-analysis of analysis, no less than the question of the·Other on that of the 'discourse of the Other [*l'Autre*]', is plausible, but it is too early to tell.

5   Nor, on the other hand, is the *wider stage* a mere extrinsic appendix to the Freudian text which one could grasp without any psychoanalytic outlay and to

any socio-political or philosophical ends. It is not outside of analysis, and yet it does not quite fit inside. It may well be the place where the division of the outside and the inside of psychoanalysis is blurred. Such a place always has the nature of a limit. The limit is not negative: it traces an identity – and this tracing excludes itself from what it traces out, simultaneously carrying along with it the identity outside itself. There is no limit which is not both internal and external: the political is at the limit of psychoanalysis, or is its limit: its origin, its end, and the line of an intimate fold which crosses it. In the text which we quoted, this line passes through the obvious opposition or contrariety (it is not a contradiction) between the two relations of psychoanalysis to the analysis of culture which Freud simultaneously establishes: one of which is a relation of mere 'reflection', the other, one of 'repetition on a wider stage'. Rigorously, the two are irreconcilable (a reflection cannot be 'wider' without being distorting). Consequently, Freud never did reconcile them.

In a word: Freud was *never* able to derive, from the psychoanalysis of a subject presupposing the plurality of subjects (parental imagos or the instances of the second topic), the analysis of this very plurality. And to go straight to the political register: from the analysis of a subject presupposing the authority which assigns it, Freud was *never* able to derive the analysis of the institution of this authority. Moreover, he himself very clearly indicated this. Even if it means coming back to it later, let us immediately recall here two texts which stand out:

> It [i.e. remorse] relates only to a deed that has been done, and, of course, it presupposes that a *conscience* – the readiness to feel guilty – was already in existence before the deed took place. Remorse of this sort can, therefore, never help us to discover the origin of conscience and of the sense of guilt in general. . . . But if the human sense of guilt goes back to the killing of the primal father, that was after all a case of 'remorse'. Are we to assume that [at that time] a conscience and a sense of guilt were not, as we have presupposed, in existence before the deed?[9]

> Moreover, in the case of some advances in intellectuality – for instance, in the case of the victory of patriarchy – we cannot point to the authority which lays down the standard which is to be regarded as higher. It cannot in this case be the father, since he is only elevated into being an authority by the advance itself.[10]

On the contrary, Freud always sought in the analysis of culture to point, in numerous ways, to the emergence of a subject neither from other subjects nor from a subject-discourse (whether it be of the other or of the same, of the father or of the brother), but from the non-subject or non-subjects. Now, the non-subject (insofar as one can name it), the without-authority, the without-father (the phrase *we must recall that the father too was once a child* is found in *Moses*[11]), the without-super-ego and thus without-ego, anterior to every topic as well as to every institution, of an anteriority with which no regression can properly catch up, and 'wider' than every founding agency – the 'non-subject' forms, as one sees, the joint limit of psychoanalysis and of the political.

6   Let us thus introduce here without further delay, a hypothesis, indeed a thesis, which quickly turns out to be indispensable: if the limit of psycho-analysis is that of the subject, the same limit, insofar as it traces the contour of the political, is that of power. Power is neither the last question nor the first instance. With the question of the non-subject, that of a non-power or of an *unpower* necessarily arises.

In short, Freud instantly takes us to the common limit of a double question which is as old as metaphysics:

● how does the subject support itself? (if one recalls that the sub-ject, the substance, is the support);
● how does authority authorise itself?

Consequently, the very limit through which psychoanalysis overflows, the space of the 'wider stage', is not culture and politics as an apparatus ready to assign, to control and to evaluate psychoanalysis. It overflows, it overflows itself on the limit (also external/internal) of the political: If with the subject something other than the subject is in question, then, with power something other than power is in question.

7   But we shall be able to progress with this hypothesis only if we examine the way in which Freud obscurely, obstinately, and repetitively searches his own limit. Let us come back to the latter, in order to situate it better.

That this limit is external is attested to – more profoundly than in the 1935 text quoted above – by the impressive series of admissions of defeat or incompletion with which Freud supplements his writings on culture. Doubtless it would be necessary to analyse for itself the quasi-system formed throughout

6

almost the entire Freudian text by the (false/true) modesty and the hyperbolic circumspection. But even though it would be necessary to take a good number of these precautions against the grain, their insistence within the analysis of culture might be revealing: it might bear witness to the major stake, for Freud, of this analysis and, consequently, it might bear witness to the way in which psychoanalysis plays itself, plays its own stake, in its overflowing on the wider stage.

Moreover, Freud does not only make these admissions by antiphrasis (and it is perhaps in this way, in avoiding or in averting a code of polite behaviour, that Freud most amazes and sometimes misleads the reader). The long avowal which in certain respects constitutes *Civilisation* (and the famous 'pessimism' with which people are happy to label it) effectively bears the mark of the renunciation of the idea of a decisive amelioration of society (by psychoanalysis in particular) such as one found it in previous texts (*Jokes and their Relation to the Unconscious* especially). No doubt, *Civilisation* does, in concluding, evoke the hope that the cure of society will one day be undertaken. But the practical obstacle to surmount in this undertaking will be that of 'the authority necessary to impose such a therapy upon the group [*Masse*]'.[12] How could psychoanalysis endow itself with this authority? How could this authority be analysed? The political indeed encounters here its limit: for the whole, perhaps inextricable, question, in any case the *limit*-question, would thus be the following: how could psychoanalysis have power (therapeutic power, but is there any other?) if power is not analysed? And how could power be analysed if, in tackling power, psychoanalysis overflows its limits?

But one sees immediately the way in which this limit doubles or is coupled with a theoretical limit of the undertaking which the same page noted: unlike individual neurosis, collective neurosis cannot be set apart from the 'normality' of the entourage. There are many aspects to this difficulty, among which one must for the moment retain the following: collective psychoanalysis cannot refer to the already-given of an 'entourage' (except that of animals or that of angels), it is dealing neither with subjects nor with the subject.

Thus it is already confirmed that the external limit is coupled with an internal limit and that each doubtless proceeds from the other in the same movement of a passage to the limit of the Freudian stage, towards a wider *no man's land*.

8   (Before going on to verify it, let us simply indicate that one can and ought to make converge, towards this admission of *Civilisation*, a series which begins at

least with the admission of the unsatisfactory explanation of the Totem at the beginning of *Totem and Taboo* and ends with this affirmation of June 1938, in the preface to *Moses*: 'To my critical sense this book, which takes its start from the man *Moses*, appears like a dancer balancing on the tip of one toe.'[13] This dissatisfaction, this uncertainty of a too fragile equilibrium is always the effect of a limit-position.[14])

9   The external limit, the limit which psychoanalysis *shares* with the political is thus (coupled with) an internal limit. This is demonstrated in a decisive manner by the median text of the analysis of culture. The one which is *framed* by the introduction (if one can say this) of the death drive (*Beyond the Pleasure Principle*) and the constitution (if one can say this) of the so-called second topic (*The Ego and the Id*): *Group Psychology and the Analysis of the Ego*.

The title is by itself a programme and the programme of a limit. Yet in order to understand fully, one still has to understand the German: *Massenpsychologie und Ich-analyse*;[15] if 'group psychology' can evoke the association, indeed the associationism of a multiplicity of individual psychologies, and the 'reflection' of the ones in the other, Mass 'psychology' calls at once for an entity (both non-political *and* political; the Freudian *mass*, as Adorno already said, is also that of fascism: such is basically the proposition, the analysis of which, more complex than it appears, should effectively emerge in these notes) which is in opposition to the *ego* rather than forming an agglomerative plurality of egos. The *und* of the title (the most manifest intention of which is one of application, in the manner of a 'reflection') in reality forms a disjunctive conjunction. The oxymoron of this phrase traces the limit that one must explore.

But the introduction of the text takes on the task of inscribing this limit *within* psychoanalysis. This introduction inextricably blurs Freud's pretension (this term is not critical) to conquer for psychoanalysis the space of 'group psychology', and the *psychoanalytical* affirmation of the pre-inscription of this space *within* that of 'individual psychology':

In the individual's mental life someone else is invariably involved, as a model, as an object, as a helper, as an opponent; and so from the very first individual psychology, in this extended but entirely justifiable sense of the words, is at the same time social psychology as well.

The relations of an individual to his parents and to his brothers and sisters, to the object of his love, and to his physician – in fact all the

8

relations which have hitherto been the chief subject of psycho-analytic research – may claim to be considered as social phenomena.[16]

So Freud can write a few lines later:

The contrast [*Gegensatz*] between social and narcissistic – Bleuler would perhaps call them 'autistic' – mental acts therefore falls wholly within the domain of individual psychology, and is not well calculated to differentiate it from a social or group psychology.[17]

The contrast of the social and the individual *falls within* the limits of psycho-analysis. It is pointless – in any case, impossible here – to summon up the monumental and polymorphous set of justifications and verifications of this proposition throughout Freud. Let us rather directly state the following: in *one and the same* gesture, Freud includes the analysis of culture within the circumscription of psychoanalysis, while leading the latter, overflowing, to pass through its own limit. Here already, between sciences, between disciplines, between their initiators (Freud and Le Bon, McDougall, Trotter – elsewhere, it is the aestheticians, the ethnologists, the mythologists, the prehistorians and, always, the philosophers and the poets), a double, undecidable trial of rivalry and identity is played out – a process of reciprocal consumption and consummation. Psychoanalysis *is* a psycho-sociology, which is to say, a sociology; the *Ichanalyse* is a *Massenpsychologie* because it is psychoanalysis. The Freudian science is by rights a science of culture, and consequently a political science. Even and precisely if it turns out that this right gives rise to the greatest difficulties, indeed to the greatest disorder, and to the threat, as we will see, of a theoretical panic.

10   (It would be necessary to show the way in which this scientific right of psychoanalysis has been, in reality, long established: at least since 1905 in *Jokes*. For under the species of the *Witz* is analysed 'the most social production of the unconscious',[18] one should say: its very sociality which comes to double the analysis of the 'most private' production: that of the dream – each one supporting and completing the other, but without this mutual supplementarity ever reaching full clarity. Similarly, the analysis of the comic involves the first sketch of the social formation of the ego, through mimicry, the emergence of speech and of thought: it thus doubles the study of the other, sexual socialisation which the *Three Essays on the Theory of Sexuality* are at the same time

considering. The parallel between the sexual 'integration' of the ego and socialisation, which is to say, the parallel between the integration *to* society and the integration *of* society will be repeated in *Massenpsychologie* – and its difficulty displayed.

It is thus time to reread *Jokes* and its context, getting rid of the fascination exerted by the witticisms. If there is a *Witz* in Freud's *Jokes*, it is first and foremost insofar as the essay states that psychoanalysis is a sociology, and insofar as it begins to betray the fact that this double science is *neither* a psychoanalysis *nor* a sociology. Nor, consequently, a political science – except in the sense in which psychoanalysis seeks to seize socio-politio-logical power. This is, of course, what Freud wants in *Totem and Taboo* and *Massenpsychologie*. But this is not exactly what happens.

Another path, on the other hand, should be followed from the *Witz*: The double science can be foreseen on the occasion of the first incursion into yet another domain, that of aesthetics. The famous 'yield of pleasure [*ästhetische Lustgewinn*]'[19] supports and doubles the fore-pleasure (a non-integrated, non-discharged pleasure) of the *Three Essays*. A problematic of representation doubles a problematic of repetition. We shall see what the political might have to do with aesthetics.)

11 The *socius* is thus in the ego. It is the other of the narcissus. How can there be something other for Narcissus? And still worse, *in* Narcissus? Or conversely: how can the narcissus constitute only a part of the ego?

Such is the very simple and yet formidable difficulty into which is converted (but it does not immediately appear) the justification which founds the sociological authority of psychoanalysis. One surmises that this question touches at once upon the entire series of properly psychoanalytical theorems (and in particular, upon everything which sets the introduction of narcissism in motion, which is to say, upon *everything*). One must here sacrifice the examination of all these repercussions. Incidentally (but without considering this examination, which we will carry out elsewhere, to be negligible), what matters is precisely that *Massenpsychologie* does not consist only in the application of the theorems stemming from the introduction of narcissism (and what is more, a decisive question as far as our inquiry is concerned should here be raised: who [*qui*] exactly introduced narcissism? The 1914 essay which bears this title? Or in 1912–13, *Totem and Taboo* (with the analysis of animism and magic)? We shall answer, to put it briefly here, that it is neither one nor the other but in 1911,

10

Dr Schreber: the analysis of paranoia, which is to say, as Freud indicates, of the social pathology *par excellence.*[20]) *Massenpsychologie* at first represents, as Ferenczi,[21] with intentional paradox, entitled his review of the essay, a 'progress of individual psychology'. Even if, to be more specific, this progress forms in fact an advance towards a crucial threshold, the threshold of narcissism's limit as the internal limit, jointly, of the 'ego' and of 'psychoanalysis'.

This advance takes place, schematically, in two phases which together form a veritable reintroduction, this time social, of narcissism.

First phase: narcissism is recognised as the limit of the social formation, or of the *Masse* (itself a limit-concept of the social). In the first place, Freud pushes aside the pseudo-concepts coined by the 'group psychologists' to explain the social bond by way of an already social reality which comes down in the last analysis to the too mysterious 'suggestion' (the entire book must also be read, clearly, as a resumption of the question of the power of suggestion, of hypnosis – and of analysis). Sociality will thus consist in the libidinal bond of elements which in themselves are non-social: the individual narcissus. Thus, *panic* is the best and paradoxical representative of the essence of the *Masse*: It is the critical moment when, the affective bond having gradually been lost, the *Masse* breaks up into what really composes it, into narcissi which are estranged and opposed to each other. Thus is laid down the first axiom which Freudian 'sociology' will not only never disclaim but will never cease to reinforce: any relation only ever takes place on the ground of a *non-relation*, and the hatred of the narcissus is unavoidable, if not insurmountable. For Narcissus, the good *Other* is a dead or excluded Other. The earliest form of alterity which is inscribed *in* individual psychology is the suppression of the Other. By rights – by right of panic, if one dared say this – the narcissus immediately occupies the entire field of this psychology. Social truth can appear only against this ground and *on this ground*. The narcissus and the death of 'the Other' are the panic truth of the political (Freud names in this book and in Greek, the *zōon politikon*[22]), which only assembles that which, by itself, disassembles and excludes itself. A certain rereading, incidentally a canonical one, of Hobbes and of Hegel is here carried out in the space of a few pages – *via* Schopenhauer, whose part here, as elsewhere in Freud, is in no way coincidental. The proper stake of this Freudian repetition of political philosophy will appear in what follows.

Second phase: contrary to what everything leads one to expect, it does not consist in the explanation of sociality and thus in the *limitation* of narcissism by the libido. At least not the pure and simple libido of Eros. Despite the

11

impressive quantity of arguments which Freud accumulates – and right up to the end of the book – on social erotics, which is to say, essentially on the *bond of love to the leader* (in relation to whom the 'horizontal' identification which develops between the *subjects* of this Sovereign appears as derived), a decisive episode takes place (at the end of chapter 6): without warning, Freud introduces another type of 'affective bonds' – *identifications*. And we know that chapter 7 constitutes Freud's most elaborate exposition of identification. Thus is given the second axiom of Freudian 'sociology', again maintained right to the end – but whose form is not as clear as that of the first one: sociality rests on identification just as much as on the libido *or* anteriorily to the libido. Be that as it may (but we shall see that a decision is taken more or less overtly in favour of the second hypothesis), identification is the ground of the social.

Right to the end, through all the texts on culture, the articulation of the two axioms will be maintained: identification forms the limitation of the narcissistic non-relation and a (the) fundamental socio-political bond.

12   This poses at least two problems:

a How can narcissism, if it is truly narcissism, be *limited*? Which is to say, not harnessed and sublimated by love in what would basically be no more than a reduplication of itself (its speculation), but, as the very idea of identification seems to imply, truly and 'inwardly' *limited* by an *other* identity? The limit-question is the question of this limitation.
b If identification does not concern the erotic model, and not even the model of sublimated sexuality (quite to the contrary, sublimation which is social in essence, will be possible only after identification), what, therefore, is its nature? What is identification?

We shall begin with the second question, because it is the one which Freud asks or attempts to ask. (If the first is only raised in silence, and as if in the shadow of the second, it is precisely because the latter, as we shall see, remains unanswered.)

13   But before even tackling identification one should ask oneself another prejudicial question: why should sublimated erotics (since 'In groups there can evidently be no question of sexual aims of that kind'[23]) give way to identification, or at least find identification appended to it? Identification arises in an apparently empirical and heterogeneous manner: it is part of the 'mechanisms'

12

which psychoanalysis knows, nothing more. (Or rather, identification*s* are known by psychoanalysis, says the end of chapter 6; but in quickly moving on to the concept of 'identification' in the singular (chapter 7), Freud is broaching a question rather than pursuing a reminder).

The analysis of identification alone should allow one to answer this question. But to be economical, and even if it means anticipating, we will sketch right here and now this answer, the principle of which is in fact given from the first pages of the chapter on identification; this latter, 'the earliest expression of an emotional tie with the other person',[24] belongs to the order of *being* and not that of *having*. Sexuality belongs to the order of *having*, which is to say, in Freud's classical terms, to that of the objectal relation. Love is object-love. Consequently it presupposes, without any wordplay and as simply as possible, a subject, whether me or the other-subject, who, taking me as an object of love, must incorporate me into society.

Love presupposes what has yet to be explained: the relation of subjects, which is to say, the objectal relation. How, for that matter, could it not presuppose it, if nothing of the pure narcissus in reciprocal exclusion presents the possibility of such a relation? In order for love to arise suddenly as a bond, there must be a subject. There must even be *the* Subject who, in *Massenpsychologie*, takes a double figure:

First, it takes the figure of social *organicity*, of the *Masse* as 'biologically, a continuation of the multi-cellular character of all the higher organisms.'[25] The model of the *cell* – or of what *Beyond the Pleasure Principle*, making a converse use of the comparison, had called 'the cellular State' – twice implies the subject: once as a constituted individual in which each cell consists; then as the organised whole [*Gesamtheit*] which reproduces on a larger scale the individuality of the members with all the characteristics of self-sufficiency of this individuality. Love – which is actually the proper mode of regeneration or/ and of reproduction of evolved cells (cf. again in *Beyond the Pleasure Principle*) – can only take place as a positive attachment among subjects whom it integrates into a larger Subject. (Sexual integration, at the outcome of which, said the *Three Essays*, sexuality becomes 'altruistic' in reproduction, is thus both in parallel and in series, indeed installed along with socio-political integration.)

Second, more markedly, it takes the figure of the *Leader* [*Chef*]. If the subjects are initially given, these subjects are on the verge of panic. The Leader, an exceptional individual, by his fascination holds them in the certainty of each being loved.

Not only does love consequently presuppose the subjects and their relation: but one also sees that this presupposition takes very precisely the form of the Political. The two figures in question, the social organism and the loving leader, more or less cover the entire circumscription of the Political, of the nature of the *zōon politikon* which twenty-five centuries of metaphysics have untiringly redescribed or reconstructed (subject, however, to a deconstructive inventory which Freud might enable us to carry out in what follows). The Sovereign, since that is who is in question, may oscillate between the integral, organic form (the ideology of socialism which is not necessarily the thought of Marx) and the form of the sole leader, who not only orders but also assembles (in fasces) and leads (the *Führer* – Freud uses this word): it still remains a question of the same *cellular State*,[26] which can change its form (the *Führer*, Freud indicates, can be replaced by an idea) but not its structure: it is a social and political *body*, or rather, as in Plato, Aristotle, Hobbes or Rousseau, sociality *as a body*; it is the Political. And this body has a head: the Leader in Freud's text is indeed the *head* [*le* chef] (the sort which one cuts): *Oberhaupt*.

But in truth, this body is a psychical body, a body of love which the head of the Father surmounts. Hence, later in the book, the recollection of the history of the horde, and the explanation of man as a 'horde animal', of the political animal, in its Freudian version, governed by the Father.

14   One could all but forget here the point of departure, so well known is the motif of the horde, repeated *ad nauseam* as the Freudian vulgate, and first of all by Freud himself. And yet the point of departure was indeed the inadequacy of the libidinal bond announced by the introduction of identification. Consequently, in all rigour, the inadequacy of the horde as a social body of love. Assuredly, in the chapters which follow the presentation of identification, the latter finds itself brought back to the relation of love, and it is all in all the Father's power of love (or of amorous illusion) which makes possible 'a positively toned tie in the nature of an identification'.[27]

But one can guess that the difficulties are heightened rather than surmounted by this. Freud himself, a few lines later, comes out with a half-admission ('We do not ourselves regard our analysis of identification as exhaustive'[28]). Reduced to love, identification loses the specificity which was attributed to it. Brought back to an amorous identification, society, on the one hand, is by no means explained (but presupposes itself); on the other hand, it renews, intact and even reinforced, the Subject of the Political and the politics of the subject.

14

Thus and quite obviously two conclusions assert themselves: in the first place, identification is dismissed; in the second place, the model of the Political (of the horde and of the Father) cannot fulfil Freud's demand. These two things are linked: it is because identification has not been drawn out as such that the Political returns, in order to explain instead of being explained.

Let us here and now underline the hypothesis that we shall not cease to confirm: the Freudian Political, namely, the erection of the Power of the Father or of the Power-Father is nothing other than the pervasive consequence of an uncompleted operation carried out on identification. We shall soon examine this incompletion. But it must immediately be pointed out that the hypothesis also comprises its reversal: if the analysis remained suspended on identification, it is also because the model of the Power-Father obscures Freud's gaze. Already, as one knows, the figure of the Father was untenable in the Darwinian derivation of *Totem and Taboo* (which will serve right to the end, as a matrix): for a gorilla is not a father, and there can only be a Father after the event, in the 'after' of the mortal event. But here as elsewhere Freud persists in fomenting and in perpetrating, on his part, a coup which is the political coup *par excellence*: 'the coup of the leader' [*'le coup du chef'*]. To begin with, there must be a head, a leader. And whether he likes it or not, Freud wants to begin: an *archeophiliac* drive or passion which forms the very essence of metaphysical (and) political desire. So powerful an *archeophilia* that it is blind to the contradiction which it never ceases to reproduce: to locate the beginning in 'a common affectionate tie with a person outside the group' (chapter 9)[29] is to presuppose the crowd and the person, it is to explain nothing. The history of the horde, at least in this form, explains nothing, nothing but the self-explanation of the Political. And as a bonus (unless it be the ultimate pleasure of the story), the self-confirmation of the power of psychoanalysis in the analysis of culture.

15 But Freud knows this. If he adds *Massenpsychologie* to *Totem and Taboo*, and if he will further add to it *Civilisation* and *Moses*, he does so in the continuous movement of a series of displacements, torsions and finally of frustrations of his own *archeophilia*. If this trajectory is so evasive, so difficult to follow (and we shall not be able here, far from it, to track down all the episodes), and never completed, it is also because the *archeophilia* does not only proceed from the exterior, from an ideological (metaphysical) remainder in Freud. The politics of the Father is introduced as an external limit because it encounters an internal limit of psychoanalysis: that of identification.

15

Freud's avowal on this point is clear and complete: the final note of chapter 7 of *Massenpsychologie* admits that it has left intact most of the enigma of identification:

> We are very well aware that we have not exhausted the nature of identification with these examples taken from pathology, and that we have consequently left part of the riddle of group formations untouched. A far more fundamental and comprehensive psychological analysis would have to intervene at this point. A path leads from identification by way of imitation to *Einfühlung*, that is, to the comprehension of the mechanism by means of which we are enabled to take up any attitude at all towards another mental life. Moreover there is still much to be explained in the manifestations of existing identifications. These result among other things in a person limiting his aggressiveness towards those with whom he has identified himself, and in his sparing them and giving them help. The study of such identifications, like those, for instance which lie at the root of clan feeling, led Robertson Smith (*Kinship and Marriage*, 1885) to the surprising discovery that they rest upon the acknowledgement of the possession of a common substance [by the members of the clan], and may even therefore be created by a meal eaten in common. This feature makes it possible to connect this kind of identification with the early history of the human family which I constructed in *Totem and Taboo*.[30]

Freud will, more or less, tell us nothing more. And yet this chapter — the textual situation of which is one of the strangest one can find — promised with identification, 'to give the formula for the libidinal constitution of groups [*Masse*]'.[31] With identification something happens to psychoanalysis: an accident, the incision of a limit. And it happens to it on its political limit, which turns out to be both the cause and the effect of the psychoanalytical limit.

This limit, however, is neither pure nor simple. The quoted note (and the entire chapter) simultaneously proposes three tasks, opens up three perspectives which, stated in a simplified manner, should be:

a since the chapter relies on a set of established psychoanalytical facts concerning identification, it would be necessary to track down this notion from its origins in Freud;

b one must examine the concept which appears to be the last instance of identification: *Einfühlung*;

c one must go back in *Totem and Taboo*, to the *meal* rather than to the killing of the father.

16 It is on this point that we shall be drastically economical. Each of these paths leads to an analysis which it is impossible to sum up here. We shall here content ourselves with dryly disclosing the results relating to the first two. As far as the third one is concerned we shall indicate its main articulations.

a The history of the notion of identification (which crosses the majority of the Freudian texts) leads on the one hand, through the progressive aggravation of the gap between narcissism and object-choice (or the step back of narcissism towards an 'absolutely' primary phase), to a primitive *incorporation* which should be qualified both as a relation and a non-relation to the Other. The identification of the 'I am the breast' (in the famous posthumous note) designates the unassignable relation without relation of an 'I' which *is* not an 'I'. The experience of hysteria joins identification to this incorporation, inaccessible as such, as its – so to speak – analysable, phenomenal manifestation. But this only on the condition that one traces its examination, on this side of imitation and contagion, right back to an *appropriation* (*Aneignung*) of the other, who can only result from a community, from an already given being-with-the-Other (this process of going back beyond imitation and contagion which *Massenpsychologie* seeks, is already laid down in principle in the *Traumdeutung*). Through the double path of narcissistic and hysterical identifications, a path never absolutely reduced, one does not thus end up with a concept, but with the formation, which endlessly redoubles and undoes itself, of a constitution of identity through a being-with-the-Other which only takes place in the negation of the Other. This negation is indeed also an appropriation: but the one who appropriates has no 'proper', he *is* not a subject. Consequently, if there must be a question of origin, the latter takes place (or arrives) neither through a subject nor through an other, nor through the Same nor through the Other [*l'Autre*] but through an asociality, or through an altered sociality. (In the same way, the paper called *The Unconscious* slyly opposes the classical doctrines of the recognition of the Other by way of analogisms, in order to substitute for these doctrines a far-reaching and primordial identification: an opportunity to point to the thesis which we are verifying without expounding it as such – namely that the problem of the unconscious is never anything other than that of the 'collective'.)

17

This history comes to a sudden end in *Massenpsychologie*, which proves that the psychoanalysis of identification necessarily led to the analysis of the 'wider stage', of the *no man's land*, but also that the overflowing of this scene was not, immediately at least, sustainable through a psychoanalysis which has remained dependent, whether it likes it or not, upon the paradigm of the subject.

b This dependency is a general philosophical dependency which Freud shares with the entire egology of his time and of the tradition.

(It is remarkable, in this respect, that *Einfühlung* ('intropathy' or 'empathy', when it was still translated) constitutes the permanent motif, in several philosophies contemporary with Freud, of a general problematic of the relation to the Other. Furthermore, the question of the Other should be recognised as the *pregnant* question (in every sense of the word) of philosophy in the age of psychoanalysis (which is also the age of the Bolshevik revolution, of the World War and of National Socialism). This is more than mere coincidence. Durkheim, Bergson, Dilthey and others could be evoked, as could Husserl. But the latter, especially, with the help of *Einfühlung*, conducts an analysis which ought to lead on to the transcendental constitution of the *alter ego*. Heidegger will quickly indicate the inadequacy of such an analysis, which always presupposes the other as already-given, unless it simply identifies it *as* an ego. *Sein und Zeit* thus proposes the analytic of a being-with (*Mitsein*) originally constitutive of *Dasein*. This analytic will in fact be entirely sketched out upon the motif of the only mode of being-with where the being-self can be experienced: being-there-alongside (*Dabeisein*) the dead Other. The experience of death — one ought to say *of* the dead — is that of a relation without relation. As one can see, the convergence of Heidegger and Freud henceforth poses an entirely different problem from that of the introduction of a few themes from one of these discourses into the other: it poses the problem of the very status of such discourses, measured against this proximity which nonetheless refers only to their radical distance [*éloignement*] and to their reciprocal exclusion. Here too, as if by chance, it is a question of a relation without relation. The relation without relation of psychoanalysis and of philosophy also draws a common *limit*, which once more involves the political. We shall have to come back to this.[32])

Here, we will be content to point out the origin, common to philosophers, to psychologists and to Freud, of the notion of *Einfühlung*: it comes from nineteenth-century post-Hegelian aesthetics, and was particularly elaborated in the work of Theodor Lipps, Freud's favourite (and consequently most envied) aesthetician.[33] This elaboration, which we will not lay out here, aims at producing, under the name of *Einfühlung*, the concept of identification (the word is also in Lipps) as a 'passage into' the other, as the 'putting oneself in the place of' (*sich einfühlen in*), characteristic of aesthetic experience, but in the last analysis, characteristic of a quite primitive and general experience. Anterior to imitation, *Einfühlung* constitutes identity by the passage into the Other. But one must here renew the Heideggerian critique: despite everything, this *Einfühlung* always presupposes the *already* constituted relation to the Other.

Now it is at the same time possible to suppose that if Freud himself does not get as far as an analysis of *Einfühlung*,[34] it is for an ambivalent reason: on the one hand, the notion functions as a given, an established fact of psychology, which spares him a difficult exploration; on the other hand, this given, for him, is no more valuable than any other given of psychology, and he silently levels a reproach analogous to Heidegger's against it: no matter what is said in the note cited above, *Einfühlung* does not make us 'understand' the 'being posited' (*Stellungnahme*) towards another psychical life, for if this other psyche is given, so is *my* position; on the contrary, it is a question of the division [*partage*] between the other and myself. Freud and Heidegger's distant proximity is thus established around the only question which forms the *limit* of the entire metaphysical egology. It is the insurmountable solipsism, or perhaps one would have to say the *ipseism*, of the thought of the Subject which both Freud and Heidegger have in sight. But from then on the difficulty is so considerable that it doubtless explains both the reciprocal exclusion, at this very point, of psychoanalysis and of philosophy, and the interruption, in both Freud and Heidegger, of the (at least direct) questioning of this difficulty.

17 (Everything, since Freud and since Heidegger, might be brought into play upon this difficulty. The entire work of Jacques Lacan, in particular, will have so far consisted in drawing attention to it and in articulating it in a discourse woven from Freud, from Heidegger, and from a certain Hegel to which, inevitably, it will henceforth be necessary to (re)turn. For it is since Hegel that identity constitutes itself only by being-in-a-negative-relation-to-the-Other. But what then clearly poses a problem is not looking for names for this subject from *before* the subject (non-subject, subverted subject, split subject, subject of analysis, subject which does not come in its place). What clearly poses a

problem is that if it is indeed a question of a *limit*, a discourse can hold itself at this limit only by virtue of holding itself at the limit of discourse: henceforth, Freud and Heidegger's *retreat* on either side of this limit should not be considered as simply a failure. We do not have to occupy the space of a radical science with a more powerful discourse, whether this be called analysis or philosophy. We do not have to identify the limit of identification, nor to relinquish discourse either. A more powerful science is inevitably archeophiliac. This space is thus clearly that of another politics, of another politics of discourse as well as of the rest.)

18 (Before going any further, let us still hold in reserve the following: to his analysis of *Einfühlung* at the beginning of his *Aesthetics* (1903), Lipps adds a rather remarkable supplement. It concerns the identification of man to woman. Energetically refusing the sexualisation of aesthetics, Lipps analyses the *Einfühlung* in man's perception of woman's breasts as the typical case of an identification without possible imitation and without perception of movement. It is the 'most interior' identification, the one through which I experience in myself a feeling which cannot be proper to me, that of a generous and exuberant life. This feeling comes from the fact that the shape of the female breast communicates to me a particular rhythmics, generative of impulses which awaken this feeling. It is possible, moreover, that the woman does not herself experience this rhythmics. Freud does not, to our knowledge, directly allude to this singular model of *Einfühlung*.)

19 Whatever his relation to Lipps may be (and also his implicit critique of the instinctual hypothesis produced by Lipps to sustain his concept), in pointing to *Einfühlung*, Freud still leaves us a decisive indication: a sexual description of identification will never be satisfactory; its stake is anterior to the objectal relation, anterior to the Oedipal scene. The wider stage can thus not be the stage of the Political, that of the Father. And for two reasons:

The first is that what is in question is what happens *before* the Father, in the *regressus in infinitum* of the childhood which was that of every father (in the order of the myth, let us say: before the story of Oedipus, that of Laius is in question, of his homosexual misdeed punished by Hera in the name of marriage, and of the procreation of Oedipus, despite the threat, under the effect of the ecstasy and/or the sensuality of Jocasta). What is thus clearly in question is what Freud ceaselessly seeks in the order of culture: the earliest society, for example, the clan (the *kin*) which *Totem and Taboo* deems to be anterior to the family.

The second explains the first: one must go back before [*passer avant*] the Father, because the Father, as absolute Narcissus (as *Massenpsychologie* describes him), is quite simply impossible. Or more exactly: if one begins with a pure Narcissus, there will never be any reason to come out of it. No objectality can be established. The *archeophilia* implies the integral autarky of the *archē*. Theoretically, it is the insurmountable *ipseity*. Politically, it is the total sacrifice to the Sovereign in one or another of its forms. The absolute Narcissus can be neither a subject (or else it is *the* Subject, but the Subject is impossible), nor a psyche, nor a discourse, not even that of the Other [*l'Autre*]. And his tribe cannot be a social organism.

The wider stage is thus the *no man's land* of several narcissi. Which means that these narcissi are not absolute, and that they are in a relation through their non-relation. This is the scene of panic, insofar as it is thus *not* the scene of a unique totalitarian Pan (mytho-political tautology), but that of a violent disorder of identities, none of which is Identity, and each one of which nonetheless posits itself only through the exclusion of the others, each of which thereby finds itself deposed. Neither at the origin or at the summit, nor at the basis, in each narcissus there is no Pan, no *Archē*, no initial Power. Anarchy is at the origin which precisely means that there is no *archie*, whether 'anarchic' or 'monarchic'. There is not even the *archie* of a Discourse, *Logos* or Speech which would already govern the crowd of narcissi. For the relation of non-relation is not that of language either: its untenable formula, which is that of 'hatred', on the contrary designates that *on the basis of which* there can be language. But if, in effect, one cannot speak about this in the order of a metalanguage, since there is no metalanguage, Freud, despite everything, attempts to 'say' something about it, while moving elsewhere: this is the third path which it still remains to be followed by us.

20   It thus refers to *Totem and Taboo* and, more particularly, to the meal (consequently to incorporation).

But as far as we are concerned, this cannot constitute a direct path. *Totem and Taboo* must be set apart from what, within it, provokes an impasse, between the admission of the insufficient explanation of totemism and the archeophiliac edifice of the killing of the father. This book can thus only be picked up again beyond *Massenpsychologie*, on the basis of its ultimate or final engagement, on the basis, that is, of *Moses*. *Moses* is the condition of reading of the entire analysis of culture. By way of a provisional justification, let us simply note this: in each of these two repetitions of the history of the horde which are included in *Moses*, a slight but decisive perturbation creeps in. In the first this lies in the mention of a privileged relation of the youngest son to the *mother*, which for the son, 'eases' his succession of the father (this partially takes up once again, and from another angle, a motif already present in appendix B of *Massenpsychologie*, to which we will return); in the second, in this formulation by Freud: ' . . . each one of which was under the despotic rule of an older male who appropriated all the females and castigated or disposed of the younger males, including his sons.'[35] Thus they were not all sons, and the filial relation is not an exclusive one. *Moses*, the ultimate 'application' and repetition of the themes which focus on the analysis of culture, could thus well offer a reworking of these themes.[36]

21   Nevertheless, *Moses* gathers to itself, by its mode of composition, by its circumstances – 1938, Nazism, the exile – and by its very undertaking, such a complexity of determinations that it is impossible to approach it directly and naïvely. Thus, we must once again indicate here, in the most schematic way, at least the two most necessary inquiries as a precondition to the reading of the book:

An inquiry into the *autobiographical* character of the book.[37] Assuredly, the concept of autobiography, never simple in any case, is even less so here than elsewhere. It doubtless simultaneously implies autobiography and self-analysis, according to a multiple relation to Freud the man, to psychoanalysis, and to the relation which each entertains with literature and with philosophy.

To avoid having to unfold this problematic here, we shall tighten it up around a single axis: Freud's correspondence with Arnold Zweig allows one to discover the way in which *Moses* is elaborated in opposition to Zweig's project of a novel about Nietzsche. The Freud–Zweig rivalry covers the Freud–Nietzsche rivalry, the role of which (but it will be necessary to return to this) in the history of the founder of psychoanalysis is well known. The stake of *Moses* is thus one of theoretical rivalry, that is to say it is Freud's own, indistinguishably 'human' and 'theoretical', identification that is at stake in this book.

(Moreover, Nietzsche only figures the visible point of this process of identification, a situation which, up to a certain point, he also shares with Shakespeare. The process itself passes through a complex network of figures distributed simultaneously by Freud's theoretical interests, his relation to

Zweig's and Thomas Mann's literary works and, finally, his own life. It will be necessary to reconstitute this narrative which blurs Rome (the centre of idolatry), Winckelmann the converted, the Semite general Hannibal, Napoleon, Egypt, Joseph the son of Jacob (like Freud), and Freud's father, which is to say, the humiliated Jewish father. But a narrative cannot be summarised: we will relate it elsewhere.)

The result of this first inquiry should be the following: with *Moses* (the book) Freud identifies himself by identifying Moses (the figure; a historical figure indistinguishable, moreover, from the artistic one, sculpted by Michelangelo) as the truth of Nietzsche's *Übermensch*. What Nietzsche announced to be coming, Freud ascribes to the origin – and not to humanity's primitive origin, but to its adult origin: to the inauguration of a history, not of a prehistory. This inauguration is both Jewish and psychoanalytical. Through psychoanalysis, Judaism speaks the truth of culture – its non-Roman, non-philosophical and perhaps also non-political truth. Such is, at least for Freud, the 'truth' of *Moses*: in it, psychoanalysis carries out what philosophy has not been able to carry out. It is here, therefore, that it goes over to its own limit. One must examine the 'truth' of this passage.

An inquiry into the psychoanalytical procedure of the elaboration of *Moses*, since the external rivalry is coupled with a rivalry which is internal to analysis.

As is well known, in *Moses* Freud silently exploits a work by Karl Abraham.[38] This exploitation, its dissimulation and the at least ambivalent relations with Abraham which preceded it – none of this can be summarised either. It is possible, on the other hand, to point hastily to the theses which Freud takes up from Abraham (after the death of the latter), and the modifications with which he imprints them. Freud retains practically the whole Egyptological reconstitution of his disciple/rival – that is, the reconstitution of the monotheism of Ikhnaton. But he refuses to consider this character as a paranoiac in delirium: in other words, the initiator of Mosaic monotheism (a thesis which is also from Abraham, but on which Freud puts the whole emphasis) slips out of the general psychoanalytic schema of religion. With *Moses*, it may not be simply a matter of religion.

Moreover, in *Moses* Freud silently confronts Reik's text published in 1919 in *The Ritual* (a book which he himself prefaced). This confrontation and the entire problematic of the 'to retain/to reject' which it implies, is much more complex than the preceding one. Let us retain this from it: from Reik, Freud keeps what could be called *Moses*'s 'originary marks', that is to say, the repetition or reactivation, in Mosaic history, of the originary killing; Judaism's assignation as a religion of the father (notably in opposition to Christianity, the religion of the son); the determination of this same Judaism as founded on guilt; and finally the redoubling of *Moses*, but inverted in relation to Reik, which allows us to distinguish between two foundations of the religion of the father: the primitive, idolatrous and sacrificial one, and its resurgence beyond a latency period in the genuine monotheism which takes upon itself, in a non-sacrificial manner, the truth of the inaugural event.

The way in which Freud treats this last 'remainder' of Reik also indicates the general orientation of his rejections. Freud silently reproaches Reik with treating *Moses*'s history as a myth of origin. This reproach implies at least two correlative refusals: first, that of reducing *Moses*'s history to an epic (i.e. aesthetic) scheme, and second, that of leaving *Moses* to a prehistoric primitivity instead of situating him in the second moment, the moment of historical repetition. At the same time, what Freud contests in Reik is the application of the sacrificial schema of religion to *Moses*.[39]

Each of these gestures forms a system: Freud aims, very precisely, to exclude Judaism from the common law of religion to which Reik had submitted it. Freudian Mosaism (and, for the moment, it is of little matter here whether it be properly Jewish or not) is an exception to the religiosity of sacrifice, which is to say, to religion as *a cathartic and mimetic compensation for the originary killing*. It escapes aesthetics (representation) and the discharge of guilt: it is, in short, the bare repetition of the origin (which does not exclude, on the contrary, the fact that this bareness is *only* revealed in repetition and in history). At the same stroke, not only does this Judaism enunciate the truth of religion but it also enunciates the truth of the whole of culture, the ethical – and not aesthetic – truth of social guilt.

And this is what one makes the Jewish people pay for, as Freud writes. Anti-Semitism is the negation [*Verneinung*] of this bare truth, the negation of the common social guilt. And the 'absolute negativity' (Adorno) of Nazism is the political acting out of this negation, the will to exterminate the bearer of the truth of the political. In this acting out, the Political itself goes over to its limit: in turn, it itself reveals the truth that it wishes to annihilate. It will, of course, be necessary to come back to this at length. For the moment, let us simply note that Freud aims at saying nothing more than this at the end of

Moses. But this means just as well – and we will clarify this later – that this truth is not *proper* to the Jew.

Moses thus produces at last the truth of the analysis of culture (it comes to rectify *Totem and Taboo* or to allow its true reading, as we shall see). Which also means that the 'Jewish truth' of *Moses* is possible only on condition that it be a psychoanalytic truth, which is itself possible only on condition that it be, going over to its limit, a philosophical truth. There is, then, no end or ground to this 'truth'. It is without *archē*. Or more exactly, it is in one and the same gesture that Freud erects psychoanalysis and erects himself in the identity of the true *and* that he thwarts or deconstitutes this identity by means of this very truth. It thus remains for us to try to describe it.

22   *Moses* falls entirely under the sign of a problematic which is inscribed in the first pages of the first essay as a problematic of the *proper* or of the *being-proper*. It connects two motifs:

First, the motif of *Moses*'s belonging to the Jewish people, which is to say, that of the gesture of dispossession or of 'depropriation' which Freud effects with respect to the Jewish people, even if he simultaneously claims his own Jewishness and (secretly) his identification with the founder of Judaism.

Second, the motif of the *proper name* of *Moses*:[40] not only does this name make *Moses* out to be an Egyptian, but it also gives him no other name than that of an Egyptian 'child' (a 'child' in Egyptian); this name is reduced to the pure indication of Jewish non-identity and, in short, of the pre-identity of the child; but what is more, this name which is not a name, or which forms the zero degree of the name, will be split in the second essay between the *two Moses* who will be necessary in order to ensure the entire specificity of the second monotheistic foundation, providing the principle of generalised reduplication which affects every nomination, from that of Amenhotep/Ikhnaton, right to that of Adonai/Yahweh, the double name of the God who has no name.

Through this double motif, *Moses* opens up . . . and never closes up again on the indefinite loss of nominal propriety, that is to say, of propriety *itself*. *Moses* holds a truth only with respect to the de-nomination of its eponym (who is precisely not a hero but the '*man Moses*', and this man is a child).

This is why this truth must indeed appear as a de-propriation – we could say, running ahead somewhat, as the depropriation of the subject of culture, of society and of politics.

25

23 This problematic of depropriation must thus organise the reading of *Moses* and, within this reading, the rereading of *Massenpsychologie*, of *Totem and Taboo* and of *Civilisation*. We will have to limit ourselves here to presenting the general programme of this quadruple decipherment: it joins two essential interrogations, one of which could be entitled that of *death* and the other that of *the mother*. Together they in fact form the counter-interrogation of the absolute Narcissus and of the *archeophilia*. Perhaps they might even form the real (in)completion of the problem of identification.

24 Death is the primary affirmation (one would have to say 'matrix affirmation', but let us not go too fast) of Ikhnaton's monotheism. The rejection of magical thought, which determines it, entails above all the rejection of the belief in immortality. The single God is, precisely, the one who does not occupy the beyond of another life. The ban on representing him, to which Mosaism's rigour will add the ban on naming him, forms its correlate.

The monotheistic recognition of death, humanity's decisive spiritual progress (carried out by this Pharaoh who can be called 'the first individual in human history', as writes Freud quoting Breasted: the first individual conscience, the first to have identified himself), occurs as the historical repetition of what Freud had been able to reconstruct in 1913 around the *taboo of the dead* (itself essentially a taboo of *names*). This taboo, a synthesis of the taboos of the enemies and of the leader – a synthesis of the politico-cultural taboo – offered the sole access to an initial exploration of totemism – the two fundamental taboos which could not have been tackled head-on.

The taboo of the dead comprises two fundamental determinations. On the one hand, it corresponds to the recognition of the Other: if '*death is only ever a dead man*', it is also because only a dead man is *an other man*; his death simultaneously installs him into an identity and snatches him away into an absolute alterity. In Freud as in Heidegger, the experience of death forms the experience of the Other – of this other who is not 'same' and whose alterity first of all takes him away from himself; it is thus the identificatory experience of this other *Other* which 'I' am: thus, something wholly other than the specular experience of an '*alter ego*' (in the dead other, I precisely do not recognise myself). On the other hand and jointly, the taboo of the dead points to the emergence of a consciousness which Freud designates as moral conscience (*Gewissen*) while underlining its proximity to psychological consciousness (*Bewusstsein*).

26

With the identity (of the other), the certainty of a '*cogito*' whose formula is not 'I am' but 'he is/you are dead' emerges. The certainty of an anxiety, the index of a guilt which is that of the narcissus: whether or not he provoked this death, whether or not he killed or desired to do so, which, for primitive thought, is identical. It is precisely the absolute narcissistic wish which discloses the Other to me through its suppression. What is disclosed here is what *Civilisation* situates at the source of guilt: the *withdrawal of love*.

Hence, two consequences:

First, the Other only ever '*is*' its own withdrawal, its own proper-improper withdrawal, the withdrawal of its love – a love which might itself only be the form or the hollowing of this withdrawal (neither object-love nor that of subject, but this withdrawal on the basis of which there can be an object; at the origin, it is not so much a question of a loss of object, nor, moreover, of a loss of love, but of this withdrawal in which love consists). The Other is not at first the identical other, but the withdrawal of this identity – the originary *alteration*. Narcissus, insofar as he *can* be, is only ever *incised* by this withdrawal (which might involve something wholly other than the merely negative and dramatic concept of 'narcissistic wound').

Second, if the birth of society is no different to that of the individual and vice versa (as Rousseau, Hegel and Marx already clearly knew), and if the taboo of the dead succeeds in explaining totemism, then the 'killing of the father' is a killing only insofar as the death of the Other (the death of the dead, the dead as dead) is this withdrawal of love: and there can only ever be a Father *after* the death of the (first) dead. In this way, then, *nothing begins with the confrontation of the absolute Narcissus*: everything begins, on the contrary, with the infinitely originary incision of the narcissus through which their non-relation is sealed.

The Father is the re-presented or re-presentified dead: he is the cathartic mimesis of the withdrawal of love (and of hatred) which compels one, in effect, to the indefinitely repeated sacrificial killing. The ban on representing, essential to Ikhnaton/*Moses*'s monotheism, is thus a ban on killing, which itself comes down to a ban on transgressing the withdrawal of love or love in its withdrawal: which comes down to the necessity of the *incision* [*l'*entame] (Freud calls it *Anankē*). Monotheism does not take up a god (a figure of death);[41] it confronts death, the Other – my desire – a face withdrawn from all figures.

25   Then comes the second interrogation, the argument of which we will lay out on the basis of (once the preceding summmary is unfolded) what still

appears to remain part of the enigma of totemism. And, this time, it seems to relate to the meal and no longer to the 'killing'. To the meal, that is to say, to Freud's last reference in the note on identification or, if you like, by an apparently trivial *Witz* (?), to *Einfühlung* as a literal incorporation.[42]

In the meal, what is consumed is the common substance of the *kin*, and consequently, as *Totem and Taboo* indicates, the substance of the mother or the mother-substance. The identification with the father occurs only in consideration of this other identification, wholly other because it is not supported by any figure (the complete, complex process, which we cannot analyse here, is not that of a double identification: it is that of the condition of (let us say, figural) identification through an 'identification' by way of incorporation of the substance – of what is simultaneously the identity common to all – to all the Others – and no identity). The mother-substance is this immediate sensible presence-evidence (always absolutely certain, whereas the father, absolutely uncertain, can only be established indirectly, intellectually: is it not the mother who alone can designate the 'father' of her 'son'?), whose 'spiritual progress', which culminates in the Mosaic institution, consists in detaching itself.

But the mother is herself at the origin of this very progress, at the origin of 'monotheism'. The suggestion came to Ikhnaton from his mother or from this other mother [*outre-mère*: beyond-the-mother: *outre-mer*: beyond-the-sea – TN] from a 'distant Asia': the Earth-Mother herself. *Moses* the child, in his turn, emerges from the amniotic fluid of the Egyptian Nile. The history of Judaism is marked throughout by maternity and by the privileged relation of the mother with the last-born: the one whose natural dependency upon the mother keeps him as close as possible to her, even as he comes away from her. The last-born, inside/outside of the mother, relates to her by 'clinging' [*le 'cramponnement'*],[43] as *Moses* calls it.[44] Paternity only ever follows on: it is always a thing of succession. It follows on from the clinging, which is to say from the un-clinging as well. The clinging is the tie without tie, the un-tying in which originates (and the origin thus remains unassignable and only repeats itself, and detaches itself from itself) the one who is thus neither a subject nor a non-subject, neither mass nor individual, but the incised Narcissus: that which incises him is the mother who expels and retains him, who presents and conceals the father to and from him.

Or more precisely, what follows the un-clinging (which never ceases following itself: it is latency and it is history), rather than the single figure of the Father, is the *triple* social institution around which *Moses* gathers data which

Totem was as yet unable to bring together: the double totemic taboo (that of the mother, and that of the father) and the recognition of equal rights between the members of the kin. *Right* presents the nature of the double taboo: the ineluctable detachment and the impossibility of the absolute Narcissus. This right is not natural; on the contrary, it conveys the broaching of narcissism [*l'entame du narcissisme*]. More precisely, it *is* itself (right with no other content than its form of right) the tracing of this opening [*entame*], the incision [*l'incision*] which *cuts out the narcissus* in every sense of the expression: it detaches it and it cuts it off. Through a sort of 'double bind', it forces and forbids him to-be-subject. This happens in the mother's withdrawal of love, it draws the line of the withdrawal [*cela forme le trait du retrait*].

This right is not a human right, for man does not pre-exist it. It is even less an individual right, for it traces itself out only from the withdrawal of the Other. It is, says Freud, the paternal right, provided we henceforth understand that the Father can only be the unnameable, unpresentable truth of the Mother. The truth, consequently, of love which withdraws, of love which *is* this face always withdrawing,[45] a relation without relation (a relation of non-relation).

26   Panic takes place in the withdrawal of this birth. As dissolution of the Political, it reveals the absence, and more than the absence, of the Pan-Father. One can then reconstitute the Political, the cathartic and reappropriative simulation of the loss of Narcissus. Or else, since we first started by defining Religion: the Political is the will to the complete appropriation of this very simulation; the becoming-profane of religion, it presupposes that the Subject is given right here (and not in heaven): man endowed with speech and with a moral sense which Aristotle posits in his *Politics*. The *political animal* here sacrifices itself to its own image.

But one can also – it does happen, even if it has no name – substitute for the sacrifice the sacro-factio which Freud talks about in *Moses*: the keeping back, in reserve, in retreat from precisely *that* [*ça*] which it has been necessary to renounce, or from *that* which refused to keep you to in its bosom. There is sacrifice as mimicry of the Narcissus and sacrifice as its *secret*. There is the *hierarchic* sacrifice, and the sacrifice of love.

We will not say, however, that there is the aesthetic sacrifice and the ethical sacrifice. It would be no more justified, cutting through crudely from now on in Freud and in metaphysics, to oppose simply (Greek) tragedy to (Jewish) ethics, than it would be to separate right from the political. For a right 'free' from every politics converts into essence or into nature ('man', 'individual', 'subject') anyone whom right cuts out, and basically supposes that the problem of its sociality is resolved. If one can discern its rigour at all, the very structure of the *withdrawal* forbids it. Ethics and right do not propose an anti-politics, but a politics of the being-without-propriety. Despite everything, it might fall, beyond Freud, to Marx to have understood it:

> We have seen that man does not lose himself in his object only when the object becomes for him a *human* object or objective man. This is possible only when the object becomes for him a *social* object, he himself for himself a social being, just as society becomes a being for him in this object.[46]

27 There is no question, far from it, of surreptitiously slipping in, in conclusion, a political programme. It is, rather, a question of programming, with the reading of Freud, *another* reading of Marx and of Hegel. These will come in due time. But they will have to be submitted to two conditions imposed by two scholia of our Freudian inquiry:

First, this entire analysis might appear to lead inexorably to laying down the origin of society in the origin of language (in the impossible denomination of the Father). It seems to us that this is not the case, and that it is no coincidence if this origin is mentioned only in passing in *Moses*. No doubt, in the withdrawal of the mother, the birth of the first epic poet which appendix B of *Massenpsychologie* describes is *also* at stake. And no doubt, the fiction of this poet who fictions himself as the hero of the myth of origin (of the killing of the Father) indeed allows Freud to write that, 'the myth, then, is the step by which the individual emerges from group psychology'.[47] But the double process of the recognition of the Other in the dead and in the mother is instituted *before* any such 'disengagement'. The structure of language is a structure, in the strictest sense, of general identification. On the other hand, the process of what makes language possible, the *incisive* process of Freudian identification, is nothing other, as we acknowledged, than a process of *alteration*. If one must speak of myth, we will say that the-being-with-the-Other indeed constitutes the (mutant) *mything par excellence*. In the mythation which the withdrawal imprints on it, there is no doubt that it accedes to language. There is no doubt either that this language institutes power. But the *access* itself, the passage, the mythation, the withdrawal and its secret are never yet either language or power.[48] Which does not mean that another politics would not have to reinscribe them.

Second, if the withdrawal of the face of the mother forms the guilt 'in the face' of which, paradoxically, one *must* stand, this does not mean that one should dispense with every figure and every politics. The withdrawal requires that a figure loom up. In certain respects, to which one would have to be attentive, Hegel's *Philosophy of Right*, far from satisfying itself in the Totality-State, enunciates the necessity of this tracing, a de-limitation of power and of its (re)presentation. Its condition might be the following, as simple as it is formidably demanding: that no Figure, no Power be what they cannot be, namely the exhibition of the face itself (neither Leader, nor Nation, nor Fatherland); but, rather, that a figure be drawn and be determined through the withdrawal. Not a face of love, but its contour which withdraws and re-draws itself from the withdrawal. The withdrawal of panic.

28 *Retrait de la panique*, the withdrawal of Panic: another politics alone can confront the Political. The most peculiar thing about Freud's 'lesson' is probably that it evades any construction of a political model, and thus declares that no mythation occurs through a Model, but only through an incision. If, on the one hand, Freud irresistibly reconstitutes the instance of the archetypical Power, he also makes it tip over onto its limit. On the other hand, Freud does not erect the model of an individual freedom, of a pure Ethics purely confronted with Power. In fact he lets us – this is the end of *Moses* – interrogate the difficult 'identity' of a 'people'. Which should not be a purely theoretical task, but one which implies a practice – itself a practice of the limit, neither psychoanalytic, nor political, nor moral, nor aesthetic. But all at once, at once wholly otherwise. There where it [*ça*] withdraws, it [*ça*] ought to happen to us.

Translated by Céline Surprenant

31

2

The Free Voice of Man

Jean-Luc Nancy

Among many other possibilities, I could kick off with a statement in which a motif can be heard or understood as self-evident, that is, as things in general are understood, a motif that today makes itself heard at the heart of the latent question or open crisis of the 'ends of man'. Partly by chance, I will take up this statement, for example, from Henri Birault's recent book, *Heidegger and the Experience of Thinking*. Birault writes: 'What indicates the distress of our world is the reiterated appeal [*l'appel*] to an ethics which might come to exorcise it.'[1]

This is the easiest thing in the world to understand and, moreover, directly or indirectly, we have already heard it many times since the beginning of this colloquium. And yet, it needs to be understood in at least two different ways. Either our distress comes from the lack of an ethics, and manifests itself by appealing to the ethics it lacks (in fact, this is a common conclusion today, yet I would not dare say without further qualifications that it is one that has been *thought* through). Or else – and this is the more decisive and problematic reading – the appeal to an ethics or the demand for an ethics as such, is *itself* a manifestation of distress; to require an ethics or, at any rate, some ethical dimension is a sign of distress, and of total distress, a distress that does not even know what it lacks. Already, this can be understood less clearly. It is also what makes it worth pausing here.

If the appeal to ethics is a distress call [*un appel de détresse*] in the sense that, instead of demanding what we might truly be said to be lacking, it transforms distress itself into the object of its demand, then this is because such an appeal is unaware of the fact that, in this statement, the ethical as such is a part of what is interpreted there as 'the distress of our world', and which is clearly nothing

32

other than the modern destiny of the West. Or, in Heideggerian terms which I am invoking somewhat hastily and simply by way of a preliminary approximation, the history of the completion of metaphysics. Now, still staying with Heidegger, 'ethics', along with 'logic' and 'physics', appears only within philosophy, whose history and end are metaphysical. To appeal to an ethics is to remain within the closure of this end. It is not even to suspect the possibility, and still less the possible necessity of challenging this closure. It is, therefore, not even to wonder where something like ethics comes from, and whether there might not be a case for questioning, indeed whether one might not *have to* question (and I shall come to this question of obligation, to the *one has to* [on doit],[2] which is inseparable, precisely, from the very idea of an ethics) the status of what, prior to the 'realm of ethics', might, on the basis of a non-ethical reserve, withdrawal [recul] or drawing back, 'subsequently authorise all ethical law in general'. These last words are, this time, a quotation from Derrida.[3]

We could not be said to have moved back to some place prior to ethics; we would be incapable of taking even the smallest step in the direction of what alone could authorise, after the event, an appeal to ethics. Therein, it might be said, lies our distress and the bankruptcy of our human ends.

But, after all, what do we know about it? How can we know if we lack any such resource, anterior to ethics and capable of reopening its realm to us; how can we, if we measure our distress by the yardstick of an already ethical discourse, when what ought to be at issue is a *quite other* discourse? Might we not already be in touch with this resource, without realising it? And how can we *know* this if, along with ethical discourse and logical discourse, the discourse of knowledge also belongs to our distress? How can we know whether a future ethics beyond ethics has not already, here and now, arrived early, in a guise that is still misunderstood? Or, to put it somewhat provocatively, how to know whether the realm of ends is not already given to us, beyond its end?

If these questions are not, in principle, unacceptable, and if, moreover, what we are scrutinising, here and now, is the thought of writing – if we are questioning Derrida – there are two sorts of demand, or two forms of appeal that we should discard from the outset:

- the demand that the thought of writing, which is also to say, the general problematic of the *proper*, should produce or engender 'an ethics', something which would *properly* be an ethics;

33

● and the demand that such an ethics be produced as the *practice* of a theory (however one takes this genitive: as having the value of an application, generation, conversion, transposition, realisation, etc.).

These demands are impossible; not because there can be absolutely no question of an ethics under the heading of the thought of writing – we simply do not know – but because indeed we must keep [*garder*] the possibility that this thought already thinks something on the subject of ethics, without knowing it, but wholly otherwise.

We know that Heidegger was once asked the question: 'When will you write an ethics?' – and it is basically the essence of his response that I was recalling a moment ago. Now imagine, simply by way of opening and over and above Heidegger's response, what Derrida might do if we asked him the same question. Let us imagine that he might answer: Write an ethics? But what does it mean *to write* the law? Is it a matter of copying out its pure and transcendent utterance, or is it rather in writing that the law might be said to trace itself? Could writing legislate? And if so, how?

This is precisely what we do not *know*. And this knowledge, as such, is also absent from Derrida's texts. And yet, despite everything, we *should* have some idea about it. Whatever our reservations concerning the nature and modality of such a knowledge, *we should* 'know' how things stand with our ethical non-knowledge. At the very least, it is necessary *to be finished* with the demand for the production of an ethics, with the demand of distress. *It is necessary* truly to be done with it: this '*Il faut*', this 'It is necessary', is unjustifiable, it anticipates everything that it would be necessary 'to know'. But there is no getting around it. (And this is basically the '*Il faut*', the 'It is necessary' of this colloquium.)

How, then, can we exercise, at least to begin with, this '*il faut*', this 'it is necessary'? Let us move and take a step backwards, and play the game of this obligation which befalls us. Let us practise the ethics of the demand for an ethics, let us play at distress, and demand to know – that is to say, let us obey the traditional philosophical obligation of asking the question of obligation [*devoir*]. Let us ask Derrida, then, without further ado[4] (it will already have the form of a trial, and the form of a requirement to appear in court; but, at the same time, there is no tribunal, no law as yet): What is your ethics? What is the evaluative competence and the axiological end of your thought? What do you obey? What is your obligation?

(We will understand shortly that this question is perhaps less crude than at first it appears, once we have the chance to hear it as the question posed by Derrida's *own* conscience, as the inner voice of a subject supposed to be the author of the thought of writing. We will then see how much it changes.)

For the moment, let us make do with this: Derrida has at least once given an explicit, and *philosophical*, response to this question of obligation or duty (because, for the moment, it goes without saying that the moral, political, etc., choices of Derrida the man are not at issue; it is not a matter of the contingences or the distress of his behaviour).

Before taking up this response, in its own place, I should put to one side all the places in relation to which one might be tempted to ask this question. By this I mean, all those places where Derrida's discourse, no doubt like any philosophical discourse, sets itself in motion – so to speak – on the authority of an '*Il faut*', of an 'It is necessary', of a supra-, para-, or infra-logical obligation. All the places, if you like, where Derrida declares, in sum, that *it is necessary* to think writing, or rather, that *it is necessary* to think (and act) according to the thought of writing. We cannot, by definition, question this non-discursive obligation of discourse, directly present and modalised in each and every discourse (and, of course, not merely in that of Derrida), so long as we cannot even establish an *obligation* of conducting such a questioning.

Must one interrogate the '*Il faut*', the 'one must' or the 'it is necessary'? This is the general form of the difficulty. Let us pause a moment upon its circle, so as to be better placed to grasp what I call the statement, by Derrida, of his philosophical duty.

A non-discursive obligation can clearly be read, for example, in a passage such as this one:

> Deconstruction cannot limit itself or proceed immediately to a neutralisa-tion: *it must* {my emphasis}, by a double gesture, a double science, a double writing, practise an *overturning* of the classical opposition and a general *displacement* of the system. It is on this condition alone that deconstruction can give itself the means of *intervening* in the field of the oppositions it criticises and which is also a field of non-discursive forces.[5]

This passage needs no commentary: there is indeed here an extra-discursive duty, with a view to an extra-discursive practice. A whole ethics is implied here. Equally, and to take just one other example, in the following passage, where a *practical* teleonomy the work of writing imposes and affirms itself – in a word, imperatively:

> In order effectively and practically to transform that which one decries (tympanises) *will it be necessary* {my emphasis} to be still understood within it, and henceforth to submit oneself to the law of the internal hammer?[6]

We must now give up summoning this entire axiology or axionomy to appear before us as though before a tribunal, because this gesture of a summons would, for the moment, be no different from that required by any philosophical discourse. Because philosophical discourse also, if not primarily, always consists precisely in determining its obligation by itself, in producing the knowledge of its *end*, and thus the *theory* of its *duty*. Consequently, Derrida has had to (this time, by a logical necessity, which would be the necessity of what he himself calls 'deconstruction') exhibit the *reverse side* of this self-legitimation and self-obligation. He does this when he writes later on in the text just cited:

> Certainly, one will never *prove* {my emphasis} *philosophically* that *one must* {Derrida's emphasis} transform a given situation and proceed to an effective deconstruction in order to leave irreversible traces.[7]

Certainly, one will never *prove*: this certitude, here, anticipates the general end of the deconstructive operation. There is an '*Il faut*', a 'One must', and one must obey it, but it is certain that it will not be proven ('philosophically' – but is not the expression redundant in this context?). Indeed, philosophy will not be able to provide the *knowledge* of a *duty* in order to put an end to its knowledge.

Certainly, we will say with Derrida, and *yet*, we can also add with him – and I am still quoting, now from elsewhere (running texts together, but respecting their deep continuity as a single discourse, which I cannot take the time to explicate):

> It must indeed be understood in this way, but also differently: differently, that is, in the openness of an unheard-of question opening neither onto knowledge nor onto a non-knowledge understood as a future knowledge.[8]

In short, this proposition – whose entire context, in its very general import, would be citable here – still superimposes an '*Il faut*', an 'It is necessary', on all our '*Il faut*'s, on all our 'It is necessary's. It is necessary, in the broadest generality, to hear doubly. Therefore, it is necessary, *at the one and the same time*, to understand both the impossibility of going behind the back of the philosophical *and* non-philosophical (or post-philosophical) *'Il faut'*; *and*, at least so as not to set up this non-knowledge as being knowledge-to-come, to understand the unexpected possibility that philosophy – in actual fact, philosophy between itself and its outside – certainly does not *prove*, but rather 'shows' itself having to (and having had to, and still having to) deconstruct itself.

(Furthermore, this possibility is open from the moment that one can also show – and this is what, since Heidegger, shows itself, which is to say, deconstructs itself – that, in reality, philosophy *cannot* philosophically prove its own necessity any longer. Philosophy cannot do this without, like Hegel – in whom this problematic reaches its peak, going back either to the 'empty sign' of the *Logic*, or to the arbitrary decision of a 'subject' at the beginning of the *Encyclopedia*: that is, to two forms of disturbance within the *very foundation* of self-legitimation.)

It is therefore possible that in the 'opening of an unheard-of question' there comes to be lodged a singular and un-reasonable necessity without reason, a demonstration without proof, an *'Il faut'*, an 'It is necessary', which *it is not necessary* to legitimate in discourse; a *duty*, consequently, whose status is perfectly ambiguous or indecisive, theoretical or moral, but just as easily neither theoretical nor moral. This would be a duty which, whilst still remaining a duty, would *decidedly* (there would be nothing undecidable here) turn aside from the philosophical duty that philosophy has always deduced or wanted to deduce from theoretical reasons – and, even better, a duty which, while remaining a duty, would decidely turn aside *from* philosophical duty, that is to say, from this obligation and from this end that philosophy always gives itself on the basis of the Aristotelian model: namely, *sophia* as supreme *praxis* of *theōria*, or *theōria* as the very *praxis* of *sophia*. Thus we will not produce this 'discarded' duty philo-*sophically*. But it is not impossible that it might come to 'demonstrate' itself – that is to say, perhaps, to impose itself.

Now, Derrida will have responded at least once to the question of duty. He has given a *response* in every sense of the term, and that is to say not only has he employed the discourse of duty, but he has pledged his *responsibility* to it – at the beginning of 'Violence and Metaphysics'.

This text opens with the impossibility of responding to the questions that philosophy addresses to itself at its end and from the perspective of its end. I am quoting this text, picking out sentences here and there:

37

That philosophy should have died yesterday . . . or that it should have always lived in and through the knowledge of its mortality . . . ; that it died *one day* . . . or that it should have always lived in its death throes . . . ; that beyond the death or this mortality of philosophy, perhaps even thanks to them, thought should have a future . . . ; more strangely still, that the future itself in this way should have a future, these are questions which have no possible answers. {And, a bit further on} . . . Perhaps these questions are not even *philosophical*, perhaps they no longer *belong to philosophy*.[9]

This impossibility of response either *at* or *to* the end of philosophy, and to the question of its end or *ends*, is evidently tied by structure and by nature to the impossibility of proving that the end or ends of philosophy *are necessary*. And it is here, precisely, that duty emerges. The text continues:

'Nevertheless, these questions should . . . ' (This '*should*', this apparently prudent, conditional or hypothetical duty, upon whose unjustified irruption and decision the entirety of what follows in fact rests, will swiftly reveal itself to be categorical. It will manifest its decision as the absolute duty of deciding in favour of the question without answer, in favour of, if one can say this, or with a view to, again if one can say this, the ends of philosophy.)

Nevertheless, these questions should be the only questions today capable of founding the community of those who, within the world at large, are still called philosophers.

A community which, a little further on, is to be found referred to thus:

A community of decision, of initiative, of absolute initiality, but also a threatened community, in which the question has not yet found the language that it has decided to seek . . . A community of the question about the possibility of the question. This is very little – almost nothing – but within it, today, an unbreachable dignity and duty of decision are sheltered and encapsulated. An unbreachable responsibility.[10]

There is, therefore, a duty – or, if you like, a duty is decided upon; a *final* duty in every sense of the term, the duty of the question, of maintaining the question of the ends or of the questions of the end of philosophy. Such is the answer given.

(Let us dispose in passing, and in parentheses, of one objection which would point to the date of this text – 1964 – and which would want to engage us in the problematic of the 'young' or the 'early' Derrida. This type of simple perspective would be no more relevant here than elsewhere. And let us simply note that, collected in 1967 in *Writing and Difference*, this text is thus *also* contemporary with *Of Grammatology* and *Speech and Phenomena*.)

One might be tempted quickly to submit this response and this duty to a classic grid of interpretation: the duty in question would be to philosophise in and about the end of philosophy; in other words, the supreme – both pre- and post-ethical – ethics would be that of the act of thinking, understood in this case as an infinite 'questioning'. But even the Heideggerian version of this schema (which would be basically still that of Aristotle, and of *theōria* as *praxis*), the version that establishes thinking as supreme acting or doing, and gives to the thinker the sole duty of thinking, even this version does not seem able – at least according to its most simple letter – to be exactly reaffirmed here. At any rate, not entirely. (Which does not prevent Aristotle and Heidegger being taken up, repeated, displaced here.) 'Questioning' does not, by itself, make for an ethics of thought, because here the question is itself in question. Thus, the obligation is not to unravel an infinite number of successive questions, which would be assured of their non-response as a formidable absolute response to come (or never to come, which amounts to the same thing). The obligation is, more simply, more modestly, one of *maintaining* [*garder*] the *question*, as a question. This is made clear by what follows:

> an injunction is announced: the question must be maintained. As a question. The freedom *of the question* (double genitive) must be stated and sheltered.[11]

More radically, this imperative is determined not as being *one* ethical commandment among others, but as *the* commandment prior to any conception of the ethical whatsoever. Derrida writes:

> If this commandment has an ethical meaning, it is not in that it belongs to the *realm* of ethics, but in that it – subsequently – authorises all ethical law in general. There is no stated law, no commandment, which is not addressed to a freedom of speech. There is therefore neither law nor commandment which does not confirm and *enclose* – that is, does not dissimulate by presupposing it – the possibility of the question.[12]

The commandment – and the beginning, the *archie* – of ethics has meaning only in addressing a freedom and, consequently, only has meaning in not

39

responding, in not summoning meaning and value but, on the contrary, in opening, in reopening the question – precisely the question of the end or ends of meaning.

In this response – in this response which responds by way of the question – it was therefore a question of a duty and a freedom, of duty and freedom as question, and of the opening or pre-opening of ethics – at the same time, note, only of ethics or its *archie* as the opening or re-opening of philosophy in its end. It was a question, if you like, of an *ethos* of the posthumous inscription of philosophy.

Therefore, if the *maintained* question can precisely only cut short *theōria*, it was not a case of *theōria* as *archē* and as the *telos* of *praxis*. What is important is the reverse side, the first beginning or the end of Aristotelian ethics, and doubtless also a displacement, a continuation of the Heideggerian motif of thought as doing or as acting. Philosophy must maintain itself in losing itself. But what might seem to be an economic calculation – and which, indeed, will always necessarily and inevitably be so, in Derrida's discourse as in anyone else's – overflows its own borders once again: for, in maintaining the question, it is a question of maintaining the possibility that philosophy is no more. Philosophy must maintain its end, it must protect its being-finite in the future of the question.

What is at least revealed here – doubling, so to speak, the economy that always maintains philosophy through *Aufheben* – is that if there is a duty bound to philosophy, and consequently an originary condition of ethics, this can only be in and through the *end* of philosophy. Duty belongs, in effect, to the structure of finitude. Heidegger has shown this in the *Kantbuch*:

A being that is fundamentally interested in a duty knows itself in a not-yet-having fulfilled, so that what indeed it should do becomes questionable for it. This not-yet of a fulfilling, which is itself still undetermined, gives us a clue that a being whose innermost interest is with a duty is fundamentally finite.[13]

The duty to maintain the question is not an ethics *of* finitude or of finite philosophy. Rather it indicates, in a still enigmatic pronouncement, finitude as ethical, as the opening of ethics – at the very point at which (that is to say, here, with us, with Derrida, in philosophy) ethics has only ever been the *properly infinite* teleonomy of a merely provisionally finite being, albeit one promised to the appropriation of its end. Finitude, on the contrary, is the depropriation of the end. Hence duty might thus be said to indicate the opening – and the question – of the proper *ethos* of the non-proper. The opening and the question of an *unheimlich ethos*, that is to say, a *contradictio in adjecto*, if *ethos* means (whatever the etymological debate about it) *Heim*, a home, familiar place: the animal's lair, man's cavern or cave.

Of course, the reconstitution and the sublation, the reappropriation of metaphysical *ethos* are always possible here. And as always, they are even guaranteed. *Philo-sophia* is always at work, just like the *Trieb* of reason in Kant, and the *ethos* of Derrida is also inevitably, philo-sophical.

However, *one must* maintain the question. Which means, henceforth: one must interrogate the duty of the question as to its propriety and its impropriety. The thought of writing has not written the ethics of this duty. It has let us know nothing beyond the response that we have just read. But could it be said, for all that, to have maintained responsibility intact? This is what we must know – since, naïvely, we still demand to know. But also, since we can make this demand a little less naïvely, insofar as Derrida himself, later on in 'Violence and Metaphysics', will have defended the possibility and necessity of a theoretical consideration of ethics. Indeed, the risk here, analogous to the one Derrida locates in Levinas, would be to claim an absolute autonomy for ethics in relation to the theoretical, to put it out of the reach of theoretical closure. Such autonomy could only confer upon it, precisely, an absolutely closing function, an archeo-teleo-logical and, *finally,* philo-sophical one. Maintaining the question cannot be reduced to exalting the mystery of a transphilosophical *Unheimlichkeit*. On the contrary. One has to make the question more acute, and with it both philosophy and discourse. Thus Derrida writes:

> there are two meanings of the theoretical: the current meaning, the particular target of Levinas's protest {i.e. – let me remind you, the protest against the theoretical subordination of ethics}; and the more hidden sense in which *appearance* in general is maintained, including the appearance of the non-theoretical (in the first sense) in particular . . . I know {and here this knowledge is for Derrida that of Husserl and of phenomenology} the meaning of the non-theoretical as such (for example, ethics), with a theoretical knowledge (in general), and I respect it as such, as what it is, in its meaning. I have regard for recognising that which cannot be regarded as a thing, as a facade, as a theorem. I have regard for the face itself.[14]

One must try to attain this sort of regard or allow it to approach: a knowledge regarding duty, a knowledge of which Derrida was thus once able to write, and surely not by chance in the first person, 'I know . . .'

Now, the fact is that this regard, this *respectful theōrein* of the *ethos* (what might be opened up here, in accordance with an indispensable Kantian resource, is a whole problematic of *respect* as respect *of theōria for praxis*; this will have to wait until some other time) – the fact is, then, that this regard could not have been attained with Husserl. For it will have been attained, precisely, in the deconstruction of theory or of phenomenological theoreticism. Perhaps this is why Derrida himself will not have *seen* this regard, or in any case will not have made it visible or discoursed upon it – or why his discourse will have lost sight of what, nonetheless, it was looking at.

How might a regard for ethics, and the responsibility of duty, be said to have been maintained in the opening of the question of writing? Let us see.

I will take only one text, but it is perhaps the 'founding' or matrix text: namely, *Speech and Phenomena*. And I will take only one, limited episode from it. I can do no more here. But I again start, in this text, from the moment at which the inscription of writing is definitely decided, in the opening and the difference of pure voice.

By force of necessity, I am going to go quite quickly, presupposing this text to be fresh in your minds.

The penultimate chapter of *Speech and Phenomena*, entitled 'The Voice that Keeps Silence', sets out to carry the analysis of the Husserlian position of the pure sphere of pure sense in 'inner life' to its conclusion.[15] In order to distinguish this sphere, this pure core of sense [*sens*] and meaning [*vouloir dire*], Husserl proceeds to the reduction of the two determinations of the sign whose examination, since the beginning of the book, is centrally at issue in Derrida's reading: indication and expression [*Anzeichen* and *Ausdruck* – EN]. It is by excluding each of these from the monologue of 'inner life' that Husserl establishes the regime of pre-expressive pure self-presence, or the regime of signification reduced to the self-presence of the intention to signify.

In order to do this, Husserl submits to reduction various examples of inner monologue, which he therefore has to show as being 'false language', essentially reducible to the silence of a pure voice. For example: 'You have acted badly, you can't go on like that.' This is, therefore, an example of a 'voice of conscience'[16] – and we can immediately add the remark (which is as silently present in Husserl's text as it is Derrida's) that nothing has ever been metaphorised so much by the voice as moral consciousness, unless things are the other way round. The being-conscious-of-self of consciousness, *Bewußtsein*, seems to show itself most inwardly, most intimately, or most originally as

42

moral conscience, as a *Gewissen* (which would tie in with one of Freud's analyses in *Totem and Taboo*). The voice of (moral) consciousness is thus declared to be the pure originarity of a pure self-presence prior to language and signification.

Derrida's reading gives itself the task of showing that, in reality, neither expression nor indication can be absent here; that they are interwoven with each other also in the supposedly pure sense; and that this interweaving affects – so to speak – the pure auto-affection of the voice of the self-present subject. I will not dwell on this familiar demonstration, the matrix for the thought – or question – of writing.

Of course, in so doing Derrida will have in passing noted the specific modalities of the statement (the *false* statement, according to Husserl, since for him it is a false language) which provides Husserl with his examples: he addresses himself to a *you*, to the 'ego' or 'self' as 'you', and he is *practical*. The first moment of the examination, therefore, consists in showing that:

1 The examples of inner discourse are chosen from *practice* in order to show, first of all, that it is a non-indicative discourse (it apprehends nothing), and then that this is a false language because the axiological is, *de jure*, always reducible to 'its logico-theoretical core'.[17] This last aspect, moreover, finds itself developed by Derrida in the same year, in 'Form and Meaning', where the convertibility (in Husserl) of 'affective or axiological experience . . . into an experience in the form of being-present', 'the desired as being-desired', etc., is underlined.[18] In this way – and according to a movement which, in sum, doubles and inverts the theoretical respect evoked in 'Violence and Metaphysics' – practice, for Husserl, 'offers itself without reserve to the logical discourse watched over by predicative form, that is, by the present indicative of the verb to be'.[19] For Husserl, inner discourse, the practical mode of which seems to furnish the type, is false as language; it is only true as or in the silence of a logicity, in the core of pure sense anterior or exterior to practical factuality as such.

2 The second person, the 'you' of this discourse, participates in its falsity, because this 'you' can only be fictive – and for Husserl, Derrida writes here, 'fiction is only fiction'.[20] Relieved of this fiction, inner life and its silence must offer themselves without *alter ego*, and even without *ego*, or according to an *ego* of a purity such that its pure voice *hears itself* prior to the 'I' of language, which is only ever a simple '"occasional" expression'.

43

In a word, and to sum up, the specific facticity — acknowledged elsewhere — of praxis and the other (the double face, quite definitely, of one same and complex facticity) is reduced as *ficticity* within the problematic of pure sense and of its 'originary generation'. The effacement or exclusion of this ficticity releases, prior to the sign, the pure origin, the voice of the 'absolute silence of self-relation'[21]

As you know, Derrida goes on to show that this originarity cannot but be 'contaminated by what it seems to exclude'.[22] The essential move in this analysis is the critical insistence brought to bear upon the impossibility, under-lined by Husserl, of naming the *present* of originary generation other than by metaphor — the silent present of the voice. This present, the source of time and time of the source, implying the relation to a 'new' present which is another and yet the same *now*, can only implicate its sameness in a 'non-identity to itself'. 'It is always already a trace', and its metaphorisation 'can only be originary'.[23] This originarity, different from itself and deferring itself from itself, is what Derrida calls 'archi-writing'. Archi-writing forms the originary interweaving of indication, expression and meaning — or again their originary supplementarity, which can also therefore be called originary ficticity or fictionality. 'Writing' fissures and fictions the silence of the voice which is supposed not to say to itself 'You have acted badly', but merely — at least, insofar as one can say this — hear itself as the theorem of a being-having-acted-badly — assuming that 'badly'[24] would here still be determinable *purely*, that is to say, assuming that the voice which keeps silence could pronounce something other than judgements of existence.

It is here, I believe, that it is *necessary* — for me, in any case — to take from the conclusions of *Speech and Phenomena* (in which, admittedly, everything I have just put forward remains more or less implicit) a point of departure, or to start out from them once again. This will be done by reinvesting in these conclu-sions, as I have outlined them, the initial givens — which are *practical* — of Husserl's example, and by trying to regain from this something like the regard for ethics to which claim is laid elsewhere.

Indeed, a simple consequence seems inescapable: just as Husserl's example was not chosen by chance, so it is not by chance that ficticity goes hand in glove with the double motif of praxity and alterity (understood in the sense of the *Other*), that is to say, with that which must surely reassemble this duality in the general motif or question of *ethicity*.

This would mean, in a simple but decisive way, that ethicity – and I do not mean ethics, at least not directly – is what may be said to be at stake in archi-writing. If 'You have acted badly' cannot be reduced to a pure silent predication, if this sign 'contaminates' sense, *it is because the 'you' and the 'badly' are originally involved in the origin of sense.*

Such ethicity, let me add immediately, would have nothing to do with a morality of writing, nor with a writing of morality in the sense of the question: 'Will you write an ethics?' It could be said to join together, implicate or interweave writing, *praxis*, the Other [*l'écriture, la* praxis, *l'autrui*] – or rather, because nothing here allows itself to be substantiated nor predicated as a *being*, it would interweave writing, *praxis*, Other [*écriture,* praxis, *autrui*]. And this interweaving of irreducible instances (an interweaving to which, for many reasons which are impossible to develop here, I would like to give the theological name of the 'communication of idioms'), this originary communication between discursive persons, as well as between discursive and non-discursive ones, would furnish the – atopical but not utopian – place of a non-theoretical, non-reductive regard for the *ethos* or for *ethos* – or again, and instead, the place of a regard *for the sake of ethos.*

This hypothesis, as you can see, seems to be deduced rigorously. Can it be confirmed? Can one validate, justify and assume this *praxical* consequence of what, already, from the very first thought of writing, was no longer simply theoretical?

Can one introduce or interweave into this situation something of the philosophical knowledge of ethics? Can one do this? But, much more importantly, *ought* one not to do it, in accordance with another necessity, another cardinal '*Il faut*', another 'It is necessary' of the thought of writing, one which can, for example, be formulated in the following way: 'In order to exceed metaphysics it is necessary that a trace be inscribed in the metaphysical text'?[25] Thus it is necessary, in order for an exceeding ethicity to be seen within writing, that this excess leave a trace in philosophy; and that, as a result, it become possible *to regard* philosophical ethics in another way, that it become possible to have a *regard* for that which has perhaps already *practically* exceeded the metaphysical *ethos* in its ethics.

To put it another way: can one (should one?), on the basis of the hypothesis just advanced, repeat the metaphysical ground of ethics; *that is to say in fact the ethical ground – or the Abgrund – of metaphysics*; or again, to go straight to what is essential, Kant, at least for the reason that in Kantian thought it is unknowable (non-theorisable) *freedom* which is expressly 'the keystone of the whole archi-tecture of the system of pure reason'?[26]

Can one repeat, therefore, on the basis of this thinking of writing, what Heidegger called the Kantian institution; which means, can one repeat Hei-degger's repetition of this institution – but, in doing so, shift it onto a register which it hardly indicated?[27]

Can one (must one?) replay anew the thought of writing within an ethical repetition of Heidegger's repetition of Kant?

All these questions clearly imply a '*Faut-il?*', an 'Is it necessary?', which might well be nothing other than the '*Il faut*' or the 'It is necessary' of deconstruction. And which, furthermore, might well secretly depend on a 'You must, therefore you can'. Whatever the answer to this question, all I am able to do today is to uncover a single trail through what is, by rights, a quite vast programme.

If it is a question of a duty or obligation – if it is a question, as we understand it at present, of maintaining the question of duty – it is a question of finitude, as we have seen. Now *Speech and Phenomena* shows that *différance* (of writing, or as writing) is finite: 'Infinite *différance* is itself finite'.[28] And that is to say, the infinity of the deferring of presence *ipso facto* constitutes (if this word applies here) finitude; that is to say, it excludes the dialectical recourse of finity (which is not finitude) to infinity, and opens the without-recourse of an *end* bereft of the *telos* of presence. Difference, which *is* nothing, *is* therefore finitude, which in its turn *is* nothing (this 'nothing', this thing, *res*, would have to be analysed; but perhaps what would be at issue in any such analysis would be duty).

Thus, and by a highly simple syllogistic path: if duty belongs essentially to finitude, then duty essentially submits itself – so to speak – to difference. Which means, on the one hand, and most obviously, that the *telos* of duty (the being of having-to-be in general) differs or defers itself, *but also*, and on the other hand, that difference brings forth duty by itself. Or that, like nobility, *différance* obliges, that *différance* (if it has anything) has the structure and nature of an obligation, prescription, and injunction, even if these terms can no longer be understood in accordance with its ethico-metaphysical concept. Difference obliges differently.

The imperative would thus be here. And here, even before – so to speak – its being Kant's imperative in all its determinations (but Kant is, at the same time, the only one to have displayed the imperative philosophically, in which, moreover, he has until now been followed only by Nietzsche), the imperative, as formulated by Heidegger, has given rise to an explication of the relation of duty to finitude: 'the concept of the imperative as such shows the inner relation to a finite being . . . This transcendence too still remains within the sphere of finitude.'[29]

Against the background of this determination by finitude and with respect to finitude, the imperative quickly displays several remarkable features. Even in its most formal structure, and its greatest proximity to language, the imperative *obliges* us to a series of observations which, all in all, precisely come to reverse Husserl's determinations of the *voice*, or else echo them.

Admittedly, nothing resembles a voice, *the* voice of conscience, the voice of a *Bewußtsein* as *Gewissen*, more than this imperative which, for Kant, is to be found everywhere and in everyone, and which is heard prior to all moral choices. Although Kant does not always speak of it as a voice (at any rate, not in an emphatic way in the major texts on practical reason), one can say that 'the moral law within me' is *the* absolute voice of absolute consciousness. It is perfectly self-evident. The imperative is the proximity to self where reason hears itself. With the result that Kant was able to describe freedom – which, by definition, is bound up with the imperative – as '*Selbstbewußtsein a priori*'.[30] The imperative is also the absolute proximity of reason, in man, to its end, to himself as its own end. It is the voice of the freedom of man, or the voice of a free man, essentially and properly free. The categorical imperative is perhaps the pure and matricial *phōnē* in which, with Kant, the whole of metaphysics is regenerated. But having, moreover, no other *telos* – in the 'universal law of nature' – than that of *theory* itself.

However, the self-evidence of this claim is immediately put into question; not by an external circumstance, but by itself, or by the appearing – which is the whole of its being – of freedom within the imperative. Indeed, this voice does not let itself be reduced to the voice which keeps silence – still less than Husserl's example of 'You have acted badly'. If this voice is indeed the free voice of man, it does not convert itself into the voice of free man, the voice of the self-present subject in the essence and the sense of his freedom. Therefore, Kantian freedom does not found a being, and does not assure a presence – it *bestimmt*, determines and destines man, which is something completely different. This is why it is inconceivable. And its voice, the imperative, operates conversely to the Husserlian reduction. The command '*Act*' does not allow itself to be transformed into 'You are having-to-act' [*Tu es devant-agir*]. The man who hears this voice, perhaps without listening to him-*self* in it, is not a being-

47

having-to [*un étant-devant*]. His being-ness is not predicated; it is at once admonished, posed, and deposed by the order that it receives. And this order, this '*Act*', is doubtless, in a manner analogous to pure sense in Husserl, neither indicative nor expressive. It is false language if, as Benveniste has shown regarding the imperative in general, it is 'not even uttered', if it bears 'neither temporal mark nor personal reference' – and more generally, still in Benveniste's terms, if it is not a performative, although, as the most recent pragmatics tends to suggest, every utterance is, in some way, also a performative. The imperative is reduced, in Benveniste's terms, to being the bare semanteme employed as jussive form with a specific intonation. The imperative is false language, but this false language is irreducible – and it gives a true commandment.

At the same time, the imperative is irreducible to the logicity of the present indicative, and to the present in general, for it does not even indicate something like a future present. Rather, it ruptures the present of its commandment in an originary manner; by the infinite postponement of the actuality of the act ordered, an actuality or actualisation for which the imperative itself supplies no guarantee, no efficacy, no mastery. It is not subordinated to the full presence of sense, nor to the general relation to the possible object. Not only is it not subordinated to them but, by a singular turn which is something quite different from a reversal, it *orders* the full presence of sense (the 'universal law of nature'), yet without having an objective, or constituting relation with it. With this ultimate, final meaning, it has, says Kant, merely a *typic* relation, the *type* being the analogon of a scheme outside of the domain of the constitution of objects (it is here, and today I note this merely in passing, that a coherent reading of the relations between the schema and practical reason – such as they are left in abeyance in paragraph 30 of Heidegger's *Kantbuch* – ought to begin; I will return to this elsewhere). Thus, the imperative is not commanded by the *archē* of sense, but rather it is the former that *commands* the latter, in another sense, from another *archie*.

Doing nothing except to command sense, the imperative defers it – or, at least inscribes its *différance*. The imperative holds by virtue of its order, and not by virtue of the completion of the sense of this order – or rather, the sense *intended* by this order. But perhaps here the order and its sense become indiscernable.

In the same way – and no doubt this is the same thing – the imperative renders indiscernable the 'indices' of the addresser and the addressee. Indiscernable from one another and for themselves. Reason there speaks to itself, it addresses itself to itself, but it does not hear itself there: it cannot call to account the theory of its freedom. As a result, it separates itself from itself. Regarding Husserl, Derrida had left in reserve a question about the place from whence the 'you' can arise in the monologue: this question would find here, not its response, but its place or its true maintenance. In the imperative, there is an 'I' and a 'you', as rigorously associated as they are dissociated, unmarkable as such, demarcating and remarking one another. It is not even a question of reintroducing an Other into the originary sphere; it is a matter of an alterity or an Other-ness of the *ego* in its egoity and even before any *alter ego*. It is heard and yet it is not heard. It remains as unheard-of in linguistic acoustics as it does in the philosophical acousmatics of sense.

On the register of sense, as on that of the subject, the imperative is only or only makes spacing. The imperative *spaces*. It spaces what it ordains by adjoining; it spaces it in organising it and because it organises it. In the most general way, the *law* spaces itself from itself as *fact*. The imperative is *factum rationis*, it is the non-empirical fact of reason, the fact *of the* non-empirical within reason and, consequently, a fact distanced from its own facticity. It makes spacing on account of man. (Elsewhere, I have proposed the old word *areality* to designate this spacing.[31])

Difference, spacing, and thus writing, would be the law of the law. But this would mean that the law is the essence without essence of writing.

Now, what does the law do? The law binds me to a realm of ends. But it does not bind me to this realm as to the promise of a pure and final advent, nor as to the necessity of a project completing itself in an object and in the appropriation of this object – that is to say in the appropriation of a final and proper being of man according to the law. The law binds me to the law as end: that is to say, at one and the same time to both the *sublime* of human existence, as Kant calls it – therefore to this existence in accordance with the law as incommensurable absolute grandeur (and incommensurable, first of all, with the humanity of the human) – *and* to this sublimity as the difference of man completed according to the law. Kant writes: 'if there must be in general a *final purpose* furnished *a priori* by reason, this can be no other than *man* (every rational being of the world) *under moral laws*.'[32] And he further explains in a note:

I deliberately say: man *under* moral laws. It is not man *in accordance with*

49

moral laws, i.e., a being who behaves himself in conformity with them, who is the final purpose of creation. For by using the latter expression we should be asserting more than we know, viz., that it is within the power of an author of the world to cause man always to behave himself in accordance with moral laws . . . Only of *man under moral laws* can we say, without transgressing the limits of our insight, his being constitutes the final purpose of the world.[33]

Man *under* moral laws: this is man doubly distanced, spaced from man: beyond the human, and on this side of the entelechy of 'Man', whether anthropological or theological.

The imperative ethicity cannot ward off distress – it is powerless, it is without empire – it cannot ward off the distress or the end of man. Rather, it might be said, in a sense, to confirm it. But to confirm it precisely not as *moral* distress. It would confirm the distress of the end as the effacement of man in man – beyond man, on this side of him. That which can efface itself, or better, that which essentially effaces itself (effaces itself from itself and effaces its self) has the property of the trace in general. But this is a property which is not one, it does not constitute an essence. Therefore, one ought not to say that the trace essentially effaces itself, but that it *must* efface itself. And that man *must* efface himself.

Thus, writing would not be absent here – if it can be present anywhere. Derrida wrote in 1967:

Here or there we have discerned writing: a nonsymmetrical division designating on the one hand the closure of the book, and on the other the opening of the text. On the one hand, the theological encyclopaedia and, modelled upon it, the book of man. On the other, a fabric of traces marking the disappearance of an exceeded God or an effaced man.[34]

What we still have to learn from this is that the 'fabric of traces' is not something which is 'discerned' by the acuity of better vision, or with purely theoretical progress, any more than through the fortuitous encounter with a new thought. Here, as elsewhere, thinking obeys what in any case commands it – from nowhere, and anywhere.

The ends of man are written because, in the multiple play of their plural writing, man effaces himself, and because it is imperative for him to efface himself. And this imperative, this effacement are constitutive of his *proper* being-ness, of this being-ness which is not properly a being-being [être-étant: *das seinde-Sein* – EN], but an *unheimlich ethos*. As Heidegger said at Davos:

> I believe that we proceed mistakenly in the interpretation of Kantian ethics if we first orient ourselves towards that to which ethical action conforms and if we see too little of the inner function of the law itself for *Dasein*. We cannot discuss the problem of the finitude of the ethical being if we do not pose the question: What does 'law' [*Gesetz*] mean here, and how is the lawfulness itself constitutive for *Dasein* and for the personality?[35]

What does 'law' mean here? Perhaps what *Gesetz* says (and which I articulate here, without recourse to what Heidegger may have said about it elsewhere): the *posited* being, the *setzen* of *Dasein* as a being de-posed in, through and upon its own trace. In other words, *Dasein* would be being-obliged, its *Da* would not be a there, but would be its summons by an order. Or the *there* would only be the *there* of the being summoned-there by the imperative.

That is, summoned by a given order; given and received. That which would always-already affect auto-affection, and which would, before all else, constitute the receiving-being of receptivity, would itself be the reception of the gift of the order, the reception of the gift of the law. The voice of the law is not self-present: it is inscribed as a receiving. Yet the imperative voice also forms a very singular *present*, which twists the indicative and expressive verbal present upon itself; it forms the present of its gift.

What does the law say? What does this free voice of man say, this voice which is indeed *his own* but also the freed voice *of* man, freed from his entelechy, and yet freeing him? What does this sublime voice say (archi-writing is a sublime voice)?

It only utters the question – of finitude. But more like a *question*. It says that the *maintained* question is an order. Derrida placed the maintainence of the question before ethics. This philosoper, then, perhaps still thought to *hold onto* something by this protection [*garde*]. In truth, he was already *obeying*. He was treating humanity, and philosophy, as an end. He was only doing his duty.

Debate

(Transcribed by Jean-Luc Nancy)

Participants: Jacques Derrida, Luce Guedj, Denis Kambouchner, Sarah Kofman.

GUEDJ asked how one could be guaranteed that the free voice of conscience is not the illusion of the law when one does not make reference to a *text* of the law.

NANCY recognised that the question of the writing of such a text must arise, but that he did not know what it implies. He was only anxious to clarify that his allusion to the third formula of the Kantian imperative does not refer to a 'text' of the 'rights of man'.

But GUEDJ pointed out that she was thinking of the text of Biblical law, already written and which we would have to 'put back into action'.

NANCY objected that he did not see clearly what 'putting back into action' would not also be a 'rewriting'; and that, on the other hand, this text cannot be considered as 'purely Hebrew', but that it is, for us, mixed with the Greek and philosophical tradition.

DERRIDA added that even the law written in Hebrew is not available to the one who knows how to read it: it is available like every order, which is never available. To receive this law orders us to rewrite it in Hebrew, into a language which is still not decipherable.

Then DERRIDA to NANCY: Not to respond now would be *de rigueur*, because you have driven, with a force which is either yours or else that of the sublime law, these questions with which I have struggled, driven them right up to the point where, precisely, I was unable to respond to them. But my keeping quiet would be an inadmissable violence, one which would signify that I had not understood the moment at which you passed into the *you*. This address in the *tu* form

52

[*tutoiement*]^{36} announced that the ethical question has to do with something that one can call the call, demand, order. Along with Beneveniste, you spoke of intonation. It is this which allows the distinguishing of how one and the same phrase is order, call, desire or demand. It is the intonation of the other who calls for the ethical response beyond ethics. I hope to have understood something of your intonation. You also said that I have done my duty (*laughter*). If this was the case, I would be excused, in advance, from a response. But I don't believe anything of the kind. I have tried to discharge or fulfil my obligations by responding to what – I am using your words – in *différance* already implicated the ethical. But at the same time, one never acquits oneself of such a call. For example, I always understand 'you must, therefore you can' as 'you must, therefore you cannot', whatever you do. I recognised in this sign of distress this voice of the other who dictates and whom it is necessary to obey. This is for me the sole imperative. This voice is recognised as coming from the other to the extent that one cannot respond to it, not to the measure of what of the other comes from the other. The very structure of the law obliges its transgression. Which can also be translated into a tragic formulation of distress, as in the irony of a *double bind*. It is when I am destitute and do not know what to do, that I am really faced with the voice of the other.

In order to interrupt this pathos in which you would be guilty of having engaged me, I will take an example of a speech act that obliges one to transgress the law: the order 'do not read me' (which, I think, is implicated in every prescription). The law says 'read me', 'know how to decipher me'. But if one contented oneself with reading, one would not obey. It is necessary to do, and 'do not content yourself with reading me' or 'not reading me' is perhaps the fundamental structure of every prescriptive. But as soon as I have fulfilled the condition for obeying, as soon as I have read this statement, I have transgressed it. The law obliges the one whom it destines to lack destination. In referring to such a figural incarnation of the law in Blanchot, I will say: the law is someone, it is an other. And its *double bind* forms the pathos or the *Stimmung* with which I view these questions. I have rarely felt with as much force as I did, in your formulation, a certain memory of these things for me, but a memory that you guide beyond itself, towards questions which do not belong to it: amongst others, the settling of accounts with Kant. This pathos resounds like the inner hammer, but one which hammers from the outside, from a completely other outside. One more detail: regarding the 1964 text on

Levinas, you were right to say that questions of dates are ridiculous here. Nonetheless, I do say: although I am always concerned with Levinas' questions, I could not write it like that today. I have recently written a text on Levinas which took the form of a dialogue between a masculine voice and a feminine voice.[37] It begins with an '*il aura obligé*', a 'he will have obliged' which is transformed into an '*elle*', a 'she' which one does not know whether it is a woman who is being referred to, God's initials or those of Emmanuel Levinas himself. Why wouldn't I write like I had in 1964? Basically it is the word *question* which I would have changed there. I would displace the accent of the question towards something which would be a call. Rather than it being necessary to maintain a question, it is necessary to have understood a call (or an order, desire or demand).

NANCY: At the end of my paper, I replaced your 'question' from 1964 with the 'order'.

DERRIDA: Yes, you gave questions and responses.

NANCY: I return to the 'you'. In the imperative – 'act' – the 'you' disappeared as such, but it is in the imperative that it is, perhaps, most 'familiar' [*le plus 'tutoyant'*]. This is equally the case in the 'come' of your recent text on Levinas. I deliberately left this text to one side: I left it for us to say 'act' to each other, and I returned a 'come' to you which you have already sent.

KOFMAN: In this text on Levinas, the voice of the injunction is feminine, and it is that of Levinas, and that of a certain name of God. Is the voice of the completely other always for us metaphorically that of a woman?

DERRIDA: I do not mean that the voice of the completely other has a unique meaning. But Levinas, who philosophically assumes – which is very rare – the place of a man, seemed to me, despite everything, to derive sexual difference from a sexual neutrality, and to drift away from woman. A very subtle exclusion, which does not efface woman from his text, but which allows it to be thought that it is the voice of a woman who sends him the entirety of his discourse in which the completely other is a 'he/it' [*il*] and not a 'she/it' [*elle*]. I have not determined the completely other as woman. I have tried to disconcert a certain organisation of Levinas' discourse by opening it up to heckling by a feminine voice that he perhaps risked muffling.

Translated by Richard Stamp

3

In the Name of . . .

Philippe Lacoue-Labarthe

Jacques, I would like to ask you a question.[1] Or rather, I would like *to address* a question to you.

It is an old and an obscure question. Old, because it near enough dates from the time when I happened to read what was, I think, the first text of yours to be published (it was 'Force and Signification', in *Critique*).[2] Obscure because it is not, at the outset, a truly philosophical question. However, it is indeed a question, but I do not know how to define – even if I feel it with an inexplicable precision – what it touches upon: perhaps it has to do with the idiosyncratic or idiomatic part of what you write, a certain climate, a strange aura, a style or a *tone*; also perhaps, but I say this without confidence (it is an impression, nothing more), it has to do with matters of profound, deep choices, tastes, a *habitus* or an *ethos* that are your own, let us say 'proper', but which one senses that you do not really master or calculate, that they are themselves brought about by carrying you along, that they inscribe you and write you when you write – or, which is the same thing, when you speak.

Today, I would like to attempt to elucidate this question. What settles it for me is, first of all, that I obstinately, that is to say passionately, believe in elucidation. I do not make myself clear, but I hear myself say, constantly: clarity is necessary. This must not – and cannot – simply be agreed.

But this is afterwards, because the occasion is here, the moment has come. I am not saying it in view of the singular circumstance of this colloquium or of your presence, here, now – which could, on the contrary, give the illusion that, addressing myself directly to you, I am enjoining or calling out to you; or that

55

even, just about, I would be summoning you to appear and give an explanation. This is not the case at all. Moreover, if you were not there (and nothing assures me, whilst writing this text, that you will be there at the moment when I will deliver it, if I deliver it), it would be just the same, nothing would change. Basically, this address is (still) a letter – through which, still, I persist (or re-offend). It is a letter because what matters, both to my question and – I think – in general, is the second person utterance. But it is a letter to which I am not asking you, in any way, necessarily to respond (it is already, in many ways, a kind of response to your '*Envois*', which are themselves one or many[3]). Despite not really knowing what must be understood by this, I will simply say: considering the situation I am in, I would like for this letter to arrive at its destination in one way or another. Or, at the very least, I would like for it to arrive – whatever the risk that lies in this type of desire.

Moreover, as I know you have already realised (and for a long time), *destination* will be my question. Or at least it is what will remain in question in my question – being probably that which can only remain in question in every question. (Although you know this, I insist on pointing this out so that no one starts to think that this is what I am settling on or fixing, immobilising or maintaining as my 'subject'. In Latin: *destinata*.)

For this, already more or less double, question, I could have started off from one or other of your texts, quite indifferently. However, if I choose to take my point of departure from 'The Ends of Man', this is not simply to play the game of this colloquium, by respecting the theme or by underlining its intentions; in the first place it is because in this text, which is evidently not (since such was not its destination) among the most fundamental of your texts, but whose character, spirited and angry, in places terse, almost brutal, and, in short, absolutely clear, will, up to a point, make my task easier – because in this text, then, three things have kept hold of or struck me.

First: regarding the political, since your preamble is explicitly dedicated to it – and in view of the circumstances: an international colloquium, in the United States, during the Vietnam war, etc.; with regard to the political gesture that you insist on making and to which you speak of having suspended, your participation in this colloquium (and consequently the editing, the delivering and the publication of this text), the fate that you reserve for or the privilege that you accord to the concept – and to the fact – of 'nation'.

I see perfectly clearly, it is true, that, being careful to inscribe this gesture completely within a 'historical and political horizon', which you point out 'would call for a lengthy analysis',[4] you also mention what is of the order of racial conflicts (the assassination of Martin Luther King) or social conflicts (May '68 in France). Still better, I see that you deliberately date your text, but this also in enigmatic fashion, 12 May 1968, it being the eve (this is your final motif) of this demonstration, which, at the time, was itself symbolic, started by workers' organisations, left-wing parties and trade unions (what I myself persist in calling, since November '56, the workers' bureaucracies – but this matters little here) and which, whatever the revolutionary chances of the movements in May, will have in any case sounded the death knell of what, therefore, could still be interpreted and acted as a real social upheaval. But I do not know, deep down, what you thought of it all (I did not know you, and you have never spoken about it); and it only obscures what, in this preamble, comes to the fore, which is the nation (national styles, for example, the question of language, institutional diversity) and this is what, for a long time, has, let us say, 'intrigued' me.

This is not, as one says, a critique. But the account of a 'utopianism', mine, which has cracked quite a bit since the first time I read this text (this was the *destinal* utopianism of the 'final' struggle and of the international achievement of 'humankind'); and also, consequently, the account of a sort of 'realism' that I recognised in you, although your remarks were always very allusive, and whose validity, nonetheless, I *also* recognised; I could not avoid thinking, to take one of your examples, that those who had opened negotiations for peace in Vietnam, in Paris in '68, were – on one side *as* on the other – the same as those against whom I always thought it necessary to fight. And above all, in spite of not being a Marxist, and never having been one (I was, like many others, simply in solidarity, through a provisional ethic or, rather, through obedience to a kind of unspoken ethical commandment, a kind of revolutionary idea, and that is to say a kind of idea of justice), I did not understand that something other than this so very overdetermined concept of the nation was possible; one not accepted by you as self-evident (your text shows that it is nothing of the kind), but as offering you the possibility for one of the most explicit political or ethico-political gestures that you have ever made, in a piece of writing at least.

I did not understand it then, and I'm not sure, even today, that I understand it now. Let us say that it remains, to a not insignificant degree, within the parameters of the question that I would like to articulate here.

Second, and on another level: even if, from the outset, you recall 'that which has always bound the essence of the philosophical to the essence of the political',[5] what struck me in the critical re-opening of the three great critiques or de-limitations of metaphysical humanism was the *extent* of your debate with Heidegger. In the two senses of this term: the place or the importance that you reserve for Heidegger, and the level of profundity at which you locate the adherence of the Heideggerean de-limitation to the anthropism or the anthropocentrism that it de-limits.

I do not want to insist on this now, except to underline the extreme importance that your *Auseinandersetzung* with Heidegger, the only one to have taken place in France, will have had for us ('us' means here: those, roughly of the same generation, that the reading and interpretation of Heidegger has decisively engaged in philosophy). I will return to this shortly. But it is clear, to me in any case, that you represent the only possible *practical study* of Heidegger. That is to say, the only possible practice of philosophy at its limit, insofar as one takes up the wager, as you put it about a year earlier in the same period, that Heidegger's thinking is the most recent of the West's 'great thinkings'.

In which case, however, the question for me remains (and not merely in regard to this text) the fact that, to the best of my knowledge, you have never said anything about the enormous weight nevertheless of the political in this 'philosophy'.

Third and finally: there is in this text – in accordance with a movement which, basically, is not uncommon with you, although, on the other hand, you might say that much of this comes from Heidegger – the relative univocity of your reading, of your critique.

And even if much has been said about Heidegger in the course of the last decade (but this had to be done), then that's just too bad; for, in turn, I am entering my question through him: both because I do not see any other way and because there is nothing that appears to me to be as decisive. If this is still obstinacy, I ask that you be kind enough to forgive me.

Obviously I am not resuming the whole thread of your demonstration, but I will simply retain this: despite the strict acknowledgement of what is due to Heidegger with regard to the question of man, the question of the relation between humanism and metaphysics or onto-theology, etc. ('It is not a matter here', you say, 'of enclosing all of Heidegger's text within a closure that he has delimited better than any other'[6]; despite, in particular, the insistence that you

58

bring very vigorously to bear upon the motif of ontological distance – and that is also to say despite all your respect for this intractable difficulty that Heidegger meets with when thematising under the name of 'thinking by examples' [*pensée par modèles*] and which refers to the necessarily ontic character of every example or to the obligation of going through this metaphorics, itself ontical, in order to say being (and this is a difficulty that, right up until 'The *Retrait* of Metaphor',[7] you have made entirely your own); despite of all this, your argumentation happens to be fastened, formed and fixed upon two points:

1 On the one hand (and I am taking up your terms) 'the hold which the humanity of man and the thinking of being maintain upon one another',[8] that you take or pick up, relieve or lift up [*relèves . . . lèves*] on the basis of the 'subtle' privilege attached to the position of the *we* (that is to say, of the 'we-men') in the Heideggerean discourse, and first of all in the breakthrough towards *Dasein* which opens *Sein und Zeit* and the question of the 'meaning of being'. And you rightly say on this subject, 'in the question of being such as it is put to metaphysics, man and the name of man are not displaced'.[9]

2 On the other hand, what you call the 'magnetisation'[10] of the Heideggerean text by the motif of the proper, which is not merely responsible for maintaining the question of essence or of the proper of man but which, going by way of the 'passage between the *close* and the *proper* [*le proche et le propre*]' (whose Latin element you nonetheless acknowledge: *prope/proprius* is 'interrupted' in German), explains the constant and heavy valorisation of proximity and of proximity to self, of propriation (appropriation and reap-propriation) – in brief, so as to speed things along, presence. In short, *Ent-fernung, l'é-loignement*, 'de-severing', at the end (and at the end of ends) always comes back down to the closest (as you write on the subject of Heidegger's trajectory: 'Everything happens as if it were necessary to reduce the ontological distance recognised in *Sein und Zeit* and to say the proximity of being to the essence of man').[11] Or indeed, since you also cite long passages from *Zeit und Sein*, *Ereignis* always bears upon *Enteignis*.

I do not believe this reading to be the only possible, strict and correct one, but I believe that it is still absolutely necessary. A necessity which is indissociably philosophical and political.

It touches, among other things, on the essentials of what (still today) founds Heideggerianism – and, this needs to be pointed out, of what founded the Heideggerianism of Heidegger himself. No one apart from yourself has –

without recourse to external, simply empirico-anthropological criteria, criteria as such invalidated and disqualified in advance by the Heideggerian de-limitation – no one apart from yourself has been able to flush out from their truly philosophical depth, and from the very centre of the Heideggerian questioning, the secret weight of preferences, the metaphorical insistence, the insidious return of the ontic which (inevitably) does not cease to weigh down upon the pure thought of difference, and perhaps in the first place because this thought also wished to be so pure. All of which does not make of it, as it has become customary to say, an 'idolatry' (idolatry as such is explicitly denounced and dismissed, for example in the final lines of the inaugural lecture of 1929[12]). But which definitely, or almost – and considering the rigorous archaeology of the occidental eidetic (eidophilia or eidocentrism) as well as the extreme vigilance shown by Heidegger towards all of the metaphysical concepts derived from *eidos / idea*, *Gestalt* included – which makes of it, therefore, almost definitely, an *ideo-logy*. In spite of everything. And as you have shown, it is a fundamentally 'economistic' ideology, systematically organising itself on the basis of the values, themes and motifs of the 'house' and of the 'dwelling-place' or 'abode' (of the *oikos*), of 'dwelling' and of 'building', of the 'guard' and of the 'safeguard' (of *Wahrheit*), of the closed peasant or artisan economy (shepherds and carpenters), of the 'homeland', of the 'native land', of the 'familiar', of the 'at home' – *Heimat*, *heimatlich*, *heimlich*, *heimisch*, etc. Turning, consequently, into the slightly biting, reactive and reactionary protestation against the entirety of modernity (not merely against all the forms of uprooting, of errancy, of *Befremdlichkeit* and devastation, but also, at the weakest moments, against technology in the sense of industrialisation, cities, mass culture, means of information, etc.). And, moreover, appealing, in a prophetic or messianic mode, to the hope of a mutation, a turning or renewal – the appearance of an 'other thinking' or, of course, a new God. In short, as Lyotard would have said some years ago (and as he still says today, perhaps), 'pious thinking' *par excellence*. I would say instead: pious *discourse*.

This reading had to be carried out, therefore – if only in order to save Heidegger from his 'faithful' interpreters or even from his own self-interpretation; if only, then, in order to restore to this thinking its impact, its irreducible force, and to undermine a certain propensity, which has not been sufficiently contested, towards idyllic inanity (or towards a manner of slightly outdated and vain aristocratism, which is not excluded from the former), with all the political consequences that this is, was, or will be capable of having.

This is why the deconstruction (the *Ab-bau*) of the proper will not have been simply critique but will have constituted, in its very difficulty, the stakes of what I was evoking before, deliberately making use of the Heideggerian term, as a real *Auseinandersetzung* — on the basis of which alone it seems to me possible thoroughly to engage the questioning of what, for convenience, I will continue to call the political or the ethico-political.

I do not believe, any more than you, in an alleged *Kehre*, still less in an improbable 'break', within the trajectory that originates in the faultline of *Sein und Zeit*; and, in order not to abandon the terrain of 'The Ends of Man', it seems to me incontestably legitimate to draw *Sein und Zeit* and the 'Letter on Humanism' into relation, whatever the importance of the successive reorientations which take place between them. The abandonment of the project of 'fundamental ontology', the substitution of the question of essence or of the truth of being for the question of the meaning of being, the appearing of *Ereignis*, etc. — all of this in no way prevents the thematic of the proper from being already entirely present in *Sein und Zeit*, and constituted there in principle.

That said, I believe nonetheless that it is possible to date a certain accentuation of this motif and, along with it, a certain precipitation of the motif into an ideologeme or into a quasi-ideologeme, at least for those texts that were made public by Heidegger himself, from the years that follow the war. I do not say this out of a concern for exactitude, but because, in the direction that I am attempting to follow, what also interests me is the weight that circumstances, historico-political conjecture and a context can have upon a thought. Philosophical vigilance and rigour never prevent naïveté (or worse), and sometimes thinkers are also, as they say, 'easily influenced'. This is why it seems to me that, without even speaking about the Rectorate episode for the moment, one cannot fail to pick up the trail, precisely from the 'Letter on Humanism' (which is, however, an offensive text on every level, one which allows Heidegger to break, internationally, an almost total silence of over ten years and allows him to practise, between the lines, but without humbling himself, the first 'clarification' of his political standpoint[13]). Thus it seems to me that one can, from this date, track down all the elements of a kind of 'reaction' to the post-war German situation. And something, in any case, like a turning in on itself (but not a retreat, about which I will say something later).

Let us put things plainly and, so as to cease being evasive, take the risk of proving ourselves to be inadequate: for an academic and an intellectual who was unquestionably 'of the right', strictly hostile to Marxism (at least up until 1946) and not especially democratic; for a friend and constant interlocutor of those close to National-Bolshevism, like Jünger or Carl Schmitt; for a reader of Stefan George and Knut Hamsun; for a man who had believed in 'the greatness and the inner truth' of Nazism and who, awakened and disappointed (principally because of the racist ideology, it must be stressed), nonetheless continues to profess a tragic heroism of self-sacrifice, of self-renunciation and of staring death in the face, all in order to safeguard the 'metaphysical people' and the institution, ever since Europe, of an 'other beginning'; for an opponent, certainly, and since 1934, to the Hitlerian regime, but whose opposition, after the resignation of the Rectorate, will never go much further (outside of the academic enclosure) than the support given to the *geistige Überlieferung* of Grassi, Otto and Reinhardt – it almost goes without saying that the entire economistic thematics of the house or the hut, the ontological pastorale complacently developed in the days following the military catastrophe (and, already perhaps, following the catastrophe *tout court*), putting aside the 'country path', the 'inconspicuous furrows', Heraclitus in his kitchen, ancient wisdom and peasant artfulness, in short everything which communicates, each time very profoundly, with the 'magnetisation' of the proper; all this was not a crude way of 'clearing his name', this would be to say too much, but, rather, a kind of release or outlet for culpability and the (painful but accepted) implicit recognition of having lost one's way or of an error. A difficult serenity: 'Whoever thinks greatly, must err greatly.'

I do not think saying this 'overdoes it'. I know that a differentiated analysis of Nazism would be necessary – as would an analysis of its unanimous condemnation (which in certain cases does not fail to perplex). I know that it would be necessary to understand, in effect, a certain 'destiny' of Germany (even so, ever since my first reaction to your text, I have thought a great deal about what, in the phenomenon of nations, resists and which one cannot dismiss with a simple shrug of the shoulders). I also know that, even with its limitations, Heidegger's posthumous gesture (the interview granted to *Der Spiegel*[14]) is not nothing. And I can even say that what emerges, in the later Heidegger, as a sort of acceptance or completion of 'modern tragedy' (Hölderlin would have said: 'in the style of Oedipus at Colonus'), as a kind of calm and lucid confrontation with finitude, in no way leaves me cold. In spite of everything, I object. My objection is less political (who, if not Heidegger, enables us to begin to comprehend what is going on in 'total domination'?) than, let's face it, 'ethical'. It is true, and I think that 'thinking only works insofar as it thinks' (I am citing approximately). But why doesn't thinking *also* think the mass-extermination? Why this or that *silence* of thinking?

But this is not what I am driving at. Still less would I want to add to the confusion which reigns on this point (a question of circumstances and of context): if I pose such a question, philosophically, it is obviously not in the name of the 'rights of man'. On the contrary. I am only posing such a question because I do not know in the name of what to pose it. And it is this non-knowledge concerning man which seems to me today worth questioning, philosophically.

What I am getting at is really this: the incontestable and constant privilege accorded to the proper, such as you have thus driven out in Heidegger, also has it's 'reverse' (but the word, precisely, is improper). I mean two things by that:

1 Just as I believe it possible to locate, on the basis of the 'Letter on Humanism' (and, in all probability, deriving from further back, in particular from the turn taken in the commentary on Hölderlin in the years 1942–43 – see the texts on *Heimkunft* and *Andenken*[15]) a certain accentuation of the thematic of the close and of the proper, so it seems to me that what earlier, and notably in the decisive period which follows the resignation of the Rectorate, occupies the foreground is, on the contrary, the whole thematic of *Unheimlichkeit* and *Ungeheuerlichkeit* which is tied, in a very precise way, to the question of man (or, rather, to the re-elaboration of the question of man). I will return to this shortly. But I also mean that:

2 As you yourself have shown on many occasions, it is doubtless impossible, in principle, to settle or fix (*destinare*) a 'logic' inherent in the *Entfernung* and the *Ereignis* on a single term, the close or the proper; a 'logic' which, in its most rigorous sense, cannot be brought back down to any (philosophical) logic of identity and of opposition, even dialectical logic, because it refuses to ensure the *relève*, the *Aufhebung* of difference, and does not cease to maintain what Hölderlin would have called the *Weschel*, the in-finite exchange or alternation of opposites, or (and the parallel, I think, is not improper) what you yourself call the undecidable.

How is the thematic of *Unheimlichkeit* tied to the question, or the re-elaboration of the question of man?

One must note, first of all, that since 1929, since the inaugural lecture at Freiburg, *Unheimlichkeit* (let us render it as dis-orientation, the un-canny, the un-usual or the un-accustomed, even, because the 'logic' to which I have just alluded obviously does not exclude what Freud, using Schelling and dictionaries as excuses, thought of as an 'ambivalence': uncanny familiarity – but it is better not to try to translate) – since 1929, therefore, *Unheimlichkeit* defines the 'relationship to' being or the 'revelation' of being, and that is to say the fundamental ordeal or experience, the *Grunderfahrung*, in anxiety, of the nothing.

I take these suggestions from 1929, from 'What is Metaphysics?', because it is, moreover, the first of Heidegger's texts that can be considered as a political text or even as a political proclamation. Politics, here, in the first place concerns the academic institution: the question is about knowing whether the University will be capable, by itself, of overcoming its division and its dissipation into diverse sciences, disciplines and specialities, and of regaining the not simply regional unity of Science, its 'rootedness' in its 'essential ground'.[16] As we know, this is a problematic stemming from speculative idealism and from the reflections on the meaning and the vocation of the University provoked by the foundation of the Berlin University. But politics is also, as a result, what touches upon the 'totality of human existence': science, which must submit to beings in order to leave to beings 'the job of revealing itself' and whose role, therefore, is first of all to serve (Heidegger speaks of *Dienststellung*), equally represents 'the possibility of a proper though limited leadership (or a guidance: *Führerschaft*) in the totality of human existence'.[17] Or as Heidegger again puts it:

> Man – one being among others – 'pursues science' {'*treibt Wissenschaft*'}. In this 'pursuit' nothing less transpires {in the sense of the historical: *geschiet*} than the irruption {*Einbruch*} by one being called 'man' into the whole of beings, indeed in such a way that in and through this irruption beings break open {*aufbrechen*} and show what they are and how they are {*was und wie es ist*}.[18]

And this is a theme which, treated with more brutality and harshness, and also politicised (in reference to the 'irruption' of the new German State), will reappear in 1933 and which will serve as the guiding thread for the Rectoral Address and to the call for the self-assertion, the *Selbstbehauptung*, of the German University.[19]

Thus, in 1929, *Unheimlichkeit* defines the 'relation' – if it is a relation – to being. Rather than lay myself open to ridicule with a laborious paraphrase, I prefer to let the text speak for itself. I am going to try to translate it as closely as possible. It is absolutely lucid – and absolutely abyssal:

In anxiety, we say, 'there is something strange', 'one feels strange', 'one feels ill at ease' {'*es ist einem unheimlich*' – this is untranslatable}. What is 'it' that makes 'one' feel ill at ease? We cannot say what it is before which one feels ill at ease. As a whole it is so for one. All things and we ourselves sink into indifference. This, however, not in the sense of mere disappearance {*Verschwinden*}. Rather, in this very receding things turn toward us. The receding of beings as a whole that closes in on us {*umdrängt*} in anxiety oppresses us {*bedrängt*}. We can get no hold on things. In this slipping away of beings only this 'no hold on things' comes over us and remains.

Anxiety reveals the nothing.

We 'hover in suspense' {'*wir schweben*'} in anxiety. More precisely, anxiety leaves us hanging because it induces the slipping away of beings as a whole. This implies that we ourselves – we humans who are in being {*diese seienden Menschen*} – in the midst of beings slip away from ourselves. At bottom therefore it is not as though 'you' or 'I' feel ill at ease; rather, it is this way for some 'one' {here 'one' translates the '*einem*' of *ist es einem unheimlich*, without any reference to the inauthentic *das Man* analysed in *Sein und Zeit*}. In the altogether unsettling experience of this hovering where there is nothing to hold onto, pure *Da-sein* is all that is still there.

Anxiety robs us of speech. Because beings as a whole slip away, so that just the nothing crowds round {*andrängt*}, in the face of anxiety all utterance of the 'is' falls silent . . . That anxiety reveals the nothing man himself immediately demonstrates when anxiety has dissolved. In the lucid vision sustained by fresh remembrance we must say that that in the face of which and for which we were anxious was 'properly' {'*eigentlich*', in quotation marks} – nothing. Indeed: the nothing itself – as such – was there {*das Nichts selbst – als soches – war da*}.[20]

I was anxious to reread this text at greater length because in actual fact it gives, in its matrix-like form, the entire thematic of *Unheimlichkeit*. Namely, to recall what is essential very quickly and schematically:

1 Being, in its truth, its essence or its propriety, being nothing which is, being no being – in any way whatsoever – and on this account being able to define

itself as 'the condition of possibility {*die Ermöglichung*} of the revelation of beings as such for the human *Da-sein*', if it appears, approaches or propriates itself (properly happens), this can only be as 'nothing', that is, as that which could not in any way appear, come near or properly happen. The revelation of being or of the nothing, which is simply the equivocation of beings in the vertiginous experience of anxiety, is infinitely paradoxical: it is the revelation of the unrevealable, the presentation of the unpresentable.

2 The access to being, that is, to the nothing or to nothing, this relation without relation to the properly nothing [*le proprement rien*] which could not be exclusively nothing [*rien en propre*], depropriates man absolutely and abstracts him from everything that might qualify him as such: it abstracts him from singular and subjective indexing or assignation ('me', 'you'), as from the power-to-speak. Only the pure 'someone' remains, struck by silence (not even the empty subject of an utterance), the pure existing or being-there, and that is assuredly to say, a being, but also, as such, one subject to the equivocation of the whole of beings. If there is some manner of 'appropriation' of *Da-sein*, this appropriation is in turn infinitely paradoxical and, in any case, it passes through the depropriation of being-man (or, more generally, being-this or being-that, being-such or such-a-being). If man is a being, the fact remains that *Da-sein* – 'that is to say man' – is not a being. The question of man is the *question* of the non-beingness of man.

3 Yet this revelation without revelation – regarding which one should rigorously refrain from resorting to the entire properly phenomenological lexicon – takes place: through one more turn in what, for want of anything better, I call a paradox, it takes place there: *Das Nichts selbst – als solches – war da*. The 'there', a pure 'there' – like Heidegger says, the pure *Da* of pure *Da-sein* as it transcends beings or as it is 'outside' of beings, another way of saying eksistence – is the place without proper space, non-localisable as such (and which nonetheless remains a place), which being needs in order 'to be itself', that is to say not to be or to be nothing. And if being, as *Sein und Zeit* (you will recall) succinctly labelled it, is the 'the transcendens pure and simple', *das Transcendens schlechtin*,[21] the *Da* of *Da-sein* thus signifies nothing other than the *finite* transcendence of being. Finitude – and, as a result, temporality, 'happeningness', historicity, etc. – is the final 'outcome' of the paradoxical revelatory nature of being.

I am not going back over these motifs – which you know better than I and which you have so often gone back over – simply in order to advance or foreground depropriation. Once again, I remain persuaded that the 'logic' at work here (that is also to say Heidegger's *writing*) is such that nothing, proper or improper, could definitively prevail. But I am going back over these motifs because it is here, essentially, that something like Heidegger's 'ethics' roots itself.

We know quite well that he never uses this term or, if he does, it is to dismiss it without appeal. Nevertheless, in the 'Letter on Humanism' (where his indictment of ethics is most explicit) he will take up Heraclitus' *ēthos anthropō daimōn* as his own. And it is not by chance, as far as what interests me here, that he will propose the following translation of it: 'The (familiar) abode {*Der (geheure) Aufenthalt*} for man is the open region for the presencing of god (the unfamiliar one [de l'in-solite] {*des Ungeheuren*}).'[22] The *ethos* – that which is *geheuer* or, since it amounts to the same thing, that which is *heimlich* (this equivalence also derives, as we shall see, from a certain reading of Hölderlin) – the *ethos*, as the holding-oneself and dwelling in the habitual and the customary, is, in reality, the opening for the un-usual and the un-accustomed, the uncanny (*das Ungeheure* or *das Unheimliche*). Again that is to say, if we retain and group together all the values of these two words: the frightening, the prodigious, the monstrous, the colossal (the enormous and the excessive), the incommensurable – in short, the sublime. (We could add the demonic and the divine, but I prefer to leave this question in reserve.) And anyway, it is from the direction of a certain heroism of the sublime, although the word never appears, that the traces of what one must resign oneself to calling Heideggerian 'ethics' furtively become clear. In any case, being-oneself, *Selbstsein*, and freedom derive from the original ordeal of *Unheimlichkeit* and from the 'revelation' of the nothing. Also delivered from this *ethos* are the fundamental existentiales (transgression, abhorrence, refusal, defence, etc.) that subsequent texts will share in accordance with the 'polemic' dichotomies borrowed from Heraclitus: greatness and vulgarity, victory and defeat, mastery and servitude, etc. And it is from there, finally, that courage and daring – *Dasein*'s confrontation with its unmasterable dereliction – whose 'secret alliance' with serenity (*Heiterkeit*) and the 'gentleness of creative desire'[23] was again (or already) recognised in 'What is Metaphysics?', also originate.

Now, if all this indeed proposes a determination, a *Bestimmung* of man in his essence (but the essence of man is itself nothing human), if all this really can be defined as an ethico-praxical field for *Dasein*, Heidegger's radicality is, however, such that one could draw nothing strictly 'positive' from it. Not even when freedom is affirmed. The 'ethics of finitude' is abyssal. I cite, once again, a very famous passage:

> Being held out into the nothing — as *Dasein* is — on the ground of concealed anxiety makes man a lieutenant of the nothing {*der Platzhalter des Nichts*}. We are so finite that we cannot even bring ourselves originally before the nothing through our own decision and will. So profoundly does finiteness entrench itself in *Dasein* that our most proper and deepest finitude {*Endlichkeit*, as different from *Verendlichung*} refuses to yield to our freedom.[24]

The question of man, the question of the essence or the proper of man, will have to be considered in (and in accordance with), and through the thematic of *Unheimlichkeit*. As well.

And I will say right now — I will endeavour to justify myself very quickly: in (and in accordance with) and through the thematic, which is the *tragic* thematic, of the incommensurable.

And, in fact, after the Rectorate episode; after the various and dismaying 'proclamations' (an attentive and serious analysis of which is nonetheless always in abeyance); after the Address itself, about which it is necessary at least to underline the fact that it repeats, to a large extent, the inaugural lecture of 1929, but *positively*, without the least allusion to the problematic of the nothing, to anxiety or to the experience of the *Unheimliche*; and consequently the period of disappointment and of the 'retreat' (which is also the period of the 'remonstrations' towards Nazism) inaugurated in 1934 by a course, the first of many, on Hölderlin, followed immediately by a seminar on art, and that is to say on *Dichtung* — an openly political gesture and, moreover, one clarified as such; after all this, or accompanying it, man — the question of man — once again makes its return to Heideggerian discourse, to the discourse always dedicated to the question of being. And, again, it is the *Unheimliche* which returns to the fore.

I am constrained, through lack of time, to hurry along analyses which should be developed at a suitable rhythm, and to retain only a strict minimum. In any case, it is not a matter of reconstituting a history; and I am relying on your familiarity with all these texts — as I am on your work which has continually developed from out of them, and which cannot be ignored here. I am going to proceed, therefore, very brutally.

Whilst initially marking the question of man as reopened and maintained as such, and that is to say, as the question of the essence or of the proper of man, it receives, nonetheless, a new formulation ('Who is man?' substituted for 'What is man?'), a formulation which imposed itself upon the reading of Hölderlin – I refer here to the second section of the lecture on 'Hölderlin and the Essence of *Dichtung*'[25] – and of which the almost contemporary *Introduction to Metaphysics* offers the following justification. I am taking this passage from the third section ('Being and Thinking') of the chapter dedicated to 'The Limitation of Being' which, moreover, comprises the sections: 'Being and Becoming', 'Being and Appearance', 'Being and the Ought'. It is not by chance that the question of man crops up in this third section which is, for all that, the most fully developed: in an identical movement, it is a matter of wresting the question of being from its modern (Cartesian or Hegelian: being as thinking, that is to say as Subject) interpretation, and of getting back behind the corresponding interpretation of man.

Once again I am going to try here to translate as closely as possible. It comprises a series of seven reasons:

1 The determination {*Bestimmung*} of the essence of man is never an answer, but essentially a question.

2 The asking of this question is historical in the fundamental sense that this questioning first creates history.

3 This is so because the question as to what man is can only be asked as part of the inquiry about being.

4 Only where being discloses itself {opens itself} in questioning does history happen historically {*geschiet Geschichte*} and with it the being of *man*, by virtue of which he dares to set himself apart from and contend with {risking himself in setting apart from [*l'explication*]: *sich in die Auseinandersetzung . . . wagt*} beings as such.

5 It is this questioning contending that first brings man back to the being that he himself is and must be. {To bring back is here: *zurück-bringen*. Consequently, the being being or the beingness of man as such derives from the 'settling of accounts' with beings in general, that is to say, prior to this, from the questioning of being through which man comes – historically – into his being. Whence, moreover:}

6 Only as he comes historically into this questioning does man come to himself; only as such is he a self {or a him-self: *ein Selbst*}. Man's selfhood {*die Selbstheit*} means this: he must transform the being [*das Sein*] that discloses itself to him {*hat er . . . zu verwandeln* – this is an obligation, if not an imperative} – he has to transform it into history and constitute himself (arise or stand) in it. Selfhood does not mean that he is primarily an 'ego' and an individual. He is no more this than he is a 'we' and a community.

7 Because man is himself as a historical being, the question about his own being *must* {my emphasis} pass from the form 'What is man?' to the form '*Who* is man?'[26]

One must not ignore in all this, and, above all, in this *necessary* transformation of the question of man, the political significance – I would rather have endeavoured to say 'apolitical', if one is, at the very least, willing to agree to differentiate this term from the sense that it has been given in the context of the 'total domination' of the political (I am deliberately taking up Hannah Arendt's expression), and to detect within it the first indication of an *active* deconstruction of the political. A deconstruction which had already been started, as paradoxical as this might appear, in the Rectoral Address (but lengthy analyses would be needed in order to show this[27]) and which, in the *Introduction to Metaphysics* – the time of the 'retreat' having arrived – again comes to rest upon the same notion, prior to every anthropologico-political determination (nation, community, State, etc.), of *the people*. I cannot linger over this here. I will simply recall, echoing the sixth reason that I have just given (the one dedicated to *Selbstheit*), and in order in some way to set the tone, these lines from the first chapter of the *Introduction*:

We are caught in a pincers (between Russia and America). Situated in the middle, our people incur the severest pressure. This is the people with the most neighbours and hence the people most endangered. And with all this, it is the most metaphysical of peoples. But this people will only be able to make itself a destiny {*ein Schicksal*} from this destination {or determination: *Bestimmung*} if first it creates *within itself* a resonance, a possibility of resonance for this destiny. . . . All this implies that this people, as a historical people, exposes itself to itself {*sich selbst . . . hinausstellt*} in the originary domain where being reigns, and thereby exposes the history of the West, from out of the middle {or the centre} of its future 'happening'.[28]

Whatever the 'resonance' for us of these propositions or these phrases — that is, let us acknowledge it again, whatever their 'political' resonance — one must at least recognise that they attempt, with the greatest possible clarity, to tear the 'we' ('we-people') away from every ontical determination, including that of the 'centre' — as a geographical or spatial determination — in order to subject it, as to the precondition of a destiny in general, to the pure requisite of *Selbstheit*, this selfhood prior to all singularity and all community, to every 'I' and every 'we', and which is the ex-position of being, through which alone a history can happen.

For this reason one will always be able to interpret the mutation of the question of man, the passage to 'Who is man?', as a political gesture. But one will only be able to do this if one knows beforehand how to relate the false evidence of 'the political' to the radical strangeness of the historical or of the advent of being. I cite the *Introduction* once again — these lines are from the final chapter:

> *Polis* is usually translated as city or city-state. This does not capture the full meaning. Rather, *polis* means the place, the there {*das Da*}, wherein and as which *Da-sein* is as historical. The *polis* is the place of history, the *Da in* which, *out* of which and *for* which history happens.[29]

The essence of the political, in other words, is by itself nothing political. No philosophical investigation can take the measure of its 'retreat'. Which enjoins me to add that if one has to maintain this word 'political' — which I believe one must, out of a concern for clarity — then this can only be on the condition, as Heidegger invites, of completely re-elaborating the concept.

Moreover, in the texts of 1934–36, the question 'Who is man?' already no longer awaits an answer from philosophy in the sense in which its space and capacity are delimited by Heidegger. It addresses *Dichtung* alone — even when it addresses 'thinking', and in this case that is to say when it addresses the still *dichterisch* thinking of the pre-Socratics. And *Dichtung*, in spite of the extension that Heidegger grants to this word (which is the word for art in general), is still, essentially, poetry. And consequently, it is also language, which is, conforming to a certain tradition issuing from para- or post-Kantian idealism, the first or the originary work of art — and, for this same reason, it is the only recognised determination of being-people.

One could show this quite easily: Hölderlin — even when, as in the *Introduction to Metaphysics*, it is Sophocles who is summoned forth — is the sole representative, during this period at least, of *Dichtung*, the essential determination of which, incidentally, he makes possible: it is poetry insofar as it thinks. Which would commit me to saying, quite willingly, that it is in the reading of Hölderlin that one would in the first place have to locate the text of Heidegger's *Auseinandersetzung* with the question of the 'political'. It is no surprise, moreover, if, in the logic of the determination-destination of the people or of the historical-being of a people, Hölderlin is designated as the *Dichter* 'whose work still confronts the Germans as a test to be stood' or whom 'it still remains for the Germans to face up to, to withstand' (*bestehen*).[30] These are the last words of 'The Origin of the Work of Art'.

This is why it seems to me possible to point out that what Heidegger attempted to rethink or re-elaborate by way of the question 'Who is man?' and the motif of destination, is the Hölderlinian problematic of the tragic. That is to say, I am at last coming back to this, the problem of the *Unheimliche* or the *Ungeheure*.

The *Unheimliche*. One knows that it is a matter of the word by which Heidegger chose to translate the *deinon* which provided the dominant theme or fundamental tonality for the chorus of Sophocles' *Antigone* dedicated to man. *Polla ta deina* becomes: *Vielfältig das Unheimliche*, multiple the uncanny.[31] As for Hölderlin, he translated: *Ungeheuer ist viel*, but Heidegger will often have had the opportunity to indicate the fact that the two words say the same thing. And they also designate, beyond the values that I recalled earlier and which one can always suspect of being still ontic (the uncanny or the un-usual, the disorienting, the monstrous, etc.), what, for want of anything better, I take the risk of calling the incommensurable or the without-common-measure. With regard to which, but this is thinkable only in the pure form of the paradoxical (or, with Bataille, the 'impossible'), every relation — and *there is* relation — is, as Blanchot would say, 'relation without relation'.

I am alluding in this way, and first of all, to the fact that Hölderlin did not reserve *das Ungeheure* for the sole translation of the Greek *deinon*. He also charged the word with defining, in its essence, the tragic relation or 'transport': namely the *ungeheuer* coupling — the coupling without coupling — of the human and the divine, of the finite and the limitless, which separation alone, itself boundless, or death can 'accomplish'. And it was thus that, in the language of the speculative, but in accordance with a logic or a syntax proper to dis-locating it, to holding it in abeyance or — to adopt one of his own terms —

'to caesura' it, he was able to reinterpret in his own way (but which is no one's way) the thematic of *hubris* and the Aristotelian doctrine of *katharsis*:

> The presentation of the tragic rests primarily on this: that the *Ungeheure*, that the God and man couple, and that, with every limit abolished, the power of nature and the innermost of man become One in fury, conceives itself in that the limitless becoming-One purifies itself through limitless separation.[32]

Now, on another level, which does not (yet) bring the divine into play but, rather, stays with being, and without aiming at, behind the question of man, an explicit determination of the tragic (but throughout taking account of such a determination which, rightly, belongs to the definition of *Dichtung*), it is the philosophical (or thoughtful) re-elaboration of the tragic 'relation' that the Heideggerian reading of Sophocles attaches itself to or tackles. (I insist on this privileged link to Hölderlin's work on Sophocles all the more because I believe that Heidegger did not want to take it into account.)

The result of this operation is totally surprising. For if man in his essence is really determined as *unheimlich*, the *Unheimliche* as such is, in reality, that which defines the essence of the work of art.

One ought not to cut short this sort of journey. Above all, one ought not to speak the language of results. I resign myself, however, to breaking the matter down with scant ceremony:

1 While basing his analysis upon the distinction between *deinon* and *deinotaton*, such as it appears in the two first lines of the chorus:

> Manifold the uncanny {*das Unheimliche*}
> But nothing, beyond man, more uncanny {*Unheimlicheres*}

Heidegger begins by defining *deinon* as 'the terrible' (*das Furchtbare*) – in the sense he says, playing on the semantic network of *walten* (to reign, to dominate, to do violence, etc.), of 'that which dominates by overpowering . . . which provokes panic-stricken terror, true anguish, as much as respectful, collected, balanced, secret fear' (this is the lexicon of 'What is Metaphysics?').[33] In such a way, and it is here that the overpowering or the essential violence of domination resides, that the *Unheimliche* is to be understood 'as that which throws us back outside of the *Heimliche*, that is to say outside the innermost (*das Heimische*), outside the habitual, the familiar, the unthreatened security'. The *Unheimliche* is that which 'does not let us be "at home"'.[34]

2 It is in relation to the *Unheimliche* thus defined or redefined, in relation to this overpowering or this original violence that is nothing other than the incommensurability of being or the nothing, that man himself is determined as *das Unheimlicheres*, that which is more uncanny. This is, Heidegger stresses, his 'fundamental trait'– and not a particular quality 'as though in other respects man was also something else'.[35] It is his fundamental trait because 'the tragic saying about man' does not exactly say man, but *Da-sein* (the Greek historical *Da-sein*), and in this way the tragic saying 'seizes man by the extreme limits and the abrupt abysses of his being'.

Now if man in his essence – and the essence of man, here, is thus indeed the *in-human* or the (in)human – if 'man' (in his essence) 'is' *das Unheimlicheres*, it is because of two reasons (I am schematising again):

- on the one hand, and one will recognise in this an echo of the motif of transcendence (out of) beings that was developed in 'What is Metaphysics?', it is because man 'leaves, escapes from the limits which are customary and familiar to him, and which for the most part remain so for him'; Man can also be defined as the one who 'does violence', that is to say as the one who 'transgresses' (this is *hubris*, obviously) the limits of the *Heimliche*, 'and precisely heading towards the *Unheimliche* understood as the overpowering';[36]

- yet on the other hand, what also matters is that by being 'the violent one', man exercises violence against the overpowering (being or the nothing), 'gathering' it and 'letting it come' into the opening, to the manifestation, to revelation. Man is the 'prodigy', as the usual translations of Sophocles put it, insofar as he effects this impossible event: the presentation of the unpresentable.

This is why the essence or the being of man is not man, but *Da-sein*: the fact that in man and through man, absolute paradox, being (the nothing) is there. Hence:

3 (I am going straight to the main conclusion) the essence of man, the inhuman, is *technē* – or the *mekhanē* of Sophocles' text – which, as we know, for Hölderlin represented the essence of art, and that is to say, that which also renders calculable the rule or the statute (*Gesetz*), the law of the work. And in fact, for the Greeks, *techne* is art. Or it is *instead* art, if one remembers

74

that the Heideggerian analysis of the work of art from the same period concluded for the first time with the putting into place of the *Ge-stell*, through which, much later, the essence of technology will be defined.

In other words, *Da-sein* – that about which you yourself say: it is not man, but it is nothing other than man (this is why I risk the term *(in)human*) – *Da-sein* is art or the work of art. Or, more rigorously, and because it is still necessary to nuance things: the *Da* of the *Da-sein* is *first* art or the work of art. I am thinking here of the subtle hierarchism of various modes of the 'installation' of being that Heidegger lays out many times (art, thinking, the founding gesture of the city, religious veneration, etc.). But I am also thinking of what is said quite explicitly in the *Introduction*:

If the Greeks called both art in the true sense and also the work of art *techne*, quite precisely and in the strong sense, it is because art is what most immediately brings being to a standstill {to the *Stehen*} in something present (in a work). . . . It is only through the work of art, considered as being-being {*das seiende-Sein*} that everything else that appears and can be found in front of us is first confirmed and made accessible, meaningful and understandable, by way of being or as not being {and as not counting: *als Unseiendes*}.[37]

In another language, that of the lectures on the work of art, this amounts to saying that the essence of man, the *Da* of *Da-sein*, is the *thesis* of being or of truth (of *aletheia*) which, henceforth, is *in the first place* the work of art because art is essentially *Dichtung*, and that is to say language. For this reason, the essence of man is just as easily language, 'the most dangerous of all possessions', as Heidegger recalls from Hölderlin precisely when he invokes him in view of the question 'Who is man?'.[38] And if, in effect, still leaning upon Hölderlin ('Man dwells poetically upon this earth') or giving way to other formulae of that kind ('Language is the house of being'), the contours of a fundamental 'economy' are evoked, it must not be forgotten that the work of art itself will have been called *unheimlich* and *ungeheuer*, so executing the shock, or delivering the 'blow' (*Stoss*) by which it is revealed that there are beings (and not nothing) and in what these beings consist.[39]

Obviously one could, on the basis of this – but it would require rather a lot of time, and force – weave between 'Heidegger' and 'yourself' (between the two texts, and in spite of the two languages, at least, and the two styles) the closest of ties. In any case, on the level of the 'philosophical' and 'philosophical questions'.

I am not saying this simply because you have already shown or said this – as, for example, when you took up the entire problematic of the *trait* internal to *alētheia*, whilst wrenching it away from its weakest context (the one that you dismantled in 'The Truth in Pointing'[40]), this *Zug zum Werk*, this attraction or gravitation towards the work, which doubles and displaces the 'will to *parousia*' of the Absolute and redefines the truth in its essence. That is also to say, for it comes to be determined in one and the same movement, when you took up the whole problematic of the incision, of the trait as *Riss*, the trait through which the work of art, *Dichtung* and language (and therefore *Da-sein* and the (in)human) had finally to be thought, behind the very 'thesis' of truth, as this tracing in re-treat that you call archi-writing.

Nor am I saying this because, *on the basis of your thinking*, it is possible to accentuate a certain number of motifs in Heidegger and to become attentive to 'logical' matrices, displacements in the syntax of thought and the effects [*les jeux*] of writing. However, there is, on the basis of your thinking, something to decode, for example, in the abandoning of fundamental ontology (contemporary with the political 'retreat' and the passage to the question of art), the rise of a general mimetology (which also drives all the texts on Hölderlin), which does not simply amount to making art and the work of art the condition of possibility for the revelation of what is, but which represents, rather, the intrusion of this paradoxical 'logic', modelled on Hölderlinian paradoxy, endlessly separating–relating the two poles of opposition or of difference, the one to the other and the one from the other in the syntax of the 'more . . . more . . .': the closer it is, the further it is; the more proper, the more improper – and vice versa. Consequently, there is also the matter of paralysing, of putting the speculative movement out of order or in abeyance – or indeed, of throwing it into disarray, it all comes down to the same thing; the matter of thinking the *Da* neither as a position, nor as a moment, nor as a sublation of (the) being (of the nothing), but as the presentation (without presentation) of being in retreat. There is even, up to a certain point, the matter of following, through the hasty substitution of ontical privileges, through the sort of submission swept up (in spite of all the efforts at fixation and the desire for a 'destination') into an obscure *pollakōs to einai lēgētai*, through the indefinite linking and exchange of metaphors – and the impossible assignation of a *proper name of being* – the multiple, divided, decomposed course of a dissemination.

I am saying this – I am addressing myself to you – because I cannot see that the thought of writing thinks anything other than being.

At the end of 'The Ends of Man' – much has been said here about this text – you appealed, through an interrogative mode and against the Heideggerian reading of Nietzsche, to an '"active forgetting"' of being.[41] You asked yourself whether it was not necessary to hear 'the question of the truth of being as the last burst of the superior man'[42] (which you identified in the man of humanism and anthropology). But from where, moreover, is it possible to de-limit humanism, beyond the Hegelian and Husserlian delimitations, if not from the question of being? And what, if not the question of being, could have allowed one to re-delimit a Heideggerian 'humanism' and, in spite of every-thing, to reduce Heidegger to Hegel and Husserl?

You will answer me – yet I am not asking you to respond, because I do not know what this ('to respond') means – you will perhaps answer me: there are weak moments in Heidegger, one must learn to read him *against* himself, in the precise manner that he himself advocated a good many times for the reading of the greatest and the closest (beginning with Nietzsche).

But how decide upon the weaknesses, in a text subject to the abyssal 'logic' of the question of being?

Such is, if you like, the question that, reading you, I have always asked myself, and which I am posing as much to myself because something has (always) bothered me in reading Heidegger (and it is for precisely this reason that I began to read you) and because, once again, I am absolutely convinced of the necessity of your gesture with regard to him.

However, this still remains unclear to me: in the name of what must one do this?

I could say to you – but this is still something obscure (the obscurity of my old, not properly philosophical question bearing upon idiom and choices, style or tone): up to what point can one 'mess with' the tragic? In the sense that he, Heidegger, gives it to us to be thought? And why, if it is true that there was no more radical movement of thought in his work?

Is it because the tragic thematic would communicate with this political loss of way which makes you bristle and outrages you? I do not think so: the political loss of way – a fault, a 'wound to thinking' as Blanchot says, nothing that could be referred to 'naïveté', nothing like any other 'weakness' – the political *mistake*, this is precisely the abandonment of the tragic. The sole preservation of heroism lies in tragic heroism. And eventually in the pathos, for it is indeed a pathos, of daring and courage, of pure decision – the pathos which is always that of 'optimistic tragedies'. That is to say, very simply, the saturation of the hiatus of the incommensurable (the recovery from chaos), the repudiation of the *Unheimliche* and the (in)human (the hurried humanisation and politicisation of *Da-sein*), the communitarian intoxication and the forgetting of tragic sobriety, the assignation (and the assignation in the face of every dictate) of a destination.

But can one escape such a mistake? Or, at the very least, evade the general form of such a fault? Will perpetually changing the terrain – as we all try to do, more or less lucidly – suffice? Will a sort of erratic installation in beings suffice? Will it suffice, in our discourses, to substitute ontic privileges *ad infinitum*, to throw every assignation and every destination into turmoil? And if so – and its name is 'writing' – *in the name of what*? In the name of what is it '*necessary to*' [*le faut-il*] if this is not, as Heidegger will have (almost) always maintained, obedient to this call without call [*appel sans appel*], to this voiceless injunction to whose excessiveness no response can correspond, and yet against which *it is necessary* to measure our impossible 'responsibility'?

From where could one refuse – say no to the question: *in the name of* . . . ? From where might one – from where might *we* – avoid saying: *in the name of* . . . ? *Obstinément*. Obstinately, relentlessly. In Latin: *destinate*.

Debate

(Transcribed by Philippe Lacoue-Labarthe)

Participants: Françoise Clévenot, Alain David, Jacques Derrida, Luce Irigaray, Gilbert Kahn, Denis Kambouchner, Jean-François Lyotard.

KAHN opens the discussion by asking for clarification about the relation which Heidegger weaves between the motif of the *Unheimliche* and the whole *heimich* or *heimisch* thematic of the house, of the at-home, of the native, etc. – that is to say, between the tragic discourse of the *Introduction to Metaphysics* and what one can describe as 'pious discourse' (that of the *Feldweg*, for example, or that of the text on Hebbel[43]). The same question might be posed with regard to technology, sometimes accepted as the destiny of being, sometimes challenged in a kind of movement of recoil or of terror.

LACOUE-LABARTHE concedes that his analysis, in many respects, remained schematic. All he wanted to indicate was that there is a trajectory in Heidegger, a precise route which, in fact, is organised through the opposition between the *Unheimliche* and *Heimichkeit*, and that this route also has a political logic. But this in no way amounts to saying that the 'young Heidegger' – the 'tragic' Heidegger – would be the 'fascist' Heidegger. In reality, the Heidegger of 1933 (who is no longer so young, however, and who in any case is not fascist) is precisely not tragic. The tragic thematic only appears (or only reappears) in 1934–35, in the moment of the 'retreat', that is to say the moment of disappointment with respect to Nazism; and it is progressively, towards the end of and after the war (in accordance with a movement that could be shown as being tied in an precise way to the commentary on Hölderlin), that one can detect a relative accentuation of the *heimisch* thematic, that is, the thematic of the proper and of the close (such as it dominates the 'Letter on Humanism', for

79

example). But we must not forget that, taken in its fullest rigour, the logic at work in Heidegger is such that it is, in principle, impossible to settle upon either one or the other motif: proper or improper, close or distant. Moreover, it is this logic, what one could call the logic of *Ent-fernung*, which explains Heidegger's permanent double gesture, for example with respect to technology. However, the important point here was not to be directed to the most rigorous part of Heidegger's questioning, but to break with a certain silence and to speak openly, from a position which is in no way anti-Heideggerian, about ideology (there is one, inevitably) or, more precisely, about Heideggerian politics. Doubtless Heidegger challenged the word; but nothing precludes one also reading his discourse after 1933 as the 'rumination' on a mistake (mistake meaning a fall in relation to the greatest rigour of questioning), and even as a partial admission, which one can admit was difficult but which, being far too implicit, remains equally unpardonable. ('To my knowledge, says LACOUE-LABARTHE, there is not a word about the extermination.')

But is this difference of accentuation, insists KAHN, tied to the fact that *Dasein* is not man?

The whole difficulty, LACOUE-LABARTHE responds, stems from this fact that a *Da* is necessary to the *Sein*. Therefore, it is a question of the privilege granted, for the thesis of being, to such and such a being. With the always possible danger of a stoppage, or of a fixation upon a determined being. When it is a matter of art, after all, as Lyotard has said, this is not dishonourable. But art is never simply art; it implies all sorts of other ontic valorisations – and it is there, inevitably, that the political problem comes to be posed. However, the secret chance of such a thinking is that other positions follow (or can follow) which are perhaps always just as much de-positions, the substitutive series of ontic privileges being, strictly speaking, unstoppable.

CLÉVENOT then intervenes to pose the question of Heidegger's relation to Marx: does the Heideggerian interpretation of Marx, and in particular the fate reserved for alienation in the 'Letter on Humanism', have something to do with the problematic of the tragic?

LACOUE-LABARTHE: There is in any case a strange privilege granted to Marx, in the 'Letter on Humanism', whose thinking, Heidegger says near enough (and it is a matter of the thought of alienation), represents a fundamental experience of human *Dasein*. Now this passage immediately precedes a long exposition on Hölderlin which organises itself, similarly, around the question of the depropriation of man. Of course, the horizon of this text is preoccupied by the simultaneous challenge of nationalism and internationalism (it is a political text), and the privilege accorded to Marx still presupposes the fundamental delimitation of Marxism, recalled many times, as a metaphysics of work, of the producing subject (of the Subject in the age of technology). Yet this does not prevent this kind of recognition of an – in order to do things quickly, let us say 'ethical' – Marx, and the recognition of a rather tragic Marx as well.

KAMBOUCHNER: Independently of the question that several of us, already, have asked ourselves – that of the relation (without relation) which the thought of writing maintains with the thinking of being – I would like to pose the question of a word that doubtless I myself have used, but one in which you yourself have invested far more: the word 'positive' (or 'positivity'). You spoke, for example, of the most radical Heideggerian gesture: 'One could not draw anything positive from it; the "ethics of finitude" is abyssal.' What concerns me about this, however, is that I would be tempted to say that Kant's question 'what is man?' is positive, at least on a certain level. But the impossibility for us, in the site that we share, of assigning a determined meaning to this word, made me step back. I would like simply to know, therefore, whether you have been able to overcome this difficulty, which I feel to be a substantial one.

LACOUE-LABARTHE replies that he does not actually appropriate this term but that he utilises it so as to make it communicate with everything that pertains to the motif of the thesis, of the position, of the installation – *Setzung, Stellung, Gestell,* etc. – and that is to say with what necessarily lures being into beings. The danger, as he has underlined already, is one of a possible stoppage upon such and such an ontic privilege. But, beyond this, there remains the question which he would formulate, provisionally, in the following way: why are we always caught between a questioning in the name of nothing that one could assign (in the name of the incommensurable) and, on the other hand, the constant, but doubtless never sufficiently vigilant, attempt at de-position? 'Such is perhaps the "ethical" question which gathers us all together here.'

MARIE-LOUISE MALLET (who was chairing the session): Everything that has been said brings us directly to J. Derrida's question: in the name of whom?

DERRIDA: I don't know if, like you,[44] I will say that the moment has come. What I am most grateful to you for, grateful beyond measure, is your having yourself addressed to me in an incommensurably exuberant fashion, that is to say

81

without asking me to respond – which is, I would not call it the surest way (there is no security here), but the most faithful and most generous way of being addressed. Thus, I will not respond, here and now, so as to allow your address to happen, not merely to happen to me, but, well beyond me, to happen and happen again. (You asked yourself whether it would happen: it is not up to you to decide, I believe that it has happened; tomorrow I will repeat in my way what you have said about the terrible and unpresentable revelation without revelation to which your whole address was addressed – I call it: the apocalypse without apocalypse.) Nonetheless, you have put me before the impossible responsibility – I am using your words – of an immediate response: I shy away, not like I did from Jean-Luc's questions (in an analogous but not identical situation),[45] but when you say in conclusion, 'from where might we avoid responding to the question: in the name of what?', I ask myself: From where, in fact, might we respond to it? And I ask you: Why 'in the name of what' and not 'in the name of whom'? (Thus I am naming the 'whom' that you yourself reconstructed earlier.) I cannot respond to such a question, either here today or tomorrow – in a certain way I have responded to it in advance, without wanting to or knowing that I have done so; no, I simply ask myself whether it is nameable, I mean whether it can give rise to one name or to one word. The question that I am asking is about what escapes unique naming. But by saying that I am perhaps messing, as you put it, with the tragic . . . To finish, to finish with not responding, and since you have questioned me, not about my own idiom, but about what speaks behind this idiom – about those (male or female) who speak behind the idiom: I understood what you said about Heidegger's idiom, and I am totally with you on this; but I am not sure whether the idiom as such, as with the name, exists in all purity. An idiom seems to be made from a multiplicity of traits and this ensemble, the adjoining of this multiplicity, is precisely what can only appear to the other. And perhaps this is the way in which, briefly, I would justify my non-response: I have nothing to say about what you have called my idiom.

LACOUE-LABARTHE: But if I have asked you this question then I have done so because, for many reasons (anxieties about the idiom as much as suspicions about tragedy or the tragic) it is a question which I am always asking of myself. It is, I know, an impossible question. You reply: it is necessary to respond, every response is lacking. I hear this response without response, I think I hear it . . . What more is there to be said now?

The debate now slowed down. Then two interventions (*David*, *Irigaray*) give the occasion for a more rapid exchange.

DAVID, first of all, without wanting to speak in the name of Levinas, asks, nonetheless, whether the question 'in the name of whom' is not an appeal, against the violence of being, to the transcendence of the other, to the 'otherwise than being'.

LACOUE-LABARTHE'S answer is articulated in two parts: his reading of Levinas (which he considers to be insufficient), the impossibility of someone in his situation referring to the Jewish tradition, and his foreignness in relation to every space of belief, all of this should prevent him from responding; however, whilst recognising that the question of the 'otherwise than being' is a limit-question, he cannot help thinking that the aforementioned limit is equally a limit in philosophy itself, an ancestral limit, and he asks in turn whether the question of being, in its most rigorous sense, is not – in respect of the philosophical determination of being – precisely the question 'otherwise than being'.

IRIGARAY: A simple question: given the stakes that you have designated, to pose the question 'in the name of what (or of whom)' to someone (whomsoever it is), isn't this to ask for a guarantee, to want to give yourself safety barriers against the tragedy of your own destiny?

LACOUE-LABARTHE: Certainly, one can always say that; but I cannot see what that might mean: the tragedy of my own destiny. (*Laughter*)

But this response, which is not one, clearly relaunches the discussion. DERRIDA intervenes to say that the unbounded extent of Lacoue-Labarthe's address destined it to recieve an answer from no one. But, he adds, what Irigaray has just said is what he himself was tempted to say beforehand in returning his question to Lacoue-Labarthe: 'And you?' After IRIGARAY has immediately refor-mulated her question (is not the demand 'in the name of' equivalent to 'giving oneself safety barriers against the unnameable'?), LACOUE-LABARTHE clarifies his intentions by distinguishing the 'what' and the 'whom': the 'in the name of what', which doubtless carries the risk of brutality and naïveté, nonetheless remains a philosophical question, one which it is possible to pose to a philo-sopher or to a thinker; the 'in the name of whom', on the other hand, cannot be pronounced nor addressed from within philosophy. There is no disavowal of the 'philosophical profession' in this, but another 'practice' is most certainly at stake. This is why Lacoue-Labarthe can echo Irigaray's 'no one can answer in your place', by saying that nothing or no one can be a guarantee against the risk of the 'in the name of whom?'

In concluding, the debate structures around a long intervention from LYOTARD. After reconstituting Lacoue-Labarthe's problematic (in which he particularly notes that the political is introduced as the will to reduce the incommensurable and to seal off the tragic), he presents an initial objection:

LYOTARD: Your question is basically: the political must not forget the tragic. But when you propose, paraphrasing Aristotle, your 'The *Unheimliche* is said in numerous ways', that is, when you counterpose your refusal of an ontic fixation, I wonder whether you are not retreating in relation to something that Nietzsche attempted to think. You will say to me, quite rightly, that there is no Nietzschean politics or that, if there is one, it is catastrophic. But all the same: in place of the tragic, for Nietzsche, there was gaiety – a way of saying: enough with piety, let us stop thinking the '*pollakōs*' in terms of impossibility; let us think it in terms of possibilities instead. It is Napoleon who said that 'tragedy, today, is politics'; this was not too effective, it lacked a little gaiety. In short, I understand your 'in the name of' perfectly well, but for my part I would say instead, simply: 'in what name'. I think less about what Derrida objected to (the division and multiplication of the name) than about the situation of the Aristotelian judge. I agree with you, even if you were indeed brutal earlier on: doubtless, the 'otherwise than being' cannot get one out of the problem. I believe that we must speak in terms of justice, of judgement. What is eminent in Aristotle's view is the fact that the judge must judge without name, but he must judge – and from that moment, there is a politics.

But a question also clings to this objection: it concerns Heidegger's university politics as it is defined in the inaugural lecture of 1929 and the Rectoral Address. Would it not correspond to a return of the speculative? Would it not inscribe itself in the weave of the great founding texts of the University of Berlin? If this was the case, it perhaps would allow Nazism to be thought as an end (in every sense of the word) of the speculative.

In response, LACOUE-LABARTHE declares himself to be conscious, in Lyotard's objection, of the theme of justice and of the juridical: if he compared tragic thinking and politics, it is not because of the isolated effect of his (doubtless hardly Nietzschean) idiosyncrasy, but so as not to misrepresent the Heideggerian problematic. A problematic which can indeed be thought of, between 1929 and 1933, as a 'return of the speculative'. On the condition, however, of distinguishing between the 1929 text (where Science itself, and not merely the sciences, is measured by the fundamental question of the nothing and brought back to its ontic register) and the 'Rectoral Address', which keeps a much more positive historico-philosophical language with respect to Knowledge (as with respect to Germany, the German people, the West, etc.). It is this kind of speculative fixation that, soon after the resignation, will be disrupted by the passage to Hölderlin and to the question of art. DERRIDA intervenes to say that he also subscribes to the thesis of the speculative problematic of the University.

DERRIDA: But I think that if something is displaced after the Rectorship episode, it is due less to a political displacement (or to a political remorse) on Heidegger's part than to what occurs in the very process of his thought, where something is going to render impossible not only the re-employment of the problematic of Knowledge, but also the maintaining of fundamental ontology upon which, in each of the two texts, Heidegger precisely wanted to found the university by organising all regional forms of knowledge through it. When he speaks again of the university, much later (for example, in *What is a Thing?*[46]), we will no longer find this speculative gesture that he repeated before in order to reconstruct the university around a philosophy, around ontology. But if there is in this way a displacement, and this is where I join Lyotard, this displacement does not give rise to a dispersion. On the contrary, the abandonment of ontology, the disappearance of any higher authority, leaves a gap or a hole. It never becomes the *yes* said to a multiplicity. To affirm the multiplicity of the name, as I did earlier, can be tragic, but this tragedy is not strictly incompatible with gaiety (which is opposed, rather, to piety), although it is tragic enough to associate gaiety and tragedy in this way.

DERRIDA, returning to an earlier response by Lacoue-Labarthe, poses a final question: up to what point, in the succession of ontic privileges, can one designate certain theses or positions as less abyssal, less equivocal than others? Would Heidegger have accepted that every '*unheimlich* trembling' had disappeared, in 1933, in the reference to the German people?

LACOUE-LABARTHE subscribes to the terms of the question but maintains that, without even recalling the diverse disquieting proclamations of 1933 (which, moreover, Heidegger renounced), the trembling that Derrida evoked tends, for all that, to disappear in the Rectoral Address. Then he returns to the motif of gaiety:

LACOUE-LABARTHE: Rather than gaiety, it is joy (which is the word for saying the destination, from Spinoza to Bergson, passing through Fichte) that I associate with the tragic. I am thinking of Hölderlin's couplet 'Sophocles':

> Many have tried, but in vain, with joy to express the most joyful;
> Here at last, in mourning [*in der Trauer*], wholly I find it expressed.

And I think that when he comments on this text, Heidegger says of the passage that it testifies simply to a moment of Hölderlin's itinerary (the moment of the problematic of the tragic and the confrontation with the Greeks), as if he is refusing to take responsibility for this exchange or this alternation, this endless *Weschel* of mourning and of joy — let us say *Trauer-spiel*. This is perhaps why Heidegger's tragedy is pathetic: it is a pathos, and not an *ethos* in the sense in which Nietzsche, it seems to me, came to understand it.

Translated by Richard Stamp

4

'Political' Seminar

Christopher Fynsk and Philippe Lacoue-Labarthe

Contribution I: Christopher Fynsk

In the initial suggestions that I sent to members of the preparatory group I took up the question of the political as a *limit-question* for philosophy in the period of its end.[1] I suggested that in our respective contributions we try to approach this limit by different, even heterogeneous paths in order to try to bring it to life (to define it if you like), but to do so always with the suspicion that it is not a question of a simple limit.

It was in these general terms that I proposed we approach the question of the political in the work of Jacques Derrida and in relation to the theme of 'the ends of man'. After Philippe Lacoue-Labarthe and Jean-Luc Nancy's opening remarks and the discussion which followed,[2] it became perfectly clear that my initial suggestion was – up to a certain point, at least – philosophical. For instance, I could have proposed that one treat the question of the political as a limit-question for the work of Derrida himself. Implicitly, however, I determined this work as philosophical, or I suggested that one determine it as such. In this way one can, I think, detect in these notes a sort of implicit response to one of the questions that I posed there: I want to speak of the question concerning what one can designate as a retreat in (or of) Derrida's text in relation to politics or to political questions. Today, I would want to clarify somewhat the decision already approached or sought after in these notes, stressing the fact that if there was already in them a sort of response to the question posed, it was not exhaustive nor would it want to be so (it was, at most, a revival of the question).

But before continuing, I would want to say that if I persist in following the path already opened by these notes, and if I allow myself to refer to them now, I do so simply in order to allow the possible resonances between these interventions to appear. Distance has prevented us from preparing a collaborative piece of work, but some of us did manage a few exchanges, and these will not have failed to mark our respective positions. I underline the common aspect of this work in order to suggest that our common goal is indeed to conduct a seminar. If there are resonances between the contributions (whether they are due to these first exchanges or not), our task here will be to produce their text.

The relation between Derrida's work and politics could be called, then, a relation of *retreat*. Such a retreat is legible, firstly, in a certain silence or hesitation which, for example, manifests itself in what Derrida refers to in *Positions* as 'lacunas' in his text, places which indicate a 'theoretical elaboration' of deconstruction and a 'conjunction' with the Marxist text which remains 'still to come'[3] (we will have the opportunity, perhaps, to reflect upon the status of this 'still to come', both in retrospect and today). This hesitation can also be seen in the multiplication of the precautions which spring up the moment a political question is broached, just as in the appeal (itself linked to the gesture by which the 'settling of accounts' with [*l'explication avec*: *die Auseinandersetzung* – EN] Marxism is deferred) to a sort of theoretical patience. (It is more *effective*, Derrida says in *Positions*, to not hasten to bring about this conjunction between his text and the Marxist text or texts.[4]) This appeal is accompanied, moreover, by a certain insistence (the allusions to the political are brief but frequent); but this insistence is, in turn, stamped with suspicion: in the interview published in *Diagraphe*, for example, Derrida remarks apropos the question of time:

> and if I say, if I rush to say that this question is also a political one, if I say that politics is always allied with whatever regulates the time to look for one's words, or the words of others, I will have allowed myself to be hurried along by a determined urgency of our 'epoch'.[5]

Now, if Derrida thus hesitates to engage himself in immediately political questions (if he does not *politicise* his thinking), he nonetheless affirms that his practice *is* political, that philosophical activity is, in general, a political practice. One could cite various statements to this effect, beginning with the first words of the essay 'The Ends of Man', whose relevance for us is self-evident:

Every philosophical colloquium necessarily has a political meaning. And not only due to that which has always linked the essence of the philosophical to the essence of the political. Essential and general, this political import nonetheless weighs upon the a priori link between philosophy and politics, aggravates it in a certain way, and also determines it when the philosophical colloquium is announced as an international colloquium. This is the case here.[6]

We will, perhaps, return to these lines. But I will also cite another statement of this type which is to be found in the second half of the interview that Derrida gave to *Diagraphe*. Responding to the question: 'Does philosophical practice necessitate for you a political practice?', Derrida says:

Philosophical activity does not *require* a political practice; it is, in every way, a political practice. Once one has struggled to get that recognised, other struggles begin that are both philosophical *and* political.[7]

At first glance, this remark would seem to respond to a common or shared obviousness. It is obvious today that philosophy does not exist outside of the system of power and knowledge which structures our institutions. And that politics forms the horizon of every practice is perhaps, for modernity, *obviousness itself* – hence our difficulty in assigning a proper meaning to the term 'politics' (a difficulty which, in another sense, would define the 'retreat of the political'). But the term 'philosophical activity' is no less obscure if what is being sought is a designation of the essence of what takes place under the name of philosophy, and that is to say if what is being sought is what gives an identity to the multiplicity of discourses which, in the university or on the far larger media stage (or beyond even this), evoke the name of philosophy *as such*. In fact, this diaspora seems to testify to the impossibility of ever realising such an identification – it seems, in other words, to testify to the end of philosophy. Now that it is no longer possible for philosophy to furnish itself with a centre or a fundamental domain on the basis of which it could think both its own unity and that of the entire field of cultural understanding and practices, then this impossibility, as Lacoue-Labarthe and Nancy reminded us in their Opening Address to this conference,[8] remains to be thought. What thus begins to take shape is what Derrida referred to in 'Violence and Metaphysics' as the question of the end of philosophy.[9] For the impossibility of philosophy can indicate to us its 'impossible', and that is to say, the *possible of thinking*. And it is in the affirmation of this possible, or in its reaffirmation as critical, philosophical movement, that what Derrida in the remark in question calls 'the philosophical act' begins to take shape. Whence our working hypothesis: it is on the basis of this act as 'correspondence with the question' that one can begin to think the relation between philosophy and politics in Derrida's text and determine the meaning of the phrase: 'philosophical activity is a political practice'. This is why I will say that if Derrida's text is political, if – before every possible political translation (and the possibility of any such translations remains to be thought) – it has a political meaning, then this is, first of all, insofar as it is philosophical.[10]

In saying this, I am not ignoring the fact that one can read Derrida's text entirely differently in order to judge its political meaning. One could, for example, attempt to situate it in the socio-political context of the last fifteen years, and extract from it a lesson wholly different to the paradoxical and difficult teaching that it actually advances – a little like Rancière had done, somewhat brutally moreover, with Althusser's teaching. One could do this, for example, on the basis of the theme of 'the end of man' and its political operation. One can still, and perhaps one should (this is what I proposed in my preparatory notes), read this text on the basis of interests which are not its own or which remain ill defined within it, in order to raise what we can hastily call its *proper* interests – and this is even inevitable in every reading. In short, one can try to take up a position in relation to this text by assigning it to a position in the politico-philosophical field and thereby decide upon its meaning. But if we do not subject ourselves from the start to the ordeal of the text, our reading can only remain ineffective – or effective merely in the tautological reinforcement of its point of departure. If, on the contrary, the text is encountered in its singular movement, if one engages *with* it in allowing oneself to be engaged *by* it, one must, in one way or another, respond to the affirmation to which I have already alluded. One could always refuse to do so but, in any case, one would still be led to recognise in this engagement or explication that Derrida's most fundamental political gesture is, finally, the affirmation (but in the active sense of this term – in its performance in a discursive practice) that the end of philosophy is not the end of thinking. Or if, because it would indeed be necessary to give another meaning to the term 'political practice', one hesitates to call this gesture political (and if this gesture is to be repeated, as politics or as political, it is always in its being articulated in relation to concrete political situations); if, then, one hesitates to call this gesture political, one still has to see that, essentially, it determines every political act insofar as every such act would be deconstructable.

Consequently, the philosophical act would take shape within the 'community of the question' of which Derrida speaks in the opening pages of 'Violence and Metaphysics' – the community which founds itself upon an injunction to protect the question *as* a question, and that is to say to protect the freedom of the question (double genitive) in its very asking. As Derrida makes clear:

> If this commandment has an ethical meaning, it is not in that it belongs to the *realm* of the ethical but in that it – subsequently – authorises all ethical law in general. There is no stated law, no commandment, that is not addressed to a freedom of speech.[11]

Answering to its possible as a question, but answering to it without answering it, and that is to say answering without closing off the question, philosophy would also be answering to what founds the possibility of every ethical law and every politics. What opens up here are the dimensions of another problem, one which poses the formula: 'Philosophical activity *is* a political practice.' This problem would be the following: in accordance with what regime of meaning, by what measure, can the identity posited by the copula in this remark be thought? What is the measure which founds the translatability of these terms?

On the basis of the determination of philosophical activity just evoked, we see that this common measure cannot be the one supplied by modern metaphysics – that is to say, the measure whereby the common element of the two terms, the value of praxis, would be determined on the basis of the notion of production. Philosophical activity would not be an instance of this 'representing production' through which the 'dominance of subjectivity', as Heidegger calls it in the *Letter on Humanism*, imposes itself.[12] Rather, philosophical practice would be this work of reading or of writing which brings to light that point where every representing production – and that is to say, every practice which implies language – fails. Every practice, then, including its own. Philosophical practice would work to define what Gérard Granel calls the 'practical finitude' of all human production, and that is to say the relation to its grounds which it does not succeed in mastering and upon which it closes itself in order to install an ideal mastery over a specific realm of beings. Doubtless one of the best examples of this philosophical practice is the analysis of linguistic science in *Of Grammatology* where Derrida locates the point at which linguistic science would open itself to a 'science' of writing which would look for its object in the root of scientificity – which, as everyone knows, Derrida thinks in terms of the idea of archi-writing or the movement of the trace. This is what is referred to in the *Grammatology* as the 'common root' of every human practice: art, science, politics, economics – a root which, as Derrida writes, 'is not a root but the concealment of the origin and which is not common because it amounts to the same thing only with the unmonotonous insistence of difference'.[13] It is this common root which we have designated as the possible of philosophy and of politics, and that Derrida, in 'Violence and Metaphysics', calls the freedom of speech. It would thus be on the basis of this thought of difference that we are reminded schematically of the fact that we would have to think the ground – but, as we shall see, it is without ground – of the translatability of the terms 'philosophical activity' and 'political practice'.

In order to think the meaning according to which philosophical activity would be a political practice on this level, it would be necessary to ask how this 'common root' of every human practice determines a community; or, in the terms with which we began, how this 'community of the question' of which Derrida speaks in 'Violence and Metaphysics' is formed. The question, clearly, is that of the Other. Granel articulates it in the following manner:

> philosophy 'as such' today, insofar as it is no more able to dispense with totality than with foundationality, can be only the conscious pursuit of a community affair, in other words a political one. Indeed, there are only (determinate) form*s* of the nothing with which all occupations of *Da-sein* are preoccupied and 'philosophy' properly occupies itself in recasting this. But if, as a result, there is an ultimate homonymy of practices, if all forms of praxis ultimately have the same name, there is no general praxology. To put it more simply, the philosophy *of* this and the philosophy *of* that are not parts of philosophy 'as such', which would be torn apart within them. This does not mean that it is not possible to assemble fragments (fragmentarily), and on each occasion as though in anticipation of the 'whole' or of the World, but rather that the idea of world is not yet an idea to be put to philosophy: once again it is a *banal* idea of *Da-sein*, one that constitutes it as 'politics'.[14]

At the heart of this affirmation would be the idea that the decision to be which is at the origin of every practice, and that is to say this enclosing decision where the incompetence or finitude of a practice indicates itself, this decision is not the concern of a solitary or single being. No more is it the decision of a community, of a people even, as a homogeneous and autonomous body. The heteronomy of the subject that Derrida describes in *Of Grammatology*: 'the access to writing is the constitution of a free subject in the violent movement of its own effacement and its own bondage',[15] this heteronomy ought also to be thought as a social fact – one which means that the *politeia* is fragmented.

This remains largely unthought by Heidegger. And if he does manage to describe this social heteronomy in *Sein und Zeit* (see the descriptions of *Mitsein*),[16] then this is almost in spite of himself; and he suppresses it in his call to a self-affirmation of the teaching body and the student body in the Rectoral Address. It is only at the cost of such a suppression that an individual or ecstatic identity can in this way assert itself, something that he recalls in the *Letter on Humanism* when he maintains that, like collectivism, nationalism is a subjectivity and, as such, metaphysical. He writes: 'Collectivism is the subjectivity of man in totality. It completes subjectivity's unconditional self-assertion (*unbedingte Selbstbehauptung*), which refuses to yield.'[17] The call of the Rectoral Address to will the essence of philosophy and, through this, create a world of spirit wherein the identity of a people would affirm itself, remains firmly embedded in a thinking of the production of the subject. What it thus teaches us – this is a painful lesson and one which would merit still further reflection – is that philosophy or thinking, if it can be determined as the struggle for a world, cannot be directed towards this world as an object or work to be produced. Or else, it would be a matter of producing this world in its fragmentary nature: which would itself shatter the very notion of production.

The struggle for a world can thus only be that philosophical practice which we defined earlier and which, in our socio-historical context, assumes only a negative appearance. In the world of production, this struggle is devoid of effect, devoid of positive result, working to frustrate the imaginary security of the different fields of knowledge which, in their positivity, seek the certainty of their liberation from philosophy (thereby ensuring the completion of philosophy in this period of its end). It would be political practice as historiographical and as historical, working towards the exposition of the constitution of the different cultural practices and fields of knowledge – and working, therefore, counter to the political and economic powers that do everything to suppress such a reflection. This is why there emerges in this analysis another image of history, one which calls into question the socio-economic structure of power, and this contributes towards defining a politics for philosophy. But philosophy is also something other than this sort of *theoretical* practice – and that is to say,

93

something other than a practice which would consist of producing a representation of the field of conflict whilst still representing (in the sense of a delegate,
a spokesperson) a given position. Such effects of representation are, up to a
point, inevitable, and one might say that, up to a point, they should not be
avoided. On the contrary. But philosophy also affirms itself as being both more
and less than such a representing production. Because both historiographical
and *historical*, this work on the grounds or the limits of cultural knowledges and
practices would seek the conditions of an effective alteration in these practices;
it would seek to open itself to what, from a past inaccessible to these practices,
gives a future. It would seek to produce political possibilities for communities
still to come.

Contribution II: Philippe Lacoue-Labarthe

I want to make clear, first of all, that my intention is to speak here only very
briefly – and then from a position somewhat external and marginal.

The idea for this contribution was hatched in the course of one of the two or
three conversations which Chris Fynsk, Rodolphe Burger and myself were able
to have in Strasbourg over the last few months. It was settled on the basis not
of a common interest, but of a common *fear* for the political[18] – by which I
understand the *question* of the political. Despite everything, from age to
nationality, that separates us, the three of us have a sort of strange 'passion'
for the political (the word here being taken in all its various senses). It is from
this position, very simply, that I want now to intervene.

It was also agreed that my intervention would follow on from Chris
Fynsk's introductory note. Not in order to 'take it up', or to try to draw
out some general orientation for the seminar, but, by dwelling on the questions
which he raises, to mark out a *position*. As such, this is of course questionable –
and is so in two ways: firstly, because this position can only come within the
scope of the restricted context of the French situation today; and, secondly,
because any such move can refer only to my 'own' position or to what has been
so for, let us say, the last twenty years or so. This is, moreover, one of the
reasons why my intervention will instead take the form of a *de-position*, which
obviously I would want to be the measure of the general 'distress' (although
clearly it relates only to myself); but, above all, I would want this de-position
to be simple, direct and clear so that we finally stop 'drowning' the problems,
with greater or lesser virtuosity. This even at the risk, which I am fully

prepared to assume, of oversimplification. I recall, then, the following from Chris Fynsk's exposition:

1 That he poses the question of the political as a (if not the) limit-question 'for philosophy in the period of its end'. Which, in his eyes, implies that, in all rigour, we cannot take this limit as being a simple one; and that the 'end of philosophy' is also, as Heidegger showed us, the opening of what he calls 'the *possible of thinking*'. The political – in other words the *question* of the political such as Fynsk understands it – forms the extreme boundary or horizon (perhaps in the process of effacing itself) of what is still, for us, philosophy.

2 That he observes a certain 'retreat' by Derrida in relation to the political; or, more exactly, in relation to politics and 'political questions'. Which in no way prevents him from recalling that it is Jacques Derrida who has managed to pose explicitly the problem of the conjunction between, to put it quickly, deconstruction and the Marxist text; or, more expansively, who has posed the political as 'a determined urgency of our epoch' and recalled the essential co-belonging of the political and the philosophical (see the lines from the start of 'The Ends of Man' cited above). More generally, however, it is the 'retreat' which dominates. As Fynsk says, the allusions to the political in Derrida are both frequent and distant – and they remain allusions. .

I am schematising in the extreme, but I do so in order to try to get as quickly as possible to what is essential. And what is essential here, as far as I am concerned, is the question of the link which indissociably unites the political with the philosophical.

By this I mean, first of all, that I believe profoundly in the necessity of the 'retreat of the political', at least insofar as it is defined – in an initial sense – as a 'retiring' of the political (and that is to say of politics and of the world henceforth determined, in quasi-exclusive fashion, as political). On condition of not immediately referring this 'retreat' to the current political situation (in France, for example, to the type of 'rehabilitation' which has followed May '68, with all the phenomena of dejection, of weariness, of disarray, which it supposes); on condition, also, of taking all the requisite precautions as regards the unity and homogeneity of the philosophical (and of the political); on these conditions, then, it is still necessary, for all that, to take account of the fact that, in the modern age, the unconditional (or, as Arendt puts it, 'total') domination of the political, whether it is achieved and realised or not, represents, in every instance and in all its forms, the completion of a philosophical programme. In the political, it is the *philosophical* which today holds sway – which is equally to say: *technology*, in the sense in which Heidegger intended (even if, as I am firmly convinced, the concept or the essence of this remains unquestioned). Historiographically – and that is to say, historically – a limit has been reached, and this is the *totalitarian fact* as it accompanies the movement of philosophy drawing to a close. Which does not mean that the gulag is in Hegel or Birkenau is in Nietzsche, but that we have to cease denying the actuality of the various modes of the completion of the philosophical: from the Party State to psychological dictatorship.

In this sense, any gesture of dissociation with regard to the philosophical can only take the form of a 'retreat' of the political. I would say that there is a necessary mistrust and suspicion – without which, as everyone knows, deconstruction would mean strictly nothing. This is why I am wary, on my part, of taking such and such an admission by Derrida as a mark of a somewhat assiduous allegiance to the political, or even as the sign of a simple political 'preoccupation'. When Derrida stresses that politics is 'a determined urgency of our epoch'; when he recalls the essential co-belonging of the philosophical and the political; even when he states that 'philosophical activity . . . is, in any case, a political practice', nothing stops us from thinking that he has not already given up on the authority of the philosophical as such.[19] If you like, Derrida's 'allusive' treatment of the political is perhaps comparable, *mutatis mutandis*, with what takes place in the later Heidegger: on the basis of a certain delimitation of metaphysics, the refusal to contemplate some action – and that is to say, some *effect* – for thinking in a world itself overdetermined, since the speculative completion, by the concept of actuality [*effectivité*: *Wirklichkeit* – EN] (see, for example, the opening pages of the 'Letter on Humanism' or the interview with *Der Spiegel*). And it is true that if 'our' task is to differentiate ourselves from the philosophical, we must also learn to renounce what has always magnetised philosophical desire: (its) practical realisation. Including when, as is still the case in Heidegger, it is thought itself (ex-theory) which passes for the highest form of practice.

This is why, moreover, the gesture of the 'retreat' cannot be a simple one. It is not a matter of turning away from the political and of 'moving on to something else' – assuming that there could still be, today, something other than the political. No 'retreat', no *safe haven*, if you like, could accommodate and protect the one who 'retreats'. Which amounts to saying that the 'retreat' has to be *active*, offensive, even – and that it has to be such all the more so given that another meaning lies hidden beneath the term 'retreat of the political', providing a different stress is placed on the genitive. Thus, Chris Fynsk has rightly insisted that the 'retreat of the political' also means that the very *question* of the political retires and gives way to a kind of obviousness of politics or the political – to an 'everything is political', for example, universally accepted/denied (and that is to say interrogated) and to which, even in so-called liberal democracies, it is demanded of us that we submit.

It seems to me that the priority of deconstruction should be to tackle such an 'obviousness'. I almost feel like saying: it might now be time to put the *deconstruction of the political* onto the agenda, hoping, however, that this proposition will not be seen as the sign of an untimely 'activism'.

To deconstruct the political implies, one suspects, an immense and difficult work. And first of all because it is indeed the whole of philosophy which is implicated in it (given the bond that philosophy is said to have essentially with the political). Thus, it is not a question of here tracing the programme, even just to demonstrate its possibility, of this deconstruction. But the deconstruction of the political does not only imply work: a course of action is still needed (the choice of words in this instance is unfortunate, but I can think of no others). And, above all, a refusal is needed: a refusal of the intimidation which, because it is 'regarded as sacred', is exercised today by the political and which forces anyone whatsoever (and, *a fortiori*, anyone who works in or *on the basis of* philosophy) to be accountable, to show their hand, to intervene, to commit themselves, etc. Just look, for example, at the type of discourses Derrida's 'retreat' has triggered.

It is true that the intimidation of which I am thinking – but here, it is my own 'position' that I am putting forward, and I am involving only myself – is, before anything else, that exercised by Marxism insofar as it still represents, I believe (and I believe that it is indispensable to say this), the most powerful of political theories or ideologies – at least in France, and that is to say in Europe as well.

By speaking in this way, I know that I am going to shock. There is, in France for instance, a vague consensus: deconstruction ('Derridism', even) is, at least tacitly, 'of the left'. This is a sort of unspoken agreement. And on the other hand, under the domination of the 'everything is political', to say that it is in any way 'against' Marxism is to fuel the opposition: the bourgeoisie, Capital, the right (whether new or not), etc. But I am taking this risk – which, providing one shows even the slightest clarity and rigour, is not one – for two reasons:

1 I am not persuaded that one does deconstruction (including the undoubtedly deconstructive element that Marxism *also* conceals) any service in keeping Marxism sheltered from it: if there is in Marxism an onto-teleology of the proper and of appropriation or of reappropriation (of the appropriation or reappropriation of man), of self-production and of effectuation, if there is a 'metaphysics of Marx' (as there is a metaphysics of Nietzsche), why should it be untouchable? And if certain political presuppositions, for example those which are at work in the theory (of the 'withering') of the State, derive from a (far too) simple critique and reversal of Hegel or from the acceptance of contestable models (the Jacobin model, among others), in the name of what do we pass silently over this?

2 There existed, and there still exists, a *revolutionary* critique of Marxism and its 'realisations' – and that is to say, for what is of most immediate concern here, a critique of all that follows from the Leninist reorientation: Soviet 'socialism' and, in Western Europe, the organisations and the parties which drew on this with a greater or lesser degree of strictness.

I am alluding here to the various 'Councilist' currents (in France, the 'Socialisme our Barbarisme' group, for example, or the Situationist International), which, their role in the events of '68 notwithstanding, cannot be ignored. Whatever are or have been my philosophical reservations regarding the Councilist theses (most notably, their focusing unduly on what could indisputably lead to 'Marxist metaphysics', on the motif of *self*-organisation, and that is to say on the conception of the proletariat as Subject), it does not alter the fact that they represented and that they can still represent the only 'provisional politics' (as one speaks of 'provisional morality') faced with the disastrous consequences of the 'bureaucratic counter-revolution' (but it is even worse than that), the pressure of which, direct or not, has invariably ended in the preservation or the consolidation, over the last forty years, of bourgeois power. Without speaking, of course, of the colonisation of Eastern Europe, of the repression of all acts of open revolt (Poznan, Budapest, etc.) or, more generally, of Soviet imperialism – which is every bit equal to that of America.

There. This is obviously a little quick but it should, all the same, serve to open the discussion — and such was the goal that Chris Fynsk and I set for ourselves.

I would not want these few remarks to be taken as a 'provocation' (this could only be to ignore or to refuse to take into consideration the decisive openings which, despite everything, have taken place over these last few years in the field of politics). I would like them instead to be seen as an 'incitement': to confront, finally, seriously, the *question of the political*, and that is to say — because nothing much has really changed — the question of the *essence* of the political.

Our submission — or our refusal to do so — to *political obviousness* depends on it.

(This text has been reconstructed from notes taken during the course of a contribution which was, for the most part, improvised.)

Debate

(Transcribed by Christopher Fynsk)

Participants: Marie-Claire Boons, Mikkel Borsch-Jacobsen, David Carroll, Luce Guedj, Sarah Kofman, Jacob Rogozinski, Gayatri Spivak.

The frequent appeal in the preceding contributions to a Heideggerian style of questioning was, for certain members of the audience, surprising; and this was conveyed in the discussion by an unevenness in the to and fro of the exchanges. The discussion of Heidegger developed intermittently throughout the whole of the first day. I will present here, first of all, the outline of this discussion, which took its initial bearings from a series of questions posed by SARAH KOFMAN. She asked how, given the enormous differences separating Heidegger and Derrida's political practices (and their respective socio-historical contexts), there could be a theoretical confluence over the question of the political. Given the political practices to which he was able to be led, how and why should we depend theoretically on Heidegger in order to raise today the question of the political?

PHILIPPE LACOUE-LABARTHE sketched an initial response by recalling that it was possible to detect in the very style of the Derridian allusions to the political something that very closely resembles *certain* Heideggerian positions, most notably those which followed the war. He noted that there is apparently nothing which can unite them if not a certain trajectory in the course of which Heidegger had, essentially, silently reworked the political question (and that is to say, in particular, his own political itinerary), thereby marking a distancing – an indictment, even – vis-à-vis the political. It is not, then, a question of reducing Derrida to Heidegger, nor of neutralising the differences between their different political situations and practices. Picking out a stratum common

100

to Heidegger and Derrida in their relation to the question of *the political* does not amount to neutralising the differences in their respective positions on the level of *politics*. (The distinction between 'politics' and 'the political' was articulated sufficiently in Lacoue-Labarthe's intervention to render it unnecessary to recall here the distinctions that were made in this regard during the discussion. One can note, nevertheless, and always concerning the reference to Heidegger, Lacoue-Labarthe's remark about the point at which politics 'trespasses' on the political, a point which would be marked in Heidegger by his silence on the mass extermination, in the fact that there is no word from Heidegger on Auschwitz. For Lacoue-Labarthe, this silence is, perhaps, the indication of the boundary which separates politics from the political, and of a sort of abutment of that which one can recognise, on the other hand, as being a deepening – and a genuinely deconstructive gesture in comparison with the whole of the political question in its most general sense, and particularly in comparison with the link, always accepted as obvious, between philosophy and politics.)

Lacoue-Labarthe's response was continued throughout an exchange with JACOB ROGOZINSKI. Rogozinski first of all posed a question concerning the relevance here of the Heideggerian concept of 'Western metaphysics': he asked, on the one hand, if the whole of modern politics does indeed allow itself to be thought under this concept; and, on the other hand, if one would not run the risk of eclipsing another dimension to which classical political reflection has always addressed itself: namely, what Rogozinski referred to as the problem of radical evil in politics – not politics as radical evil, but politics as the occasion of a crisis in community.

In order to clarify his position, LACOUE-LABARTHE responded very briefly, explaining that his intention was simply to bring together problematics which had, until now, remained foreign to one other – and that is to say, in this case, what remains today of the problematic of the far-left and Heideggerian thought. Addressing myself to the same question (to the question of the relation between the Heideggerian problematic and modern politics), I tried to explain that, with the notion of 'modern metaphysics', it seemed to me possible to think a fundamental aspect of what appears in certain Western countries as a homogeneity of political and cultural space and to think, just as easily, from this perspective, the differences which work community and which produce other places (which one can see, perhaps, in the multiplication of political discourses). In thus addressing oneself to what metaphysics would have

101

'forgotten' and which it suppresses as ideology (to take up one of Lacoue-Labarthe's terms), one would touch on one element of what constitutes a constant crisis in society and perhaps on what has been called 'radical evil'. I developed this idea (rapidly dealt with in my talk) in detail, making reference to the difference which is constitutive of *Mitsein* and, consequently, of *Dasein*'s world (the difference which *Dasein* experiences in the experience of the *Unheimlichkeit* as it is defined in *Sein und Zeit*,[20] but which is, as will be the case in the later political writings, eclipsed in certain moments of the existential analytic).

In response to these remarks, ROGOZINSKI clarified his question by referring to Sartre's critique of the Heideggerian notion of *Mitsein*, and which amounts to the suggestion that Heidegger would have lacked the dimension of conflict which is constitutive of the relation to the Other. The question that Rogozinski thus asks of Heidegger (and, moreover, also of Marx) would be that of the status of conflict. Do they pose the ideal of a sublation of conflict? Or is it a matter of persisting with conflict, of settling on a conflict without end?

As regards Heidegger, LACOUE-LABARTHE responded by pointing out that just as one can detect an 'ontological' emphasis on conflict from 1927 onwards (on everything that is, for example, of the order of the 'struggle for a world'), so in the political texts there is, explicitly, a challenge to conflict in the political sense and, most notably, to the class struggle. According to Lacoue-Labarthe, the problem is one of knowing how to articulate the philosophical with such political declarations if one is unhappy simply ascribing Heidegger's political practice to a fall or to weakness. That is why he evokes, in this context, the Rectoral Address of 1933, which takes up the problem of the university (and consequently of science) in terms of *Selbstbehauptung* as it is posed in the inaugural lecture of 1929 ('What is Metaphysics?'), but which does so without any precaution concerning the value of the *Selbst* and by ignoring the fundamental theme of the inaugural lecture, the disclosure of *Unheimlichkeit*. Everything in the Address is *positively* transformed: there remains only the 'pre-critical' lexicon of interruption, of decision, of attack, etc., which, when it was the very elaborate product of the problematic of the nothing, aimed, precisely, at giving a philosophically (or ontologically) 'un-marked' meaning to *existentialia*. And which gave the hope, consequently, of a *new* phrase, one opposed to political phraseology. Lacoue-Labarthe observed, moreover, that Heidegger never renounced the Rectoral Address and that, on the contrary, all the subsequent texts ceaselessly resume and unravel it. Up to a certain point one can indeed speak of 'rupture', but what persists is a concretely *political* discourse, readable, for sure, as a sort of self-critique, but where the question is of knowing whether it confronts, with regard to his commitment to Nazism, the problem of *philosophical* responsibility.

Several questions raised in the course of the discussion remained unanswered or did not lead to any subsequent development. In particular, it was asked how the 'passion' evoked in Lacoue-Labarthe's talk could have anything to do with what had been called the essence of the political. Equally, and as regards the relation between philosophy and politics, a question was asked concerning the object of this 'passion'. On the other hand, taking up LUCE GUEDJ'S question concerning an ethics which would be founded on a determination of community as subject, MARIE-CLAIRE BOONS remarked that what was lacking in the project of a deconstruction of Marxism evoked by Lacoue-Labarthe was a thinking of the subject of the unconscious in its political capacity. To which LACOUE-LABARTHE responded by saying that, at the price of a certain rapidity, he had limited himself to what seemed to him most urgent: namely, to raise the question of Marxism to the extent that it has become, for the discourses of Derridism, a sort of fixation, a situation which to him seemed essential to remedy. But the question of the subject, in his opinion, is today a decisive question: it is the question, for example, of *self*-determination or of *self*-organisation, and that is also to say the question of re-appropriation in Marx's sense of the word. If it is therefore necessary to criticise certain properly political effects of psychoanalysis (its role amongst the petit bourgeois in capitalist countries, a certain pessimism issuing from analytic discourse), one must recognise that there is also, in a certain analytic rigour (in Lacan, for example, in a notion like that of the fractured subject, a notion which it is possible to radicalise still further), a weapon against the often disastrous utopia of re-appropriation or self-determination. Today, the political stake is the question (and it is indeed a *question*) of re-appropriation: is not re-appropriation – in which one has dreamt of an end to alienation – itself the condition of possibility for totalitarianism?

The end of the discussion was oriented in its entirety around a contribution by DAVID CARROLL in which he asked in what sense one can take Marxism to be 'the most powerful of theories' (a question which developed into a question on the unity or the coherence of Marxism), and whether this would be true only for a particular circle, that of the French intelligentsia. The question was thus of knowing whether the political theory of *Capital* (if indeed it is one) is not, in fact, more powerful, and whether in this case one should not, first and foremost, have to tackle this question instead of turning against Marxism. Lacoue-Labarthe's contribution, in other words, perhaps responded to the French situation but not, for example, to the American one.

LACOUE-LABARTHE specified that, in this case, 'powerful' also meant 'intimidating' and reaffirmed that in France, Marxism remains the most complete, most overtly theoretical political theory. Insofar as in France 'Derridism' is, on the whole, 'of the left', the necessity of 'settling accounts' with this founding determination is imperative – which in no way precludes a precise and uncompromising critique (but a critique, rather than a deconstruction, properly understood) of the thought of the right. Furthermore, it is not a matter, within a 'programme' of deconstruction, simply of opposing, of going against or of destroying Marxism, nor is it, for precisely this reason, a matter of making it into something homogeneous – no more so in what concerns Marx's text (where, at very precise moments, one finds elements which approach the sense of deconstruction) than it is for that which concerns the general field of Marxism within which there are elements of which it would be necessary to provide another account.

This question of the heterogeneity of the field of Marxism was continued, moreover, on the basis of a comment by Derrida (drawn from an interview given to an English journal[21]) concerning the notion of an 'open Marxism' (a Marxist movement which would not be closed to discourses which are not Marxist in origin), and the problem of strategy tackled in relation to the anti-Marxist movement. Insofar as it would participate in the transformation of struggle *as such* into merely isolated struggles, would there not be a danger of the deconstruction of Marxism contributing to what remains fragmentary (in the bad sense of the term) in these struggles – something which would risk calling into question the construction of a community or communities to come? And indeed, one can see in this the horizon of a certain risk; but if, in the actual crisis of the left, the limited, heterogeneous movements have a function, we must not ignore the fact that the extent of their play is also given by this crisis.

Translated by Simon Sparks

5

Foreword to The Centre for Philosophical Research on the Political

Philippe Lacoue-Labarthe and Jean-Luc Nancy

In November 1980 the Centre for Philosophical Research on the Political was opened in Paris at the Ecole Normale Supérieure on the rue d'Ulm, under the guidance of Philippe Lacoue-Labarthe and Jean-Luc Nancy.[1] Conceived as a place of free investigation, the Centre was intended to occupy a marginal or 'withdrawn' position in relation to the places traditionally assigned in the dialogue (agreement or conflict) between philosophy and politics. An introductory statement clarified what was at stake:

> How to question (indeed, can one), today, what must provisionally be called the *essence of the political*?
>
> Such an inquiry, the imperative nature of which needs no commentary, no doubt demands the construction of a new object and should not be confused either with a work of 'political studies' or with an undertaking of 'political philosophy'. Philosophy there finds itself called into question; which, for all that, does not presuppose that one can substitute for it a positive (sociological, economic, technological) or normative (ethical, aesthetic – or 'political') discourse.

This position of retreat (this apparent 'return' to a 'question of essence') did not, however, exclude resolutely 'political' intentions. In these times, in particular, in which the most simple political despair (weariness), but also the ease or calculation of things, generated every imaginable regression and reduced political debate to almost nothing, it was necessary to give ourselves some room. Not in order to shut ourselves off from the political or to reject it but, on the contrary, to replay its question anew. If there was the chance, albeit a very slender one, of a philosophical intervention in politics (or with regard to the political), this was its — exorbitant — cost, if one considers it to be such.

One will find in this volume the initial traces of this first investigation.[2] They are simple tracks cleared here and there, without a properly predefined programme — just to see: literally exploratory. . . .

In between times, however, the political situation has itself changed. Moreover, had we had the material resources (recordings, transcriptions, the establishment of protocols), one would have been able to see the effects of this change in the course of the discussions which followed each talk. We are not saying all this in order to suggest that, in its nature and its function, the Centre would henceforth be redundant. We are saying it simply in order to indicate that, in future, it is not impossible that its work might reorient itself, at least in its aims, and that another way of replaying the political might answer a certain, very modest, revival of history, without surrendering the necessity of critique.

Translated by Simon Sparks

6

Opening Address to the Centre for Philosophical Research on the Political[1]

Philippe Lacoue-Labarthe and Jean-Luc Nancy

It is, then, today a matter – but perhaps we should say: it is today *simply* a matter of opening or inaugurating this Centre for which, for want of anything better, we have proposed the following title: *The Centre for Philosophical Research on the Political.*

For all sorts of reasons which are (or which could become) obvious, to open a Centre for research cannot be to define a programme. A Centre is first and foremost a site, a space of work – and a space of collective work. Which presupposes, therefore, that there exists an object and an aim; and that an agreement can be reached amongst the various parties as to this object and this aim (as well as to the type of work or the nature of the research to be conducted); and, consequently, that the stakes of the enterprise are determined with the greatest possible clarity. But in any case, even the most preliminary route of a programme of work cannot be supposed on the part of those who propose the opening or creation of such a Centre. Responsibility for a Centre cannot bestow this sort of authority.

It will be, therefore, for us, a question today of simply delimiting a site. Which will, in actual fact, amount to justifying our having agreed – at the behest of Jacques Derrida, for which we here thank him – to take responsibility for this Centre; or, because it amounts to the same thing, to explaining the title which we have provided for this Centre and the object that we propose for its research.

Thus: The Centre for Philosophical Research on the Political. Under this somewhat flat (and even rather anodyne) title, we in fact envisage two things.

107

First of all, and this, in a way, goes without saying, the *philosophical* questioning of the political. (And we should of course point out that 'philosophical' has here an exclusive – that is, 'properly philosophical' – value.) But also, and above all, we envisage the questioning of the philosophical itself as to the political or, more exactly, the questioning of the philosophical itself *about* the political. Which is totally different and hence demands a few justifications that we are going to try to provide. But at the very least it is necessary to show, and without any further delay, that it is precisely because of this double aim that we are speaking here of questioning the *essence of the political* (a formula which, as we are well aware, is open to confusion, but other terms are somewhat lacking), and that we even go so far as to believe that such a questioning today represents a real urgency. If you prefer, and to submit as briefly as possible to the rhetoric of the declaration or programme of intention: to pose, today, the question of the essence of the political seems to us to be a task finally – and decidedly – necessary. And our aim here would be finally – and decidedly – to render it possible.

There is, then, from the beginning, a double aim. With the first, that is to say, with the one which most obviously inscribes itself in the title of this Centre, we would want simultaneously to circumscribe a domain (or at least specify an attitude) and to dissipate an initial possible misunderstanding.

To relate the type of work that we envisage here to philosophical interrogation or questioning (making this gesture of exclusion with regard to other, assuredly always possible and in some cases even desirable, approaches to the political), does not for us mean a pulling back into the *position of the philosophical*, as if such a 'philosophical position' were today still tenable – as is clearly no longer the case. It is neither the lofty claim of some philosophical privilege (or of the privilege of philosophy), nor, even less, the pure and simple renewal of the classical appropriation of the political by philosophy. But what it does mean, above all, is that we have no pretension to *political theory*, and that is to say, to anything that could evoke a 'political science' or a 'politiology'.

This is, firstly, a question of competence: we are in no way 'specialists' in the field of politics or in the sciences which deal with politics, and nothing – beyond the work of a (philosophical) teaching carried out in common for some years (we will speak again of this later) – authorises us to venture into this realm.

But it is also a deliberate choice: the direct approach to the political (which, even if the description is a little quick, might just as well be called the empirical approach) does not interest us — and for the very simple reason that, basically, we no longer believe such an approach still to be possible (or even less that it can still be decisive). If there exists, for example, a *concept* of the political (which, moreover, we would distinguish rigorously from the *essence* of the political), if a new concept of the political or something that one could present as such could become clear, then any such concept would, in our opinion, necessarily derive from the philosophical field and, for reasons to which we shall quickly return and which are, incidentally, well known, from a philosophical field itself determined, that is to say, ancient, past, closed.

Which shows, moreover, that this 'recall' to the philosophical of the question of the political — which, contrary to what one might think, supposes no assurances as regards philosophy — is not a simply critical and 'negative' gesture. Vigilance is assuredly necessary, today more than ever, as regards those discourses which feign independence from the philosophical and which claim, correspondingly, to treat the political as a distinct and autonomous domain (or, and this does not make much difference, one tied up with or subordinated to another such empirical or regional domain). Thus vigilance is necessary as regards every positive discourse, that is to say as regards every discourse formed by a pretension to grasp social and political phenomena on the basis of a simple positivity — whether this be ascribed to history or to discourse itself, to force or desire, to work or affect, etc. (and as far as this goes, anything, or nearly anything, is possible). The project of a theory or a science of the political, with all its socio-anthropological baggage (and, consequently, its philosophical presuppositions), now more than ever necessitates its own critique and the critique of its political functions. But vigilance is not enough here; and simple critique would probably be too quick and ineffective faced with the almost undivided domination of anthropology. This is why our insistence upon the philosophical — beyond any critical exigency, which is the least of our worries — was intended to mark, before anything else, the following: that what today appears to us as necessary, and hence urgent, is rigorously to account for what we are calling the essential (and not accidental or simply historical) co-belonging of the philosophical and the political. In other words, to account for the political as a philosophical determination, and vice versa.

This reciprocal involvement of the philosophical and of the political (the political is no more outside or prior to the philosophical than the philosophical, in general, is independent of the political), does not for us simply refer, even on the level of 'historicality', to the Greek origin — it is not a shortcut to the Sophistic *polis* and its guarantor, the *anthrōpos logikos*. It is, in reality, our situation or our state: by which we mean, in the mimetic or memorial after-effect or *après-coup* of the Greek 'sending' which defines the modern age, the actualisation or installation of the philosophical *as* the political, the general-isation (the globalisation) of the philosophical *as* the political — and, by the same token, the absolute reign or 'total domination' of the political. Such is, moreover, the reason for which, in speaking of *the political* we fully intend not to designate *politics*. The questioning about the political or about the essence of the political is, on the contrary, what for us must ultimately take stock of the political presupposition itself of philosophy (or, if one prefers, of metaphysics), that is to say, of a political determination of essence. But this determination does not itself produce a political position; it is the very position of the political, from the Greek *polis* to what is deployed in the modern age as the qualification of the political by the subject (and of the subject by the political). What remains to be thought by us, in other words, is not a new institution (or instruction) of politics by thought, but the political institution of so-called Western thought.

Whence our second aim, by which we envisage not only the philosophical questioning of the political (or the philosophical critique of political theories), but the questioning of the philosophical itself as to the political or *about* the political; in short, the questioning of the philosophical *as* the political.

Which supposes at least the following:

1 that one recognises a certain completion of the political, or, to use another lexicon, that one takes note (but neither in resignation nor through vexation) of the *closure of the political*. What we mean by this is not unrelated to what Heidegger (and within the limits imposed on him, despite everything, by his own history and that of Germany) attempted to think under the question of technology.[2] In view of contextual differences and another history (in the restricted sense), in view also of our respective political itineraries and our particular political choices, which are neither similar nor assimilable,[3] for us 'Marxism is the unsurpassable horizon of our time', although doubtless not in the sense in which Sartre would have understood his own formula. In our translation: socialism (in the sense of 'real or actually existing socialism') is

110

the complete and completing figure of philosophy's imposition – up to and including what, for one of us at least, could have represented the hope of a critique and a revolutionary radicalisation of established Marxism.

Great theoretical patience would be needed here (in the course of long analyses for a demonstration which is not self-evident), and above all much political rigour. But it seems to us as indispensable today to recognise that what completes itself (and does not cease to complete itself) is the great 'enlightened', progressivist discourse of secular or profane eschatology, and that is to say the discourse of the re-appropriation of man in his humanity, the discourse of the actualisation of the genre of the human – in short, the discourse of revolution. Which in our eyes in no way authorises the tragico-mystical counter-discourse, the one which finds its authority in an always too simple 'beyond' of the human, or else in such and such an ancient transcendence, one which persists in the denial of finitude and the recognition, itself 'tragic', of the end of tragedy (since, from around 1806 onwards, it appears that tragedy is precisely politics). Whatever still remains of the possibilities of revolt – and luckily everything leads us to believe that there are still a few possibilities here and there, but rather more there than here – a certain history, which is perhaps even History, is *finished*, *finite*. In the epoch where the political is completed to the point of excluding every other area of reference (and such is, it seems to us, the *totalitarian phenomenon* itself), we can no longer decently ask ourselves what theory would still be in a position to promise a political solution to inhumanity (which is still not finished), because we now know what the desire for a social transparency promises, the utopia of the homogenisation of the 'social body', the hope attached to management or to enlightened direction.

But this further supposes, by way of consequence:

2 that we distinguish the philosophical from metaphysical discourse in general, from that discourse dedicated to founding the essence of politics (or political essence) and to instituting or programming an existence of which it would be the correlate. There is, today, a 'banal commonplace' that exposes in philosophy the gesture of political foundation which organises it or which it organises. But this exposure falls short, firstly if it does not distinguish very carefully these two doubtless very different gestures (to organise is not to be organised), and then insofar as it remains a critique – itself political (and that is to say itself philosophical) – of philosophy, instead of troubling itself with questioning the philosophical essence of the political. In deciding,

on the other hand, to respond to this exigency – and that is just as much to say in recognising the urgency of which we have spoken – philosophy immediately finds itself implicated as a political practice relieved of its own authority: not simply of its possible social or political power, but relieved of the authority of the theoretical or the philosophical as such (however one determines such a practice: critique, back to basics, thinking and distorting re-appropriation (*Verwindung*), step backwards, deconstruction, etc.).

This is, of course, precisely what for us is at stake. But what is perhaps most serious today, and first of all because it leaves the way open for the barely disguised repetition of old positions, or for the 'anything goes' mentality of supposed novelties, is that, despite everything, there has never been a questioning of the political rigorously, absolutely, comparable with these gestures of deprivation. It is as though philosophy in the movement of its own destitution had not dared to touch the political, or as if the political – under whatever form – had not ceased to intimidate it. It is, in other words, as if a part of philosophy (if not its very essence) had, to all intents and purposes, remained off limits to philosophy in the movement of its own destitution (and when this has not been the case, it is deprivation which usually finds itself abandoned or compromised – I am thinking here of Heidegger). And as if, lastly, the political remained, paradoxically, the *blind spot* of the philosophical.

It is this double exigency – recognition of the closure of the political and practical deprivation of philosophy as regards itself and its own authority – which leads us to think in terms of *re-treating the political*.

This phrase is taken here in at least two senses: first, withdrawing the political in the sense of its being the 'well-known' and in the sense of the obviousness (the blinding obviousness) of politics, the 'everything is political' which can be used to qualify our enclosure in the closure of the political; but also as re-tracing of the political, re-marking it, by raising the question in a new way which, for us, is to raise it as the question of its essence.

In no way would this constitute – and we hasten to say this in order to prevent any misunderstanding – or indicate a falling back into 'apoliticism'. The re-treat, in the sense in which we understand it, is assuredly necessary in order to render possible a questioning which refuses to confine itself to the categories ordinarily grouped under 'the political' and probably, in the long run, to the concept of the political itself. Such a questioning, which is something totally different from a trial or summary execution of the political, is, of course, dedicated to returning to the most archaic constitution of the political, and to exploring the essence of the political assignation of essence, and that is to say, to putting into question the concept and the value of the archaic in general: origin and primitiveness, authority, principle, etc. It is, if you like, the *principiat* in general which must be put into question and into questions. But into questions which ought to disturb the politics of the Prince just as much as the principle of the political. Which is equally to say that the gesture of the re-treat is itself a political gesture – by which it is doubtless a matter of exceeding something of the political, but absolutely not in the manner of a 'foray outside of the political'. The re-treat is not, above all, a foray which, under whatever one of its forms (ethical, aesthetic, religious, etc.), would always amount to confirming the domination and the *principiat* of the political. For us, on the contrary, it is a matter of what not so long ago would have been called an 'engagement' – which is something quite different from a pledge given to one politics or another.

This said, it would be futile to hide the fact that this outline does indeed presuppose a work already underway on our part – and already underway, doubtless no coincidence, in our teaching. In order that our position here be defined as clearly as possible, it is necessary to mention a few things.

It seemed to us desirable to retrace briefly before you our path through this question of the political. Desirable, first of all, and in order – if necessary – to correct certain impressions which might have been given by the first part of this talk. Indeed, such impressions will always be possible if only because we have no 'systematic' representation of this question to offer, and because the corollary today of the massive, *blinding obviousness* of the question or of the 'political' authority at the heart of philosophy is doubtless the contingent, uncertain, even erratic or fragmentary nature of the procedures which allow it to be tackled (which, we clarify this in passing, in no way means, as is said sometimes here and there, that the political *itself* henceforth boils down to an uncertain dispersion of pure effects of power). Then – second reason – this sort of 'account' or 'report' appeared to us to constitute the least false way of situating *us* in the opening of this research Centre, and that is to say of situating *our* particularity in the open space for which we intend to take responsibility without ever taking over.

Up until now our work on the political has — over the last five years — for the most part taken place, as we have already said, through the work of teaching. Which means, first of all, that the work written and published in this area is, in a way, still out of our reach. On the one hand, it is obvious that, more than any other, public work on the political has to reckon with its effects in the matter of political intervention — with politics. On the other, everything has happened as if it had been necessary for us to feel our way along for quite some time before being able to free ourselves slightly from the blinding obviousness of the political. (On this depended, moreover, at least some of the usual cautionary maxims in political matters and, so as to simplify things, the maxim of not risking any harm to the left through misunderstandings. But today, in any case, and if it is necessary to pose the problem in these terms, the risk would be of contributing, through our silence, to the extinction of every 'left'.)

We have tackled the question of the political in an arbitrary manner: I mean, without it finding a place in some determinate and explicit logic of our earlier work. We were not specialists in 'political philosophy' and our approach has, in a way, been practical and political before being philosophical. This, in passing, has not stopped us and does not stop us from considering that, between works devoted, for example, to the relation between philosophy and literature, or to the status and *Darstellung* of philosophical discourse, and a questioning about the political, there are in fact relations far more direct, fundamental and determinate than a certain spirit of the epoch is willing to accept.

Our first question is addressed to Marxism, to the question of the political in Marx and in the early Marxian traditions. This was hardly a matter of choice but was thrust upon us by its sheer obviousness. Moreover, this obviousness up to a point led us to encounter for ourselves what had already been recorded elsewhere and which has been continually underlined since: namely, what Claude Lefort, for example, has called the 'lacuna of the political' in Marxism. But in this 'lacuna' we just as much encountered the *obvious presence* of the very problematic of the political: we encountered it under the form of the negation of the *purely formal* or *abstract* State in favour of a 'material impregnation by the State of the content of all the non-political spheres', according to the terms by which Marx characterises authentic democracy in his *Critique of Hegel's Doctrine of the State.*[4]

Beyond Marx himself, it seemed to us that all the Marxist problematics, whatever they may have been and whatever the analyses they have adopted as regards the history and the displacements of Marx's thought, were tributaries of this lacuna *and* of this presence – in short, tributaries of this presence in and through the lacuna of the political – whether they have simply recorded this heritage or whether they have come up against the necessity of posing to it the supplementary, exhaustive question of a specificity of the political. In theoretical and practical contexts as varied as those of, for example, Councilism, Gramscism, Althusserism or Maoism, it is indeed the general form of such a question that has imposed itself. Not only as the question of a *transitory* political form necessary to the movement of revolution but, more radically, as the question of the singular term which one finds in the 'Critique of the Gotha Programme' when Marx evokes or invokes the 'future *Staatswesen* of communist society', the being-ecstatic, the mode of being or ecstatic essence which will be or which would be that of communism, or even the space of the state which will be its own:[5] a term which does not furnish the concept, but which opens a pure problem, the problem of the responsibility of limiting the separated State, the separated State-form, to the bourgeois State, or else, and systematically (if the *Staatswesen* designates the being of a non-separated-State), the problem of the implications of a thinking of the total immanence or the total immanentisation of the political in the social.

Of course, this location of a problem could not pass for a *reading* of Marx. It only opened the path forward. Nonetheless, the massive – too massive – character of this problem turned us away from any direct reading. It became necessary, for us at least, to pursue the indications of a specific, non-Marxist, certainly – but, for all that, not anti-Marxist – return of the question of the political. We addressed ourselves, then, both to Bataille and to Heidegger at the same time, to two groups of texts which had accompanied – in every sense of the term – the rise and fall of Nazism.

From this double reading – which was largely exploratory and which still remains to be resumed – we can, in the first instance and *very* schematically take the following:

1 On the one hand, we approached these texts as discourses specifically on the political (discourses which also included acts of political intervention: namely, the Rectoral Address or *Contre Attaque*), and in which was organised a fundamental register which one can designate as 'beyond politics' or, more exactly, as the register of a limit, of an extreme (and for this reason, decisive) boundary of the political. Thus, in particular, the two poles

115

constituted by the concepts (or by the problems) of, on the one hand, the *people* and, on the other, *sovereignty*:

- the 'people' as the place of a proper individuality, as much distinct from the State as from civil society, the place of a 'mission' or of a 'destination' (of a *Bestimmung*) itself dependent upon the general problematic of the State as destiny or as being-destined;
- 'sovereignty' as non-dialectically opposed to mastery or domination, and yet as the non-principle principle, so to speak, of political power as such, as well as its subversion.

In both – although certainly in very different ways – the question of a proper subject or, rather, of a beyond-the-subject of the political imposed itself, exceeding the absolute subjectivity that stages the Hegelian State.

We were thus forced to contemplate two *limits*, which are not those *between* which the political would confine itself (or between which it would have confined itself): rather, these are the limits upon which the political erects itself – but doing so, moreover, only while completely repressing or eclipsing their nature as *limits*, and eclipsing, by the same stroke, the *excessive* questions that they imply. It seemed to us that the moral (and/or political) condemnations hurled at fascism and at Stalinism served only to eclipse these questions.

2 On the other hand, this same excess of the political seemed, in both Bataille and Heidegger, to be closed back up, to be reappropriated (once again in very different ways: in Heidegger, this closure directly engaged the responsibility of his sinister political compromise of 1933; in Bataille, however, it also engaged, although no less seriously, the responsibility for praise of the Marshall Plan[6]): a closure or re-appropriation which takes place to the precise extent that, despite everything, a schema of *subjectivity* persists in controlling the analysis of the limits themselves. The questions opened by the words 'people' and 'sovereignty' are closed back up when the people or sovereignty are reascribed, reassigned as *subjects* (and that is perhaps to say, in fact, as *will*): the vocation (and the Führer) of a people, the vocation (and the rendering sacred) of the artist.

It was not a matter of conclusions, but of questions, of obstacles and warnings encountered along the way.

We looked upon this as implying, for the second time, the impossibility of a *frontal* approach to the problem of the political if, behind its own obviousness, was still concealed the obviousness of the subject or the obviousness of an archē-propriety always leading back behind the figures of absolute depropriation which were supposed to be constitutive of the proletariat just as much as they were of sovereignty. The question of the State, or the more general question of power, appeared to us to be unable to be engaged for itself without passing through the question of the subject. Which also meant that the question of power did not seem by itself to constitute the initial question of the political. But this did not mean that, as far as we were concerned, the question of power lost all proper relevance and that the idea of power would conceal a type of effects indissociable from discourse, for example, or from the unconscious – effects themselves multiple, diversely localised and dispersed or stratified in mobile configurations. The combinative and uncertain nature of micro-powers dissolves the nonetheless very real actuality of the great powers, whether they be those of class, of State, of monopoly capitalism, or all three at once. Now, the ruling out or sublimating of either class struggles or political struggles has never been what is at stake for us: these are the givens of the epoch of the domination of the political and technology or of the domination of political economy. But the stake could be one of no longer subjugating these struggles, in their finality, to this domination.

And no longer subjecting them, consequently, to the archē-teleological domination of the Subject. For the political obviousness of the Subject is due to the absolute *presupposition* of the *relation of* 'subjects'. This presupposition alone allows the ordering of the political as *telos*. It is through the ideal or through the idea of the *polis*, more than anything else, that the modern epoch – Romanticism, of course, and all idealism, including socialist idealism – has refastened itself to the Greek origin and finality of the West, that is to say, has tried to reassert itself as the subject of its history, and as the history of the subject.

The *polis* presupposes the relation – the *logikos* relation or *logos* as relation – which it nonetheless inaugurates – and this is what makes of it *the* philosophical ground.

It is unsurprising, then, also to see the question of relation as such arising throughout philosophy as soon as the political becomes an enigma, lacuna or limit for philosophy – which is no doubt what happened as soon as Hegel thought the completion of the political, and in the political. *Politeuein* – Hegel translates this verb as 'to lead the universal life in the city': to conduct relations as the life of the Subject alone. Henceforth, and as if in return, whether this be under the figure of the 'human sciences' or under various philosophical figures, what proliferate in the thought of the end of the nineteenth century and the first half of the twentieth century are questions of the Other, of the *alter ego*, of the 'forms of sympathy', of the agonistic, of the sources of morality and religion, of being as being-with, etc.

Consequently, what arose for us was the necessity of again taking up this question of relation, the question of the 'social bond' not as a presupposition, and yet as impossible to deduce or to derive from an initial subjectivity.

We thus wanted to tackle this question from within the most remote field (or at least what appears to be so), and remote from philosophical *habitus* and political investment: that field was psychoanalysis.

For us, it was in no way a matter of a programme-statement of the 'politics *and* psychoanalysis' sort. Rather, it was a matter of questioning the multiple and powerful motifs of sociality, of alterity, of relation as such, which trouble the specificity of the Freudian 'subject' – and which trouble, moreover, the sort of reconstruction or reaffirmation, in the same Freud, of the *zōon politikon*.

From this work, published elsewhere,[7] we felt able to retain the following: although, on an initial register of Freud's discourse or even in the psycho-analytic vulgate which has today become firmly established, the unconscious is structured like a State (or like a dictatorship) and although Narcissus is totalitarian, another register of the same discourse (and, but this is another question altogether, which perhaps will go so far as to cut into the very propriety and the autarky of psychoanalysis) corresponds, on the contrary, to the multiple weakenings and fissurings of this political and subjectival norma-tivity. And in fact, a thinking which, in principle and on principle, excludes the position of a self-sufficiency and an autocracy, has no choice but to raise the question of relation. As a *question*, and that is to say, in terms of the imposs-ibility of presupposing the solution of relation, whether this be in a subject or in a community. The question of relation is the question of the passage *to* community, but it is equally the question of the passage to the subject. And this question arises in all sorts of ways in Freud, from the problematic of originary sociality to those of bisexuality, identification, or the prehistory of Oedipus.[8]

We will be content today to underline the following: if the 'social bond' is a genuine question – and is, by the same stroke, a *limit* question – for Freud, it is in that the *given* relation (by which we mean: the relation which, in spite of everything, Freud *gave himself*, which, like the whole of philosophy, he *pre-supposed*), this relation of a subject to subjectivity itself in the figure of a father, implies, in the origin or in the guise of an origin, the *birth* (or the *gift*, precisely) of this relation. And a similar birth implies the *retreat* of what is neither subject, nor object, nor figure, and which one can, provisionally and simplistically, call 'the mother'.[9]

Behind politics (if it must be identified with the Father), 'the mother': one can easily imagine the *Schwärmerei* to which this could give rise. But this situation doubtless only arises for an interpretation already itself subordinate to the political.

For us, this sort of sharp end of the question of relation (which has, moreover, many other forms) signified this: there was, in another sense or rather on another level than that to which we have until now confined ourselves, a problem of *retreat* in relation to and *in* the installation of the political, in the erection of the political. A problem of the *retreat*, and that is to say the problem of a non-dialectical negativity, the problem of an advent (of identity and relation) by (the) abstraction (of the 'subject'); or even the problem of that which gives relation *as* relation, insofar as the nature of relation (if it ever had a nature) is the reciprocal retreat of its terms, insofar as relation (but can one even speak of 'relation' in the singular?) is given by or proceeds from the division, from the incision, from the non-totality that it 'is'.

It is not with Freud that we have pursued the exploration of this question. From this point, psychoanalysis leads back to the philosophical. In our most recent work, the question of the relation and of the retreat has been reformulated: for one of us in a questioning, via Heidegger, of the retreat of the political in the problematic of the work of art;[10] and for the other in an examination of what, building on Kant, I would call the ethical prescription of relation.[11] But these are, in all essentials, works in progress, and this is not the right place to speak of them.

This is, on the other hand, the place to say that these works brought us back to the political by bringing us back to the question of a disjunction or a disruption more essential to the political than the political itself, and which, moreover, seems to us to provide the stake, on several different accounts, for more than one contemporary interpretation. A stake which, for now, we will sum up in the following way: the transcendental of the *polis* is not an organicism, whether that of a harmony or of a communion, nor that of a distribution of functions and differences. But no more is it an anarchy. It is the an-archy of the *archē* itself (assuming that the demonstrative pronoun 'it' can still apply in the lexicon of the 'transcendental'; but, likewise, it is so as not to enter too quickly into predetermined discussions of this sort that we have simply – if we can say this – situated the whole of the Centre's work under the title of a question of 'the essence' of the political).

We can at least say, with these summary formulae, that the question of the retreat (of the essence, and thus of the 'retreat') of the political appears to us to be a matter of a general problematic of *the breach*, of the *trace* (of the trace without propriety) as it has been elaborated by Derrida. And that, by the same stroke, the question of the political appeared to us to relaunch afresh, and on the basis of other places, this problematic itself, the disinstallation of the 'textual' field (in a sense often reduced to the 'literary') to which one attributed it.

This is why the last stage was, for us, this summer, a colloquium where, under the title 'The Ends of Man', we tried to propose not an elaboration – this is not the function of a colloquium – but, let us say instead, a punctuation of this state of questions on the basis of Derrida's work.

And this is why now seems to us the right time for a new space in which to work, this 'research Centre', which should strive to function 'on the basis' of various types of work and problematics.

We are not opening this space in order to pursue *our own* directions. We will, of course, continue to pursue them and will periodically intervene with them here as elsewhere. Rather, we are opening this space to a problematic collection, and that is to say to a collection *of* problematics and to a collection which is, *as such*, problematic, multiple, heterogeneous, flexible, without absolute limits and without exclusions. Such a situation is not self-evident; little by little it will have to be thought out, worked, questioned for itself. This much is clear.

But the initial stage ought to consist in allowing the schema of these questions, and consequently the schema of the singular identity which could become that of such a 'Centre for Philosophical Research on the Political', to emerge through work and confrontation. We do not accept that its point of departure need be tied to a philosophical and/or political figure, since it is the philosophico-political figure *as such*, or the figure of the philosophico-political that we are intending to question.

For the moment, this space is delimited by only one thing: the determination to pose the question of the political for itself, and that is to say, at the same time, not to presuppose an answer, and to take it as a question of 'essence' – or as a question of a 'retreat' of essence. Which excludes the standpoint of a *foray* outside of the political. We have already indicated here that the foray, or the liquidation of the political – whether it takes an ethical, juridical, sociological, aesthetic or religious form – is always poised to confirm its domination. It may be an old schema, but it is still operative.

Translated by Simon Sparks

7

The 'Retreat' of the Political[1]

Philippe Lacoue-Labarthe and Jean-Luc Nancy

If we have asked to say something today, this is not in order to give an academic assessment or a final report of the Centre's work over the past year; still less is it to 'take things back in hand' and to redraw the contours of an orthodoxy. No; we have asked to speak simply in order to take our bearings, to see where we are as regards the questions which were, and which remain, at the origin of the Centre. Which means, of course, our own questions – the initial questions of the Opening Address[2] – but only on condition of combining or including with them the way in which they have, in turn, been questioned as well as the new questions to which they have given rise. There is no orthodoxy here, but there is a genuine problematic, even if it is a problematic in the process of formation, a problematic looking for itself. It is to this problematic, very briefly, that we want today to return.

Put simply, then: where are we in the construction of this problematic (it would be better to say: of this problematic space, that being the idea of such a Centre)? What are the contentious questions? Put another way: What are the questions which we think it necessary to ask?

In order to go quickly and not clutter things up, we have held onto three questions, but ones which clearly intersect with a whole host of others. They are:

1 The question of the *philosophical*, and of the relation between philosophy and politics.
2 The question of *totalitarianism*.
3 The question of what we have called the *retreat*.

122

Each of these are enormous questions. But nothing prevents us, at the point we have now reached, from drawing attention to several essential traits.

First, then: the question of the philosophical and of the relation between philosophy and politics. What did we have in mind by insisting from the start, and simply in order to clarify the Centre's title, on the 'essential co-belonging of the philosophical and the political' (in which, what is at stake is, moreover, and barring error, a formulation of Jacques Derrida's[3])? I recall without further delay what was said at that time:

> This reciprocal involvement of the philosophical and of the political (the political is no more outside or prior to the philosophical than the philosophical, in general, is independent of the political), does not for us simply refer, even on the level of 'historicality', to the Greek origin – it is not a shortcut to the Sophistic *polis* and its guarantor, the *anthrōpos logikos*. It is, in reality, our situation or our state: by which we mean, in the mimetic or memorial after-effect or *après-coup* of the Greek 'sending' which defines the modern age, the actualisation or installation of the philosophical *as* the political, the generalisation (the globalisation) of the philosophical *as* the political – and, by the same token, the absolute reign or 'total domination' of the political.[4]

Now, these formulae are, it seems, prone to confusion. Possibly they were not too clear, or possibly not enough care was taken to clarify the presuppositions that they inevitably brought with them. None of which alters the fact that, on more than one occasion, they have been seen as the site of a grave difficulty. Consequently, it is necessary for us to explain things further.

In the first place we would point out, as you might expect, that if we used the expression 'the philosophical', then it was assuredly in order not to say 'philosophy'. A little later in the same text, and under the pretext that this use of the term was starting to spread, we performed an analogous operation upon politics and the political. It seems, however, that this latter operation appeared less awkward or more acceptable than the first. Why, then, the philosophical? What is this sort of element or milieu which we appear to be substituting for the thing itself? And why, for example, are we not content to stick with 'metaphysics' in Heidegger's sense of the term, which no more signifies some mode or some region of what, since Aristotle, has generally been called philosophising than our 'philosophical' refers to the discipline, to the literature, to the tradition, to the scholastic category even, of so-called philosophy? There are two reasons for this:

1 Because the way in which Heidegger, on the basis of a certain epoch, usually uses the word and concept of metaphysics – even if we subscribe to this, and even if our 'philosophical' is not foreign to this metaphysics – silently but obstinately preserves a sort of 'positive value' attached to philosophy and to philosophising. Despite such and such a declaration from the 'Letter on Humanism', despite the lecture 'What is Philosophy?' – despite, even, the opposition of 'thinking' and philosophy – metaphysics too often remains that which, through philosophy, shields philosophy from thinking. One could say schematically: something of the Kantian interpretation of metaphysics still overdetermines the Heideggerian delimitation. To say nothing of the apparent simplicity (in its historical partition, for example) or homogenisation (albeit through the uniqueness of its specific traits and the manner of its deployment) of this delimitation. Whence our concern not simply to contest, but to *put to one side* the use of any such concept. We are not ignoring the fact that things are very complicated in Heidegger. But we are equally aware that no thinking is immune either from its own simplification or from epigonal simplifications. An entire code is constructed and an entire metaphysical language is elaborated on the word 'metaphysics', a language and a code from which we feel it necessary to try to escape;

2 On the other hand, our 'philosophical' is actually the same thing: it is metaphysics. If you prefer: the philosophical designates a general historico-systematic structure – which, up until recently, one could have called the West – of which philosophy is each time the thematisation, the prefiguration or the anticipation, the reflection (critical or not), the contestation, etc., but which largely overflows the basically restricted field of operations of actual philosophising. If the concepts or the quasi-concepts of civilisation, of culture, of ideology, of mentality, of representation or of symbolism were not so heavily marked (philosophically) and had not served in discourses or contexts so foreign or so barely attentive (when not outright hostile) to philosophical phenomena or to the specificity of the West, they would perhaps be usable or be susceptible to re-elaboration. Clearly this is not the case. Whence our 'philosophical', which, for all its difficulties, has the merit of clarity and pretty much shows itself for what it is.

It is for these reasons that it seems to us possible to speak, since the Greeks, of an essential co-belonging of the philosophical and the political – the political in its turn, as I suggested a moment ago, not designating politics, whether that of the Chinese Emperors, the Benin kings, of Louis XIV or of German social democracy (even though in these last two examples politics and the political are not totally alien to each other). There again a simple relation, one which is not the relation of a dogma but, more simply, that of an accuracy. In the Opening Address, these lines follow on from the passage I have just cited:

Such is, moreover, the reason for which, in speaking of *the political* we fully intend not to designate *politics*. The questioning about the political or about the essence of the political is, on the contrary, what for us must ultimately take stock of the political presupposition itself of philosophy (or, if one prefers, of metaphysics), that is to say, of a political determination of essence. But this determination does not itself produce a political position; it is the very position of the political, from the Greek *polis* to what is deployed in the modern age as the qualification of the political by the subject (and of the subject by the political). What remains to be thought by us, in other words, is not a new institution (or instruction) of politics by thought, but the political institution of so-called Western thought.[5]

Of course, beyond all these points questions still remain. And, to our eyes, principally the following: is not the political as it appears and dominates today – and, if we were simply Heideggerians, we would say: technology, but, for reasons impossible to unravel now, we prefer not to – is not the political, then, as it appears and dominates today, the effect of a certain retreat of the philosophical, and that is equally to say of a certain completion of the philosophical (in the sense in which Heidegger speaks of a completion or completion of metaphysics)?

Such a question, which we have already asked and which, consequently, I will not unpack for its own sake, suggests a joint closure of the philosophical and the political – which does not mean that it is simply a matter of a closure and, even less, of a simple closure. Like the word 'end', the word 'closure' indicates, first of all, the completion of a programme *and* the constraint of a programming. It is this delimitation and its unsurpassable character which appeared to us to warrant question.

But of what is it a question? For us – but it has become very clear that this question is, for the most part, a common one here – it is a question of what, in

Heidegger's wake, and with no less rigorously political clarity and determination, was first thought and analysed by Hannah Arendt under the name *totalitarianism*.[6] We have hijacked Sartre's formula on Marxism, but we could just as easily have said, this time without hijacking, that totalitarianism is 'the unsurpassable horizon of our times'.

But once again we must agree on what such a formula implies. And even, prior to this, on the meaning that we are giving here to the concept of totalitarianism. I thus come to the second of our three questions.

First of all I would indicate – this is still a clarification – that, as far as we are concerned, two different meanings overlap each other in this concept. Of course, it is very likely that at a certain level these two meanings are actually only one, but it is always more useful to begin by distinguishing.

There is, on the one hand, the very general meaning (too general or too loose, it will be said, perhaps) which appears in our Opening Address under the name 'totalitarian phenomena'.[7] There it designated the total completion of the political, and that is at the same time to say the undivided reign of the political (the exclusion, as Hannah Arendt says, of every other domain of reference,[8] the 'everything is political' which near enough universally dominates today) and, in this reign or under this domination, the completion of the philosophical, and of the philosophical primarily in its modern figure, the one outlined by the philosophies (or, at a push, the metaphysics) of the Subject. We were at that time given to think – and indeed still think – that, under such a domination, the political becomes *unapparent* (it has the obviousness of an 'it goes without saying') and that its unapparence is proportionate to its all-powerfulness. And *vice versa*. That is why we spoke in the same breath of the 'retreat of the political' – to which we will return in a moment.

To submit the totalitarian phenomena to this sort of generalisation is clearly to tear it from every empirical hold and from all empirical treatment. We will be reproached for this. Nonetheless, it does allow us to begin to analyse certain 'facts' of our world, at the forefront of which we would willingly place the following absolute paradox, worked over at length by Arendt:[9] the fact of the disappearance of all 'political specificity' in the very domination of the political, the fact of the political ceaselessly merging with all sorts of authoritative discourses (in the first place, socio-economic, but also technological, cultural, psychological, etc.) and, despite the 'media' circus or the 'spectacularisation' of an absent public space, everywhere converting itself into a form of banal management or organisation. In the totalitarian phenomena thus understood, nowhere do even the least of specifically political questions come to be asked, do new political questions (corresponding to transformations of the world) have the chance to emerge, if not from inside an accepted ideological phraseology, whether this ideology (in Arendt's sense of the term[10]) be that of class, the nation, the meaning of history, the rights of man, the State, etc. Which in no way ever prevents politics from being done.

But a second, more restricted or more 'technical' sense of the notion of 'totalitarianism' overlaps this first meaning: one which comes to us from and turns us back to specific politiological analyses (those of Arendt, for example, or of Lefort) of actual totalitarianism's most notorious cases: Nazism and Fascism, Stalinism (or, more generally, Soviet types of society). In a word: totalitarianism is here each time thought as the attempt at a frenzied re-substantialisation — a re-incorporation or re-incarnation, a *re-organisation* in the strongest and most differentiated sense — of the 'social body'. Which is almost always the same as saying that totalitarianism is the response to or the attempt to get out of the impasse presented by, in and as what we might call 'democratic crisis': democracy as crisis. For instance, and at random: the disappearance of the authority — tradition — religion triptych, the disembodiment of power, the collapse of ground or the loss of transcendence (mythico-religious or philosophical: reason, nature, etc.), the disruption of hierarchies and the customs of social differentiation, the de-localisation of the political (the 'empty space' of power, as Lefort has it[11]) and the rule of political changeover, the desubstantialisation of the body politic which no longer is one except in the pure dissipation of suffrage, politics eventually given over to the play of vested interests, etc. And we know roughly the terms and forms of this response or this attempt to get out of such a crisis. I do not imagine that it is particularly useful here to draw up the list of counter-measures, nor to take stock of their results.

We do not wholly reject this concept or this description of totalitarianism. On the contrary, we even go so far as to think that, failing to recognise the reality and the nature of this phenomenon, most discourses which like to think of themselves as being political do not for one second touch on the question of the political, any more than do those which are happy to 'denounce' totalitarianism — and, while we are on this subject, the political as well — as a new sort of 'radical evil'. Nonetheless, it seems to us necessary to question it further and, first of all, in its apparent heterogeneity with the first meaning of the

127

concept of totalitarianism articulated earlier. In particular (and here, near enough, is the statement of our current questions) we feel that it would be necessary to ask:

1 if this analysis is not applicable, above all, to the henceforth historical (but not entirely 'past') figures of totalitarianism, even to a sort of initial and pure figure of totalitarianism in all its radicality and brutality; and consequently:

2 if a more insidious and (as one says of some technologies) 'softer' form of totalitarianism has not since been installed, more or less without our knowledge or through the unapparence of which we have spoken. Recall, for example, Lyotard's analyses in *The Postmodern Condition* on the 'social system' conceived by the decision-makers as a 'totality in search of its most performative possible unity', and what he has to say on the new sort of 'terror' that such a system is able to impose.[12] In other words, under the very general domination of technical and productivity criteria, would there not be surreptitious reincarnations of the body politic, a relatively constant and 'unbroken' occupation of the places of power, a certain homogeneity of the 'people of suffrage' (albeit only because of the spectacularising techniques of electoral and political games), frenzied fabrications of consensus (albeit only on the level of economico-cultural consumption), a diffuse (but powerful) psychologising ideology? In short, a way of responding to 'democratic crisis' which would be internal to democracy or what we still describe as such. (But such a response would not take the form of a redress.) Let us say: a totalitarianism of crisis, whose fragility would appear to be the most formidable force. Whence one might further ask:

3 whether a certain ready-made and much circulated opposition between totalitarianism and democracy, even if it is true and if the differences between these forms are glaring, is not, in reality, a little too simple. We do not have camps and our police, whatever their 'technological advancedness', are not the omnipresent political police. But this does not mean that our democracy is that of Tocqueville. And if Tocqueville's democracy contained the germ of classical totalitarianism, nothing guarantees that ours is not in the process of secreting something else, a new form of totalitarianism. This is at least one question which arises and one for which it does not seem totally out of the question to generalise (once again, at a certain level) the concept of totalitarianism.

This said, there still remains the third of our questions, namely the question of the 'retreat'. But as you probably suspect, this question is implicit in everything that we have said. Thus we will not be able to avoid a certain amount of repetition.

In speaking of the *retreat*, we meant that something *draws back* into (or from) what, both in order to speed things along as well as to provoke, I will call the modern *city*. In the constitution of the enormous and complex unity which one can no longer even call the State – neither in the Machiavellian nor, perhaps, in the Hegelian sense – something like the city, or like the 'civility' of the city precisely pulls back. This complex (eco-socio-techno-cultural) unity can be determined in economic fashion by three traits borrowed from Arendt's description:

1 The 'victory of the *animal laborans*', of man defined as worker or producer.[13]
2 The determination or the recovery of 'public space' by the *social*, by society as such (*Gesellschaft*, as distinct from *Gemeinschaft*), and that is to say by a common-life or an interdependence regulated according to life or subsistence, and not according to a public or political end in itself.
3 The loss of authority as the distinct element of power, and which, relating itself to the transcendence of a foundation (whose model, for Arendt, is the foundation of Rome), goes hand in hand with the loss of freedom.[14]

These traits basically mark out the question of what we have come to call a 'new totalitarianism', with regard to which one can no longer be happy with the critique of 'classical totalitarianism'. Let us say (or let us say again) that if classical totalitarianism, again to use Lefort and Lyotard's terms, proceeds from the incorporation and the presentation of transcendence (as the work of art in Nazism and as the reason of history in Stalinism), new totalitarianism would itself proceed from the dissolution of transcendence, and, henceforth, come to penetrate all spheres of life now devoid of any alterity. This is, of course, an allusion to the formula by which Marx defined democracy in 1843,[15] and it was with this formula in mind that we hijacked Sartre's phrase on Marxism as the 'unsurpassable horizon of our times'.

The retreat appears, then, first of all as the retreat of transcendence or of alterity. Which clearly does not mean that it is for us a matter of repeating the appeal to a transcendence, whether it be that of God, Man or History: these are the transcendences which have installed totalitarianism or those in which it has installed itself, converting them into the total immanence of life-in-common. In this case, moreover, the question of the retreat is not one of 'regaining' a remote transcendence, but of wondering how the retreat compels us to

129

displace, re-elaborate and replay the concept of 'political transcendence'. And, in view of a transformation of the very idea of transcendence (or, if it is less ambiguous to put it like this, the idea of alterity), for us it is indeed a question, in the name of 'the essence' of the political, of a transcendence and an alterity. This is why this question cannot be an *empirical* one.

What draws back would be, then, the political itself as a specific dimension or as the dimension of a specific alterity. Where does such an alterity come from? Let us say, even more schematically this time:

1 It comes from the articulation of power, as material and constraining force, with authority, as transcendence; or else, in terms this time borrowed from Bataille, from the articulation of the 'homogeneous' power of the State with the 'heterogeneous' authority of the 'sacred' (an articulation whose reactivation in fascism fascinated him for some time).[16] Not only is this articulation lost but, again as Bataille says, all realisations of the militario-religious order have ended up only in an 'immense failure'.

2 It comes from the relation of community to an immortality which, in this world, is its own – and not that of individuals in another world – in the sense in which Arendt writes, for example, in *The Human Condition*:

> the *polis* was for the Greeks, as the *res publica* was for the Romans, first of all their guarantee against the futility of individual life, the space protected against this futility and reserved for the relative permanence, if not immortality, of mortals.[17]

It is this immortality which reappeared, albeit in a totally different way, first of all from Fichte to Heidegger in the element of the *Volk*, then in the communist Humanity beyond the *Völker*.

3 It comes from a relation of community to itself wherein it can itself present or represent (*sich darstellen*) its being-common as such. This relation is, for example, at the root of Lefort's definition of the political and of his problematic of the political as 'the manifestation of the social to itself'.

In all probability, these three determinations may be gathered together, with others, under what Bataille called *sovereignty*. And if, in turn, the term sovereignty gathers together the essential determinations of the political (not merely as the character required by a State to be worthy of the name 'State', but much more as the supreme *end* to which the political destines each and

130

every one of us), then the retreat of the political is nothing other than a retreat of sovereignty.

Such a retreat makes something appear or sets something free. At the very least, we sought to question ourselves not according to the rule of a nostalgic lamentation for what would have drawn back (we subscribe to the verdict of the 'immense failure'), but according to the hypothesis that this retreat must allow, or even impose, the tracing anew of the stakes of the political.[18]

And first of all on the basis of the fact that what drew back perhaps itself never took place. It is Bataille who showed that the glorious and transcendent sovereignty of the Sun-King presenting to all their common sovereignty had only ever taken place held and enslaved within the installation of bourgeois power, of market economy, of the modern State, etc.[19] – and perhaps one ought also to say, *mutatis mutandis*, within the installation of the most archaic sovereignties. Moreover, from this angle it would be necessary to question Arendt as to whether or not the *polis* or the Roman foundation had actually taken place. In an analogous way, the Hegelian 'monarch', of which one of us spoke last year,[20] testifies, at the depths of the philosophical ground of the political, to an extreme striving (and to the rupture of this striving) towards the sovereignty which never took place, and whose place 'to come', for precisely this reason, remains enigmatic or at the inappropriable limit. And the essence of democracy as indicated by Lefort does not, in turn, fail to imply a 'non-place' or a 'not-taking-place' of the same sort.

All of which in no way means that it would now be a matter of giving rise to what had not taken place, as if one could, quite simply, take the political out of its retreat (or as if the retreat of the political was only a simple pulling back [*retraite*]). There is no 'getting out' of the retreat, except in undergoing the experience of what the political doubtless articulates *as* or *according to* an essential 'retreat', and which is perhaps the retreat of unity, totality and the actual manifestation of community. This supposes an entire elaboration all the more complex if it is the political (or sovereignty) which must thus 'retrace' itself. But in any case it supposes – and in this regard, our intentions must not be misunderstood – that this problematic can only be the problematic of a *ground* (or of a new ground) of the political.

Correspondingly, this means that it is indeed *from* the retreat of the political that the political 'itself', its question or its exigency, arises. And that it arises, as we recalled a few moments ago, as ineluctably *philosophical*. It is in terms of this relation that, in his talk last year, Lyotard seems to us to have transcribed the progress of the Centre in an evocative way:

> The field opened by the inaugural performative {of the Centre} is equally political. Indeed, philosophy (as that discourse which has as its end the discovery of its rule) is situated by that performative as the genre of discourse, of phrase ordering, within which it is judged suitable to phrase the political in preference to many other families of phrases which also claim to phrase the political: the scientific (politiology), narrative (history of political doctrines or facts), the epidictic (praise of the political), I could go on . . . By this presupposed suitability of the philosophical to the political what is necessarily presupposed is the principle according to which the political does not give itself (or no longer gives itself) to be phrased as a presentable given according to the rules by which phrases regulate themselves. Nonetheless, and this is also part of the presupposition, it 'hands itself over' to being phrased, all the same.[21]

In spite of a lexical difference upon which, for the moment, we will not dwell, we recognise something of ourselves in this description: the political draws back into its determinable and presentable specificity; but in this indetermination, which simultaneously corresponds to its dilution or to its general impregnation, it unburdens itself anew, and delivers a question or the outline of a question. If you prefer: the retreat of the political corresponds to its *closure* – and, by the same stroke, to the opening of the following question: on the basis of what, against what, or along what, does this closure trace itself? It does not simply trace itself 'against' the non-political. That is to say, for example, it is not enough to designate 'sociality' in relation to the State, whether one thinks only of the difficulties underlined by Clastres or of Balibar's citation of the first definition of 'civil society' as 'political society'.[22] On the contrary, the closure opens onto 'something', as Lyotard says, something which would be 'the political' – or the essence of the political – drawn back from the total completion of the political in the techno-social.

The basic traits presented by this 'something' are no less determinable and, to conclude, we would like quickly to list them. They are:

1 The exigency of getting away from the metaphysical *ground* of the political, from a transcendent or transcendental ground, for example in a subject, as Lyotard was able to suggest in his question to Lefort[23] (which is perhaps no

reason to prohibit a questioning of the difference which should be made between 'ground' and 'foundation' in the sense understood by Arendt).

2 In opposition to the motifs of ground and the subject (or even, and we are thinking of Rancière's analysis, the motif of incorporation under an identity such as that of 'class'), there is the motif of *finitude*. This motif has, more or less, been evoked on several occasions, either from the point of view of the purely symbolic or regulative aspect of the Idea of political totality, or from the point of view (adopted in part by Jacob Rogozinski) of Michel Henry's *Marx*, which is that of the individual and the 'numerous one'.[24] But it is not certain, as we have seen, that one can in this way avoid a grounding gesture. Nor is it certain, let us add, that in this way one ever thinks anything else but 'liberal' democracy as we are supposed to understand it. Thus, the motif of finitude seems to us to imply, as the true place of its determination, the question of *relation*.

3 The so-called question of relation remains, to our mind, *the* central question; as such, it is even, perhaps, the question of the essence of the political. It is remarkable, moreover, that this question shows up almost everywhere in the Centre's work, independently of the accent which we ourselves had placed upon it. (It arose, for example, in the question raised by Lyotard of the 'presupposition of the *us*' in Lefort, or in what is, for Rancière, the only common predicate of class – 'being in the place of the other' – or, further still, in the renewal of the problem of 'the mother' in Soulez.) In a general way, one can suggest that this question intervened with the insistence of a theme – in truth, still not particularly thematised, if it ever could entirely be so – the theme of *desertion* or of *dissociation*, and which, consequently, refers to what we have called:

4 The question of the *mother*. For Lyotard as for Soulez, this is a somewhat 'risky' designation. We retain it, nonetheless, more or less provisionally, and, before anything else, as the index of a *question*. It is a question which comes to us from Freud and we treat it in practically his own terms. It is the question of *identification*, what one can and must refer to as a general problematic of *mimesis*: how and according to what *relation* does the identification which, according to Freud, is 'the earliest *Stellungnahme* toward the Other' take place?[25] And what might this relation – in its relation to language, art, death and eroticism – reveal about the subject of the political? Once again, we are only indicating one category of questions here: the question, for example, of identification as the social constitution of identity

(and as the constitution of social 'identity'); or that of an 'originary' or archē-originary sociality, or again of an archē-sociality, in which or according to which the entire retreat of the political is played out (this question remains, remember, the obsessive fear and the stumbling block for practically the whole of contemporary thought, from Bergson to Heidegger and Levinas, through Freud, Husserl, Bataille, and probably many others). This is why the so-called question of the mother is, first of all, the question of a *maternal retreat* − of the mother as retreat and of the retreat of the mother.

5 Finally, if each one of these traits refers us to a specificity of the political, then this is precisely *not* to a specificity of the *empirical* by which the political would be signalled, but to this 'fact' which is a 'philosophical fact' (a sort of *factum rationis* of philosophico-political reason): that, at least since Aristotle, the being-together of men, the *zōon politikon*, does not stem from the factual given of needs and vital necessities, but from this other factual given of the sharing of ethical and 'evaluative' speech in general: this 'fact' resists all assignation in empirical factuality, to the extent that such a factuality actually exists. What occupies us, in other words, is the *surplus* of this 'fact', this excess over 'living' − and over purely social 'living together' − of 'living well' which alone determines the *zōe* of the *zōon politikon*. It is, in short, such a 'good' − this 'more than' of every organisation of needs and every regulation of forces − it is such a 'good', which some of us charge with having no moral weight, it is such a 'good', today indeterminate, which lives on in the retreat and whose question the retreat unburdens and delivers.

Discussion

Participants: Alain David, Jacques Derrida, Georges-Arthur Goldschmidt, Denis Kambouchner, Philippe Lacoue-Labarthe, Jean-Luc Nancy, Philippe Soulez.

The first part of the discussion began with a remark from SOULEZ, who asked about the relation which links Lacoue-Labarthe and Nancy's remarks with the classics of political philosophy: the Arendtian theme of 'immortality in this world' reminded him of Hobbes's definition of the Leviathan as 'mortal God'; but it was above all the insistence, via Bataille, upon the 'it has never taken place' (of sovereignty, of democracy) which reminded him of Rousseau's gesture at the start of the second *Discourse*.

NANCY sketched a first response by invoking the thematic of the 'regulative Idea' in the Kantian sense: that which has never taken place is perhaps just as easily what regulates 'political reason'; and in any event the question of what actually took place rather than what had not taken place is always asked in such a way that one cannot but be suspicious of the historical actuality of what the philosophical tradition has retained as 'models' of the political. To this DERRIDA linked the question of principle: what is it that takes place? A regulative Idea, a promise – the performative of a promise, this is an event: even if 'it' is presented only in a single phrase, from the moment that one continually speaks about it, this is an event. It is indispensable, in other words, to specify the mode of the 'taking place' whenever one is faced with performative statements, doubtless over and above what Soulez evoked of the 'schema of the promise' in Lacan or the invocation, by Susanne Allen of the 'logic of the *après-coup*'. No

135

reconstruction is possible without a past (even if this past did not actually take place), and a simple promise can by itself tear a historical continuity to pieces.

Then, the second part of the discussion, KAMBOUCHNER intervened in order to point out that it is impossible to formulate any 'disagreement' which arises in the terms used by Lacoue-Labarthe and Nancy: the misunderstanding which runs throughout is the one which remains as to the notion of 'empirical'. On the one hand, the distinction that was made between the philosophical (whose determination appeared excessively broad) and philosophy seems scarcely more convincing than the distinction between the political and politics. On the other, the use of words like 'totalitarianism' or 'democracy' still remains extremely fuzzy: what is the relevance of these terms in relation to specific political systems? Is there not a formidable inadequacy between the name and the reality? An overly philosophical discourse seems to stifle any factual examination. Finally, what is left to be thought in the name of 'essence' remains still too little determined.

On the second point, LACOUE-LABARTHE conceded that there was a genuine difficulty, the proof of which lies in the use to which these words have been put in the current politico-philosophical vulgate, where they are used to dispense with analysis altogether, are applied to basically moral entities, and authorise the most arbitrary of simplifications. But this is no reason to avoid them when they have a genuine relevance or when one can grant them a precise meaning: the word 'totalitarianism' has an entire philosophical (Hegel and Marx), juridico-political (the German doctrines of the 'total State', Carl Schmitt's analyses) and ideological (Jünger's 'total mobilisation') background; since Arendt, it has given rise to detailed analyses; it allows one to name and to think political forms unprecedented in history. And if Kambouchner declares himself to be aware of the hyper-complexity of political systems in general, a complexity which can only delay the moment when very general statements become something other than provisional statements, Lacoue-Labarthe himself claims to be extremely sensitive to the opposite danger: the danger that hyper-attention to factual or empirical complexities has no other (political) end than to mask the clear-cut nature of situations and blunt the cutting edge which it is very often necessary to give to the analyses and to the taking of positions. That said, what remained essential for Kambouchner was the question of what had taken place or had not taken place: where does one locate what has taken place? in philosophy or somewhere else? NANCY responded: the type of operation that appears to us necessary to begin here is reducible neither to empirical enquiry nor to exclusively 'intra-philosophical' analyses. The political assuredly gives facts. But to raise the question of the political is to analyse the analyses to which these facts have given rise; it is to deconstruct the (political, ideological, philosophical, etc.) discourses on the facts. The discourses on Athenian democracy, for example.

An intervention by GOLDSCHMIDT on Heidegger's support for Nazism and the influence of the Jüngerian concepts of homogeneity and work (in *Der Arbeiter*) then led LACOUE-LABARTHE to recall the distance explicitly taken by Heidegger (in *The Question of Being*) as regards Jünger's 'metaphysical' conceptions, and led DERRIDA to make it clear that, in Heidegger's eyes – more or less beyond the very detailed declarations of 1933 – work, the philosopheme of 'work' (as it essentially operates in Marx), is an ontological and metaphysical determination (in, amongst others, the 'Letter on Humanism'). GOLDSCHMIDT nevertheless pointed out that Heidegger's political discourse in 1933 developed an entire thematic of work; he indicated, moreover, that Jünger was himself an attentive analyst of what Lacoue-Labarthe and Nancy had presented as a 'subtle totalitarianism', more and more easily detectable in our societies.

The end of the discussion again turned around the question of the 'factual'. DAVID asked if one could not use Benjamin's distinction between the chronicler and the historian:[26] the Messianic era comes about at the moment when all the facts of its past have become citable. But NANCY objected that the Messianic idea precedes that of the gathering of all the facts; and he asked, in turn, whether the true question of the factual is not in the appearance (and the recognition) of new facts, as, for example, the 'subtle totalitarianism' sheltered by our 'democracies'.

Translated by Simon Sparks

8

Annexe

Philippe Lacoue-Labarthe and Jean-Luc Nancy

To the record of this last session we are adding the text of a circular intended to prepare for the session of 15 March 1982, followed by a summary of the discussion to which it gave rise.

It is not by chance if the course of one of our discussions (that following Jacques Rancière's talk of 15 February 1982) brought to light the necessity to outline better the 'definition' and the stakes of what we have termed the *retreat* of the political. This expression plays a major role in the determination of the Centre's work. Which means that it needs more work. It became clear in our discussions that 'retreat of the political' could, at a first reckoning, take on (at least) three different meanings:

1 The *Aufhebung* of the political, if it is admitted that the Hegelian State *aufhebt* the political itself (an admission which remains to be clarified, and which remains to be submitted to the following counter-proof: is not the *Aufhebung* fundamentally political?).

2 The *secondarisation* of the political, if one recognises in this Marx's gesture of reducing the political to bourgeois political illusion, and if one detects in Marx – via Michel Henry – a radically infra-political 'ontology of the individual' (which remains to be confronted by the texts relating to prole-tarian politics by questioning the exclusively strategic (or not) character of this 'ontology'; and which remains to be submitted to the general question of the reading of Marx, of its conditions, of its orchestration);

3 The *retreat* in the Heideggerian sense (*Entzug*) of the presentation which only takes place as the concealment or the disappearance of what is presented

138

(this is the structure or the movement of *alētheia*) and, with the Derridian value of the 're-treat', of the 're-tracing' (combining *Zug* and *Riss*) implying in the retreat a 'new' incision or inscription, which cuts out again that which retreats.

As regards these three different meanings, it needs to be made clear that:

1 as much as they are clearly distinct, they nonetheless pose the question of what it is that could link them all together – or at least link them in groups of two – and what it is that these possibilities engage;
2 we wanted to understand 'retreat' in the third of these different meanings (in truth, the only one which justifies a philosophical use of the term). But this meaning itself, in other words the entire singular logic of the retreat, demands to be articulated *in terms of the political*. Which can be initiated in accordance with at least two hypotheses:
   a Our 'retreat' accompanies, in reality, a retreat of the political *itself* within and from the epoch of its world domination. And that is to say that the 'everything is political' conceals an effacement of the specificity of the political. This specificity implicates the political as a space (or as an act) separate and distinct from the other components of the social whole. The retreat would thus retrace the contours of this specificity, whose actual conditions would need to be reinvented (this is, for example, one aspect of Arendt's thinking).
   b Alternatively our retreat operates in relation to the political in general and absolutely, and that is to say in relation to the intrinsic political determination of the onto-theology of *Realpolitik* as it appears through the theoretical face of the Hegelian State or through the empirical face of the calculation of forces. What retraces itself, then, would be a space *other* than political (which was, moreover, Bataille's route and, no doubt, finally Heidegger's). In any case, this 'other' would remain to be named.

It is not certain that it is a matter of discerning between the two hypotheses (and, above all, not in this form, which is insufficiently elaborated). But what is certain is that hypotheses of this sort are implicit in all critical, interrogative or deconstructive discourses (for example, those which came out of the Centre) on the political, and that such hypotheses demand to be brought to light and analysed.

More precisely, this general question of the retreat involves the thought of 'dis-sociation' that we put forward this year as a regulative idea. All the contributions to the Centre's work have indeed implied, more or less directly or more or less thematically, a thought of 'relation' (or the 'social bond') as constitutive of a break or of a 'deconnection' whose nature or structure has, until now, been formulated only in opposition – let us say – to self-relation (to the Subject as self-present). It could be that the retreat is the – theoretical and practical – gesture of relation itself. But should this gesture be attributed to a retraced politics or to something 'other' – or otherwise – than the political?

These considerations were *de facto* linked to the question (underlined in January by Derrida[1]) of 'coherence', to which we did not have time to return the following session. At first glance, it would seem to be a question of the coherence between theory and practice. Under this form, it immediately highlighted two distinct problems:

1 The following is a banal statement of the question of coherence: built upon a teleology of the realisation of theory in practice, and upon a merely 'ideal' or 'regulative' status of this very teleology, coherence is thought and practised as the linking of negotiations, of properly calculated compromises, of provisional tactics. This 'incoherent coherence' is the ordinary lot of the 'left intellectual', and often for such an intellectual even circumscribes the properly political space. Is this enough to characterise a political gesture of the philosopher?

2 Furthermore, it will be agreed readily enough that the opposition of the theoretical and the practical is itself to be deconstructed. But what is most properly at stake with this deconstruction is that it is not (if it must be) 'theoretical alone'. It should be allowed to set out, for example, a work such as that of the Centre according to an actuality which is neither that of a disengagement, nor that of a militant action. An actuality which is, consequently, consonant with the retreat.

Discussion

Participants: Jacques Derrida, Denis Kambouchner, Philippe Lacoue-Labarthe, Patrice Loraux, Philippe Soulez.

The discussion unfolded around three motifs: dissociation, the political and totalitarianism:

Dissociation: DERRIDA underlined the role that dissociation plays in the ontological structure of *Dasein* in Heidegger, although *Mitsein*, being-with (or -together) is never thought as political. There is a whole series of dissociative terms at play: *Zerstreuung*, *Zerslitterung*, etc., which, in spite of their negative resonance, are not to be taken negatively. The prefix *zer* is to be understood, rather, on the model of the English 'dis': there is something like an originary dis-tension of *Dasein*: *Dasein* is originally dis-tended, and it is in such a distension that history and spatiality originate. LACOUE-LABARTHE related this dissociation to the structure of *Selbstheit*, of self-hood itself; and SOULEZ saw in Janet, Freud and Bergson the similar motif of the actual as 'dissociated'. Whence the problem of the 'phantom of unity': the social bond itself already consists in acting as if there were no dissociation. On the other hand, Soulez recalled the *clinical* origin of the concept of dissociation.

The political: LORAUX recalled that, in Plato, the political arises in the retreat of the question of the divine, and the political itself is in retreat, concealed by the institutions and the constitution, democracy, etc. He proposed the following distinction: if *the political* is that which is thus aimed at in a retreat, *politics* would be, then, the state of the 'everything is political', and *a* politics . . . organisation, bricolage, institution (*a* politics would not be a species of the

141

genre '*politics*'). DERRIDA then added that the political is to be understood as the essence of what is political; and, as KAMBOUCHNER objected that politics has an institutional determination (and not necessarily an *essence*), DERRIDA clarified that a certain unity of meaning is indeed necessary: do we actually know what 'politics' means, plain and simple? Heidegger, one imagines, would have said: politics is *technology*. If he did not say it, then this is because such a determination is insufficient (see the treatment reserved for the 'politics of culture' in a text like 'The Age of the World Picture'[2]).

Totalitarianism: The question is one of knowing whether the concept is in a position to define everything that pertains to the State today. DERRIDA: Everything that today pertains to the State is related to the same metaphysical thing: strategy between States, diplomacy, etc. imply a homogeneity. Such a proposition can certainly be nuanced, but it is still the case that the State can today be said to be *penetrating* – and a sexual connotation is not absent from this word. SOULEZ would willingly define the 'retreat' as a variant of transcendental *epochē*, destined to show at what point the State is penetrated. DERRIDA: if it is a matter of drawing back, then this is only in order to think what is to be thought politically.

Translated by Simon Sparks

142

9

'Chers Amis'
A Letter on the Closure of the Political

Philippe Lacoue-Labarthe and Jean-Luc Nancy

CENTRE DE RECHERCHES
PHILOSOPHIQUES
SUR LE POLITIQUE

École Normale Supérieure,
rue d'Ulm, Paris

Responsables:
Philippe Lacoue-Labarthe
Jean-Luc Nancy

Strasbourg, 16 November 1984

Chers amis,

We have decided, for this year at least, to suspend the Centre's activities. We will try to explain the various grounds for this decision.

There are, first of all, reasons which are personal and have nothing whatsoever to do with the functioning of the Centre: fatigue, the burden of work and of duties, the impossibility of facing up to all this. Both of us are in need of a break. On the other hand, it has so happened that those in charge of philosophy at the Ecole Normale Supérieure are themselves contemplating rethinking in its entirety the politics of philosophical activities in the establishment: from this angle also, in another way, a suspension was to be wished for.

143

Yet it is obvious that these reasons would in themselves only provide adequate grounds for closing the Centre if we deemed it unnecessary to take into account the state of its work. Indeed, this seems to us to have reached a critical point, perhaps even a limit point, in the way the Centre has functioned since its inauguration. This point is the point at which the Centre's role as a place of encounter has become almost completely dissociated from its role as a place of research or of questioning. No doubt the Centre has remained, through its 'opening' and the possibilities that this offered, which ought not to be confused with those of an eclecticism, a unique site of encounter over the last four years. Right up until the last meetings concluded, the proposals or the intervening questions made in the name of some of the more acute investigations, all the more exacting today, testified to this role. Nonetheless, insofar as a 'Research Centre' must ensure something other than the successive reception of speakers whose propositions are linked or stimulated by nothing, or nearly nothing, within a common space and in accordance with common concerns, it seems to us that, for some time, the Centre has not exactly fulfilled its remit. We had already tried to begin this critical analysis at the end of the 1982–83 session: in all essentials, this attempt seems to us to have gone unheeded.

We had said at the time how, with the recession, it became clear that the inauguration of the Centre in 1980 had coincided with a moment when the political question was near enough totally put back into play. With the collapse of certainties, with the deterioration of their foundations and the effacement of their horizons, it became possible – even necessary and urgent – to resume the question of what we had then called 'the essence of the political': to resume it, and that is to say to open it anew, and to open it prior to or beyond the political positions recently adopted by some people. Not in order to settle in God knows what philosophical no man's land of the political and of politics, but in order to reinterrogate the political and its philosophical 'position' or 'positions' as to its essence (or, indeed, if you prefer, as to its conditions of possibility). To our mind, as to that of many of the other participants or contributors, this type of work presupposed that no certainty, old or new, could hastily seal up the breach opened in what one could call the general mind-set of our time by the de-position of the political. Which, specifically, means this: that nothing of the political is henceforth established, not even and above all its liquidation or its writing off of the West and its metaphysics.

144

Now, as we also said in 1983, it appeared more and more justifiable to ask if any such questioning actually remained open within the Centre, or whether a sort of easily accepted consensus of opinion had not been established in its place. This consensus was not proper to the Centre. It was then, and remains so today, what, in eagerness and haste, occured as the after-effect or the counter-effect of what has been called the 'end of Marxism'. (This event, quickly enough taken to be unique, simple and identical everywhere and in every respect, would be, moreover, an event already remote in our history – in short, outdated – and already covered over, it seems, by the event of a (re)birth: that of an economic neo-liberalism and a political neo-conformism. The haste of disappearances and rebirths is, incidentally, the mark of the epoch: the death of God, psychoanalysis, the experience of literature, structuralism, etc., separately and as a whole, know something of this.)

This consensus bears, first of all, on the simple and vehement designation of a unique political danger: 'totalitarianism', henceforth embodied in the regimes of Marxist origin. In this respect, the consensus signals the end of questioning as to either the always incomplete and problematic character of the philoso-phical analysis and determination of so-called totalitarianism, or the distance and the proximity between its Fascist, National Socialist and Communist models, or the relevance of the concept (if it is one) of totalitarianism for grasping the actual realities of regimes or societies (and what problems, already, in this alternative!) that it serves to designate. So many neglected questions; and yet so many questions which might well risk returning one day, in the classic fashion of something repressed.

But there is more. The consensus bears also on Marxism itself. One would love to recognise in it, on some sort of posthumous basis, a certain, clearly delimited number of ethical merits or intuitions as to existence. In what is essential, however, the Marxian event is henceforth null and void, bearing the stamp of an antiquated, if not detestable and, in any case, somewhat obscur-antist nineteenth century, against which, going back a century, one hastens to oppose the Enlightenment (against speculation), critique (against questions of essence), right (against politics), and freedom (against equality). For a few, it would be *philosophia perennis* (against 'historicism'). It is not that the Centre received a great many contributions which intended, precisely, to cheapen the Marxian event, whether this be under a form which we might term purely theoretical, or under the form of certain readings of events in Poland. None-theless, the vote of confidence never really became clear: supposing that it fails to break all ties with Marx (itself a first vote of confidence), towards what and for where will it head (if not Pufendorf or Fichte)?

And even this does not exhaust the extent of this consensus: it bears also, and in the last analysis, on *the political* itself. And that is to say it refers, in the last analysis, to the political – of which Marxism would be the completed form and the total permeation – as the absolute danger or as the definitive impasse of thought and of praxis. The end of Marxism, modestly and curiously baptised the 'end of ideologies', is insidiously transformed into the end of every consideration and every operation which has in view the identity of the collectivity, its destination, the nature and exercise of its sovereignty. An intellectual attitude (for this does not amount to a thinking) which privileges the ethical or the aesthetic, even the religious (and sometimes the social) over the political, has been allowed, little by little, to gain ground.

This attitude has, according to us, two consequences:

1 By definition, it cuts short any questioning of the *essence* of the political. This essence is, at root, considered as simply being submerged in the essence of the philosophical, itself related to a vast (and vague) will to mastery to which metaphysics and the whole of the West, including that which finally awakens us from this nightmare, would obstinately devote itself.

2 It scarcely leaves any scope for a political *choice*, and that is also to say for discerning what stands in the way of such a choice, except for the obligation to choose: for example, struggle, injustice, exclusion, stupidity and intolerance, corruption – this is in no way a closed list – which are not simple accidents confined to the heart of a 'broadly' acceptable order, as from now on (?) the order of our Western democracies seems to be.

The first consequence removes its very object from an enterprise like ours.

The second turns a place of encounter into a place of *a-politicism* which in the long term, until more information becomes available, always means a place of an absolutely determined politics.

Over the last two years we have touched on these two limits in a precise and repeated manner. We also have the feeling that the real *questions*, even though more than one of them was introduced and debated during the Centre's meetings, have ended up being evaded or, to say the least, no longer finding amongst us either the place or the means of their articulation and analysis (questions of essence, of relation, of totality, of Marxism, etc.).

This state of things has probably contributed to the wearing out of a very open formula of talks which well suited the initial function of the Centre but which, subsequently, could not help but favour a certain dispersion at the very moment when it would have been necessary to grasp once again the nub or point of our questions.

It is perhaps not impossible to imagine another formula. Yet whatever the case, it seems to us necessary to prompt a rupture, through which alone — this is our feeling on the matter — there perhaps exists a chance that something else might invent itself. No 'acknowledgement of failure' here, then: rather, the usual lesson of an experience tied, from its origin, to precise circumstances, now outdated, and whose evolution one could certainly say that the Centre will have accompanied rigorously. For us this gesture of rupture clearly responds to a political exigency, even if we do not know exactly how to uphold this word, this concept, or this Idea. It is just such an exigency which appears to us to demand a pause but also, and apart from that, a new departure. When the time comes, if it comes, perhaps we will have other proposals to make.

Warmly yours,

Philippe Lacoue-Labarthe and Jean-Luc Nancy

PS The third volume of work from the Centre (the 1982–83 session) has encountered serious editorial difficulties on account, precisely, of its 'volume'. We are looking at the problem with the authors concerned.[1]

Translated by Simon Sparks

10

The Spirit of National Socialism and its Destiny

Philippe Lacoue-Labarthe

My initial hypothesis is that National Socialism is in no way an abhorrent or incomprehensible phenomena, but that it is inscribed, in perfectly rigorous fashion, in the so-called spiritual history of Germany. Only a historico-philosophical interpretation can provide access to National Socialism in its essence, to what singles it out amongst other analogous phenomena in the first half of this century (which, for convenience's sake, can be called 'totalitarianisms') and makes of it an exception.

This hypothesis is justified in turn by a clarification of Heidegger's political thinking. Heidegger is not considered here as a Nazi (which, nonetheless, he *also* was, albeit briefly), but as the thinker of National Socialism, of that which he simultaneously acknowledged and disguised.

The proposition 'Heidegger is the thinker of National Socialism' means that Heidegger tried to think – and he is probably alone in this – the *unthought* of National Socialism, what he himself in 1935 called 'the inner truth and greatness of the Movement'.[1] But nothing here is self-evident. And first of all because the difficulty was – and remains – immense (and one needs to see that the unthought of National Socialism perhaps remained the unthought of Heidegger himself). And secondly because the uncovering, or the attempt to uncover the unthought or the essence of National Socialism supposes that every simply political, historical, or philosophical (and, *a fortiori*, ideological) interpretation of the phenomena has been challenged beforehand. Put differently, Heidegger's political message is entirely encoded: it is not a political message and, in order to understand it, one has to take the step beyond – or, rather, behind – the political, a step that leads in the direction of its essence which, in

148

itself, is nothing political. Such a step, which is the step of thought itself, is more daring than that required by the fundamental ontology of *Sein und Zeit* whose project is, quite precisely, abandoned in 1934–35, when it is a matter of preparing the 'retreat' from National Socialism.

As is well known, the logic of the retreat is abyssal: in every retreat, that from which one is retreating retraces itself. Political negation [*dénégation*[2]] is the touchstone of fascism. It is assuredly at work in the Heideggerian discourse of the 1930s and beyond – even up to the end. Nevertheless, it should not be confused with the a-politicism or anti-politicism commonplace in the ideology of the 'conservative revolution' since at least 1918 (even, in its 'anti-' form, in the left's discourse on democracy). The negation of the political in Heidegger is undertaken in the name of the essence or the origin of the political, of that which I propose to call the *archē-political*. Just as, after the defeat of 1945, Heidegger – and this is, remember, his first public gesture – denounces ethics (humanism) in the name of an *archē-ethics*, and that is to say in the name of an original comprehension of *ethos*,[3] so, in response to National Socialism – which evidently implies a responsibility – he will have sought to think an arche-politics: *polis*, he says in 1935, does not refer to any sort of 'politics' (a word which he will always place between quotation marks); *polis* signifies the *Da* of *Sein*.[4] And a year later, amongst the inaugural ways of the institution or the thesis of truth (*alētheia*), alongside the work of art, the proximity of the supreme being, essential sacrifice and the questioning of thinking, he places the founding of a *polis*, the founding of a State.[5]

Such is the reason why, if, for all that, it is necessary to define Heidegger's 'political' position, I believe myself justified in speaking of *archē-fascism* (which has nothing to do with the '*sur-fascisme*' with which Breton imagined it to be decisive to accuse Bataille during the same years).

Under these conditions, what gives to thinking as regards the unthought of Nazism and the arche-fascism of Heidegger?

(A word of warning: the propositions that I am going to put forward will be extremely schematic; in reality they presuppose lengthy and detailed analyses that I cannot reproduce here. I offer my apologies, in advance.)

1 National Socialism is the completion of the Western history of *technē* – or better: of Western history *as* the history of *technē*.

One of the banal commonplaces of European reactionary thought following the First World War is that the modern age can be defined as the age of technology; one either deplores it or takes up its challenge. It is in no way fortuitous if Heidegger remains, for more than twenty years, deeply attached to the two of Jünger's books which, in his eyes, were epochal: *Die Totale Mobilmachung* and *Der Arbeiter*; or if, after the event, at the start of the 1950s, he can still clarify what he understood in 1935 by 'the inner truth and greatness of the Movement' (now amended to 'of this movement') by speaking of the 'encounter between global technology and modern man'.[6] From the perspective of the most radical of fascisms, the Marxian ontology of work and of production (or of the self-production of man) is only a first stammering of the thought to come of the modern age. Technology is the truth of Work.

What distinguishes Heidegger, however, beside the fact that he never subscribed for an instant to the 'Nietzscheanism' fabricated by the intellectuals and ideologues of the 'Movement' (from 1935 to 1941, the majority of his teaching was concerned with the deconstruction of (the metaphysics of) Nietzsche), is the 'step back' that he tried to accomplish in the interpretation of *technē*: not only does Heidegger go back from science to knowledge, by which he invariably translates the Greek *technē* (after all, was not this movement already constitutive of speculative Idealism?); but under the most commonly accepted meaning of art, it is an *archē-technē* upon which he sets his sights, and which requires him to deconstruct the entire 'Western aesthetic' from Plato and Aristotle up to Hegel and Nietzsche ('The Will to Power as Art').[7] The 'retreat' of 1934–35 leads toward 'The Origin of the Work of Art' and produces consequently the truth of National Socialism as *national aestheticism*.

2 National aestheticism (this monstrosity is forced upon me by a reading of Heidegger[8]) is a difficult notion to manage. To use an expedient which Heidegger himself employed – as regards the relation between the *Gestell* (the essence of technology) and *Ereignis* – one might say that national aestheticism is to the Heideggerian thought of art and of the 'political' (or of the historical) what a – more or less fully – developed photograph is to its negative. And even the gesture in the direction of the negative is too much here. In any event, it is because National Socialism is a prisoner not of an aesthetics, but of aesthetics itself – of the aesthetic apprehension of art – that it is National Socialism. If you prefer, to cut things short, it is because it allowed the Wagnerian din to conceal and to deaden the voice of Hölderlin.

3 Excluding the, so to speak unique, reference to Hölderlin, Heidegger's poetico-political programme resembles nothing so much as the Romantic programme, if one recognises in Romanticism, as did Walter Benjamin, the last modern – and thus revolutionary – movement which endeavoured to 'rescue the tradition'. The 'conservative revolution' precisely. (And it must not be forgotten that the only publication on which Heidegger collaborated during the regime was the more or less oppositional journal – in any event, it ran to only two editions – which was edited by Ernesto Grassi with Walter Otto and Karl Reinhardt, *Geistige Überlieferung*.) Equally, there are, via Nietzsche, certain stubborn affiliations with Romanticism from which it will take Heidegger a long time to detach himself (indeed, one will have to wait for the lecture on technology and, above all, the letter to Jünger of 1955, *Zur Seinsfrage*).

Amongst these affiliations, the principal and most resistant is that which forms the notion of *Gestalt*, borrowed more from Nietzsche than from Hegel, and which allows one to think – certainly in a complex way, since the lexicon of the incision, of the trait or of the trace: *reissen*, *Riss*, etc., constantly intrudes – the essence of the work of art beyond or prior to *Bilden* (*Bild*, *Bildung*, *bildende Kraft* or *Einbildungskraft*). It is in connection with the work of art that, in 1936, Heidegger first risks the word *Gestell* to designate the unity of all the modes of *stellen* and of *stehen*, that is of the *thesis* of truth. This motif is fundamental because it carries with it the ante-formal or 'ante-eidetic' values of modelling or of fictioning/figuration (*plassein*, *fingere*), of shaping, of the stamp (*Schlag*) – Nietzsche's 'to philosophise with a hammer' – and of *Geschlecht*, of the imprint and of the impression – or, to speak Greek, of the *type* (but *Geschlecht*, and I refer to Jacques Derrida's reading of the Heideggerian reading of Trakl,[9] also signifies genre or species, race, family or descent, lineage and sex; the semantic drift is abyssal). It is for this reason that, borrowing one of his own formulations, I have proposed to define Heidegger's arche-fascist ontology as an onto-typo-logy – precisely what he drew to a close by demarcating or delimiting it in Jünger and, consequently, in Nietzsche.

The fascist haunting is, *de facto*, the haunting of figuration, of *Gestaltung*.[10] It is a matter of simultaneously erecting a figure (this is, as Nietzsche surmised, a work of properly monumental sculpture) and of producing, on the basis of this model, not a type of man, but the type of humanity – or an absolutely typical humanity. From a philosophical standpoint, it is, at the end of the day, a matter of overturning the Platonic critique of – heroic and aristocratic – archaic education founded upon the imitation (the *mimesis*) of examples which initiates the political project of the *Republic*. In the paragraphs of *Sein und Zeit* devoted to History, Heidegger says that it is by the choice, in tradition, of its heroes – and this is a matter of a decision – that *Dasein* can open itself to its historicality.[11] In the Rectoral Address of 1933, the hero thus chosen is Nietzsche, the prophet of the death of God.[12] Several months later, signalling the 'retreat' and the explicit entry into a 'political' discourse, the hero is Hölderlin, the poet mediator or the demi-god, who is the poet of poetry (of, precisely, the essence of art) only because he is – or ought to be – the 'poet of the Germans'.[13] (That the Germans are still 'indebted' vis-à-vis Hölderlin and, consequently, have not yet come to pass, thus suffices to indicate the insufficiency of National Socialism.)

4   On virtually the same level, this haunting of the figure is a haunting of myth. In the – squalid – world of desacralisation and 'disenchantment' (of the *Entzauberung* of Max Weber but, more radically, Heidegger will speak of the *Entgötterung*, of the a-theistic world), the watchword, since the first Romanticism and 'The Most Ancient Systematic Programme of German Idealism', is that of a 'new mythology'. Wagner's *Ring* and Nietzsche's *Zarathustra* only complete the programme. Which means that, with the ending of the period of the *imitatio Christi* or the *imitatio sanctorum* from whence came theologico-political or Christian-Catholic (universal) authority, the discrediting of the civil Republic, and the denunciation, above all after the first world catastrophe, of the bankruptcy of the Enlightenment, one appeals to myth (which can, of course, as in Sorel, easily be the myth of the general strike) as being the only chance to give back a meaning and to ordain a being-in-common.

Very schematically, once again: one must see clearly that the collapse of Catholicism has produced the modern political as the contradiction between the promise of a universality (the rights of man) and the re-foundation of national communities in the form of the nation state (the rights of the citizen). The imperialist export of the French Revolution inaugurated the age of national wars – the age of wars between peoples – announced by Fichte and more powerful than that between philosophical doctrines evoked by Nietzsche. Everywhere, in this century, the new version of man will have been that of a people, even a race; and 'eternal Russia' will have quickly swept proletarian internationalism aside.

Myth – in Heidegger's lexicon, *die Sage* – has only reappeared in this way because it was thought as being originally tied to the being-of-a-people – to the 'popularity'. Myth is the originary poem (*Urgedicht*) of a people. Which means, for the whole of Romantic politics, that a people originates, exists as such or identifies itself, appropriates itself – and that is to say, properly is itself – only on the basis of myth. When Herder, Hegel or Heidegger repeat Herodotus' words: 'It is Homer who has given Greece its gods', then this is exactly what they mean. According to the mimetic logic or the mimetologic just evoked, myth is the means of identification (this idea is still powerful, whatever the complexity of its re-elaboration, right up to the last works of Freud and Thomas Mann); and the appeal to myth is the demand for the *appropriation of the means of identification*, judged, in short, more decisive than those of the means of production.

5   On this point as on others, Heidegger's thinking is at least more subtle and wily than that of Romanticism in general. He leaves to the 'thinkers' of the Party (Bertram, Krieck, Bäumler) the job of naïvely opposing *mythos* to *logos*; and to Rosenberg that of defining, in response to nihilism and the Spenglerian decline, the 'myth of the twentieth century'. But a logic analogous to this underlines both his radicalisation of the concept of nihilism (applied to the whole of metaphysics) and his determination of the essence of art (successively, this is well known, as *Dichtung*, *Sprache* and *Sage*). And thus, consequently, his appeal to Hölderlin.

But this does not merely allow him to understand what the political stake of art is in the modern age. It allows him to understand that art, *technē* – and that is to say, for Heidegger, *archē-techne* – is what is at stake in modern politics. He states the truth of Goebbels' reply to Furtwängler, which itself drowsily repeats Napoleon and Nietzsche: namely, that the true artist, the one who moulds according to the most elevated sense, is the Statesman.[14] Or, on a level really much closer to his own, he states the truth of Hegel's threefold determination of the Greek artwork: as 'athletic body' (subjective moment), as pantheon named in language or sculpted in marble (objective moment), and as City (subjective–objective moment).

But what he actually ends up stating in this way is the truth of the German destiny.

6   The modern political, in the very difficulty it encounters in instituting itself, does not begin with the French Revolution but, as Heine and Marx suspected, with the Reformation (the radicalisation of Christianity) and the Renaissance

(the imitation of the Ancients). In each case, although in different ways, what is attained is Rome – Empire as Church. But if the nations of the properly Roman region are left caught in Latinity (the French Revolution repeats the Republican *gestus*, and the return to antiquity is, in Italy as in France, filtered through the Hellenistic and Roman imitation of the Greeks), if, in these nations, the dislocation of the theologico-political leaves the Catholic religion relatively healthy, it is not the same with the – more or less confused – peoples formerly situated beyond the *limes*, which is and remains the frontier of Lutheranism, the people of Tacitus' *Germania* – and of Kleist's *'Arminius' Battle'*. Although Hegel baptised the whole Christian age since the fall of Rome the 'Germanic world', and despite the existence of the Germanic Holy Roman Empire, these peoples have never belonged to *Weltgeschichte* as politically identified peoples, and that is to say as properly national peoples. What the *spiritual* history of Germany indicates – and there is one: it is, even, its *sole* history – is that Germany (the country of poets and thinkers, as Heidegger would say) lacks any identity. 'German distress', *die deutsche Not*, has a single content: Germany does not exist. At root, it determines the elegiac essence of German art, or its melancholic genius. (Thomas Mann, in the period of *Doktor Faustus*, wrote several decisive pages on this subject.)

Modern political identification supposes and engages a severe agonistic, in the sense of this word which Nietzsche recovered from the Greeks. In the appropriation of the means of identification it comes from a 'mimetic rivalry', with its formidable *double bind*: 'It is necessary for us to imitate the Ancients', said Winckelman, 'in order to render ourselves in turn inimitable.'[15] This, at least, stated that the German agonistic had to differentiate itself from the Latin type *imitatio*, even from the cultural imperialism of Italy or France: from Rome. As Bäumler wrote in 1931 in *Nietzsche, der Philosoph und Politiker* (but he was far from being alone in using this language):

> Germany can exist, in universal history, only as Greater Germany. It has only the choice of being either the anti-Roman power of Europe, or of not being { . . . } Only Nordic Germany can be the creator of a Europe which will be more than a Roman colony, only the Germany of Hölderlin and Nietzsche.[16]

From this point of view, Germany was indeed the place of a radicalised *Kulturkampf* where, as is well known, it was a wholly other antiquity – a wholly other Greece – than that passed on by the tradition which sought to invent itself as the origin and the model of an incomparable destination.

Such is what, in the course of this century, Nietzscheanism conveyed and which, in the historical turmoil, led to the installation of the Nazi political as the 'total work of art' – and not merely to fascism as the 'aestheticization of politics', in which case we would probably have got no further than Italian opera . . .

7   This agonistic controls three fundamental motifs in Heidegger. In conclusion, I will limit myself to listing them – their examination would take too long:

a The motif of *Heimatlosigkeit* (or of 'uprootedness', if I transcribe it into the lexicon of the thought of the French extreme-right, from Barrès to Maurras and beyond). It is a matter, says Heidegger in 1946, of the fundamental historical experience of Europe which Nietzsche, prisoner of the nihilism which he was denouncing, was unable to sustain up to the end, and which Marx alone – outside of Hölderlin, of course – was able to think by placing the epoch under the sign of alienation.

   One could show, from this angle, that fascisms, just like Marxism in its Russian interpretation, are only a response to the generalised *urbanisation* [dépaysement: literally, de-countrification or being off one's home ground (*pays*); figuratively, disorientation – TN] of the modern epoch, to the mass deportation of centuries-old peasantry, organised for scarcely a century by industry and by Capital. Heidegger knew this more than he wanted to.

b The motif of *Wiederholung*, of the repetition of the grandeur of the (Greek) beginning of Western destiny insofar as – logic of the unthought – this grandeur has not properly taken place and insofar as it forms, therefore, the future or the to-come of 'our' History. (This motif comes from Nietzsche's second *Untimely Meditation*, but one equally finds it in Paul de Lagarde: 'For whilst you turn your eyes and your heart towards new things, with every breath I take I live in a past which has never been and which is the only future to which I aspire.'[17]) Heidegger takes a step behind *imitatio*, a step which indicts the weakness, the kitsch even, of mass art and the imperial monumentality of totalitarianisms. The example of the Greek temple or Van Gogh's peasant shoes in the 1936 lectures on art have been much ironised and glossed over. One would have done better by relating it to the unrestrained critique of the Wagnerian project.

c The motif of the theologico-political: what Heidegger sought, in the Höl-derlinian message – in *Sage*, myth, which is not, he will say on another occasion, *Heldensaga* – is the promise of a new God: 'Nur ein Gott kann uns retten'; such are, one recalls, Heidegger's final words.[18]

The lamentation of an existential loss, the appeal to another beginning, listening to 'evangelical' poetry: very close to, very far from, Messianic utopianism – this comprises or configures the hope of a religion. Whence can be seen, at the bedrock of totalitarianisms, the restoration – which is profane only as regards Christianity – of political religion. Or if you prefer: of religion, pure and simple. But that is another matter.

Translated by Simon Sparks

11

'What is to be Done?'

Jean-Luc Nancy

What is to be done, at present? The question is on everybody's lips and, in a certain way, it is the question people today always have lying in wait for any passing philosopher. Not: What is to be thought? But indeed: What is to be done? The question is on everybody's lips (including the philosopher's), but withheld, barely uttered, for we do not know if we still have the right, or whether we have the means, to raise it. Perhaps, we think more or less discreetly to ourselves, perhaps the uncertainty of 'what is to be done?' is today so great, so fluctuating, so indeterminate, that we do not need even to do this: raise the question.

Especially if the question were to presuppose that one already knows what it is right to think, and that the only issue is how one might then proceed to act. Behind us theory, and before us practice – the key thing is knowing what it is opportune to decide in order to embark on specific action. But this is what is presupposed most ordinarily by the question. And 'what is to be done?' means, in that case, 'how to act' in order to achieve an already given goal. 'Transforming the world' then means: realising an already given interpretation of the world, and realising a hope.

But we do not know what it is right for us to think, or even properly to hope. Perhaps we no longer even know what it is to think nor, consequently, what it is to think 'doing', nor what 'doing' is, absolutely.

Perhaps, though, we know one thing at least: 'What is to be done?' means for us: how to make a world for which all is not already done (played out, finished, enshrined in a destiny), nor still entirely to do (in the future for always future tomorrows).

This would mean that the question places us simultaneously before a doubly imperative response. It is necessary to measure up to what nothing in the world can measure, no established law, no inevitable process, no prediction, no calculable horizon – absolute justice, limitless quality, perfect dignity – and it is necessary to invent and create the world itself, immediately, here and now, at every moment, without reference to yesterday or tomorrow. Which is the same as saying that it is necessary at one and the same time to affirm and denounce the world as it is – not to weigh out as best one can equal amounts of submission and revolt, and always end up halfway between reform and accommodation, but to *make* the world into the place, never still, always perpetually reopened, of its own contradiction, which is what prevents us from ever knowing in advance *what* is to be done, but imposes upon us the task of never making anything that is not a world.

What will become of our world is something we cannot know, and we can no longer believe in being able to predict or command it. But we can act in such a way that this world is a world able to open itself up to its own uncertainty as such.

These are not vague generalities. I am writing these lines in January 1996. France's December strikes showed clearly the whole difficulty, not to say aporia, that exists in 'what is to be done?' once all guarantees are suspended and all models become obsolete. Resignation in the face of the brutalities of economic *Realpolitik* clashed with feverish or eager words that hardly took the risk of saying exactly what was to be done. But between the two, something was perceptible: that it is ineluctable to invent a world, instead of being subjected to one, or dreaming of another. Invention is always without model and without warranty. But indeed that implies facing up to turmoil, anxiety, even disarray. Where certainties come apart, there too gathers the strength that no certainty can match.

Translated by Leslie Hill

Sources

La panique politique: originally published in *Confrontations* 2 (1979), pp. 33–57.

La voix libre de l'homme: originally published in Philippe Lacoue-Labarthe and Jean-Luc Nancy, eds, *Les fins de l'homme: À partir du travail de Jacques Derrida* (Paris: Galilée, 1981), pp. 163–84. Reprinted in Jean-Luc Nancy, *L'impératif catégorique* (Paris: Flammarion, 1983), pp. 113–37.

Au nom de . . . : originally published in Philippe Lacoue-Labarthe and Jean-Luc Nancy, eds, *Les fins de l'homme: À partir du travail de Jacques Derrida* (Paris: Galilée, 1981), pp. 415–43. Reprinted in Philippe Lacoue-Labarthe, *L'imitation des modernes: Typographies II* (Paris: Galilée, 1986), pp. 229–55.

Séminare 'politique': originally published in Philippe Lacoue-Labarthe and Jean-Luc Nancy, eds, *Les fins de l'homme: À partir du travail de Jacques Derrida* (Paris: Galilée, 1981), pp. 487–500.

Avertissement: originally published in Philippe Lacoue-Labarthe and Jean-Luc Nancy, eds, *Rejouer le politique* (Paris: Galilée, 1981), pp. 9–10.

Ouverture: originally published in Philippe Lacoue-Labarthe and Jean-Luc Nancy, eds, *Rejouer le politique* (Paris: Galilée, 1981), pp. 11–28.

Le retrait du politique: originally published in Philippe Lacoue-Labarthe and Jean-Luc Nancy, eds, *Le retrait du politique* (Paris: Galilée, 1983), pp. 183–200.

Annexe: originally published in Philippe Lacoue-Labarthe and Jean-Luc Nancy, eds, *Le retrait du politique* (Paris: Galilée, 1983), pp. 201–05.

Chers amis: previously unpublished.

L'esprit du national-socialisme et son destin: previously unpublished.

Que faire?: previously unpublished.

Supplementary Texts

As regards the present volume and, in particular, the question of the relation between the political and the philosphical, the reader might be interested to note the following texts by Lacoue-Labarthe and Nancy, all of which could have been – but for various reasons were not – reprinted here. (It perhaps goes without saying that the problematics broached in *Retreating the Political* are themselves played out across the whole of Lacoue-Labarthe and Nancy's *oeuvre*.) Each of the following texts engages, more or less explicitly, more or less thematically, with the questions of the retreat and of the political.

Philippe Lacoue-Labarthe, 'La transcendance fini$^e/_t$ dans la politique': originally published in Philippe Lacoue-Labarthe and Jean-Luc Nancy, eds, *Rejouer le politique* (Paris: Galilée, 1981), pp. 171–214. Reprinted in Philippe Lacoue-Labarthe, *L'imitation des modernes: Typographies II* (Paris: Galilée, 1986), pp. 135–73. Translated by Peter Caws as 'Transcendence Ends in Politics', in Philippe Lacoue-Labarthe, *Typography: Mimesis, Philosophy, Politics* (Cambridge, Massachusetts: Harvard University Press, 1989), pp. 267–300.

Philippe Lacoue-Labarthe, 'Poétique et politique': reprinted in Philippe Lacoue-Labarthe, *L'imitation des modernes: Typographies II* (Paris: Galilée, 1986), pp. 175–200.

Philippe Lacoue-Labarthe, *La fiction du politique* (Paris: Bourgois, 1987). Translated by Chris Turner as *Heidegger, Art and Politics* (Oxford: Blackwell, 1990).

160

Philippe Lacoue-Labarthe and Jean-Luc Nancy, 'Le mythe nazi': originally published in *Les méchanismes du fascisme* (Strasbourg: Bibliothèque de prêt du Haut-Rhin, Comité sur l'Holocauste, 1981). Reprinted with a preface and revisions as *Le mythe nazi* (La Tour d'Aigues: Editions de l'Aube, 1991). Translated by Brian Holmes as 'The Nazi Myth', in *Critical Inquiry* 16, 2 (1990), pp. 291–312.

Jean-Luc Nancy, 'La juridiction du monarque hégélien': reprinted in *Rejouer le politique* (Paris: Galilée, 1981), pp. 51–90. Translated by Mary Ann Caws and Peter Caws as 'The Jurisdiction of the Hegelian Monarch', in *Social Research* 49, 2 (1982), pp. 481–516. Reprinted in Jean-Luc Nancy, *The Birth to Presence* (Stanford, California: Stanford University Press, 1993), pp. 110–42.

Jean-Luc Nancy, *La communauté désoeuvrée* (Paris: Bourgois, 1990; new edn). Partially translated by Peter Conner *et al.* as Jean-Luc Nancy, *The Inoperative Community* (Minneapolis: Minnesota University Press, 1991), chs 1–3. See also 'Of Being-in-common', translated by James Creech in Miami Theory Collective, eds, *Community at Loose Ends* (Minneapolis: Minnesota University Press, 1991), pp. 1–12.

Jean-Luc Nancy, *La comparution (politique à venir)* (Paris: Bourgois, 1991). Translated by Tracy B. Strong as 'The Compearance: From the Existence of 'Communism' to the Community of 'Existence', in Jean-Luc Nancy, *Political Theory* 20, 3 (1992), pp. 371–98.

Jean-Luc Nancy, 'Politique I', in Jean-Luc Nancy, *Le sens du monde* (Paris: Galilée, 1993), pp. 139–47.

Jean-Luc Nancy, 'De l'être singulier pluriel', in Jean-Luc Nancy, *Etre singulier pluriel* (Paris: Galilée, 1996), pp. 19–123.

Notes

Editor's Preface

[*Note*: All translations from Lacoue-Labarthe and Nancy's texts in editorial matter are my own. I have provided references to published English versions wherever possible. When cited in the text, these follow the original French pagination. All other references are to the original editions cited, although I have retranslated throughout.]

1 Jacques Derrida, 'Désistance', in *Psyché: Inventions de l'autre* (Paris: Galilée, 1987), p. 599; translated by Christopher Fynsk as 'Desistance', in Philippe Lacoue-Labarthe, *Typography: Mimesis, Philosophy, Politics* (Cambridge, Massachusetts: Harvard University Press, 1989), pp. 6–7.

2 For Lacoue-Labarthe and Nancy's 'reading notes' for the notion of *le retrait*, see the 'Annexe', pp. 138–40, below.

3 See '*La panique politique*', pp. 29ff, below. See also Derrida's 'Le retrait de la métaphore', in *Psyché*, pp. 63–93; translated by Frieda Gasdner, Biodun Iginla, Richard Madden and William West as 'The *Retrait* of Metaphor', *Enclitic* 2, 2 (1978), pp. 5–33.

4 Philippe Lacoue-Labarthe and Jean-Luc Nancy, 'Le peuple juif ne rêve pas', *La psychanalyse, est-elle une histoire juive?* (Paris: Seuil, 1981), p. 66; translated by Brian Holmes as 'The Jewish People do not Dream', *Stanford Literature Review* 6, 2 (1989), p. 201.

5 Lacoue-Labarthe, 'Poétique et politique', in Philippe Lacoue-Labarthe, *L'imitation des modernes: Typographies II* (Paris: Galilée, 1986), p. 188.

6 Martin Heidegger, 'Die Vollendung der Philosophie und die Aufgabe des Denkens', in Heidegger, *Zur Sache des Denkens* (Tübingen: Niemeyer, 1969), p. 63; translated by Joan Stambaugh as 'The End of Philosophy and the Task of Thinking', in Martin Heidegger, *Basic Writings*, ed. David Farrell Krell (London: Routledge, 1993; 2nd edn), p. 433. The reader might be interested to note that this essay *originally* appeared in French in 1966, translated by Jean Beaufret and François Fédier as

'La fin de la philosophie et la tâche de la pensée', reprinted in Martin Heidegger, *Questions* IV (Paris: Gallimard, 1976), where this passage is rendered as follows (p. 114):

> L'ancienne signification du mot allemand '*Ende*' (fin) est la même que celle du mot '*Ort*' (lieu): *Von einem Ende zum anderen* signifie: d'un lieu à l'autre. La fin de la philosophie est lieu – celui auquel le tout de son histoire se rassemble dans sa possibilité la plus extrême. Fin comme achèvement signifie se rassembler en un seul lieu.

Editor's Introduction: Politica ficta

1 Insofar as the facts are well documented in the texts which follow (as elsewhere), I have not attempted to provide any complete account (narrative *or* philosophical) of the Centre's activities, but merely to provide one possible itinerary for reading *Retreating the Political* – that of the *politica ficta*. Consequently, these introductory remarks are intended to be just that: introductory, and they seek neither to be extensive, nor to resolve any of the more glaring difficulties of Lacoue-Labarthe and Nancy's text: either *philosophical* (the operation on the basis of a – critical – Platonic inheritance of the political which is never confronted with its Aristotelian critique, the use of Arendt or the over-reliance (albeit disavowed) on Heidegger, or *economico-political* (put simply: the lack of any direct engagement with the question of economics or Capitalism as such).

To the best of my knowledge, there are only two studies available in English concerning the Centre, which while excellent on the history of the Centre's activities, should be treated with caution as to the readings they put forward regarding its philosophical importance. See Nancy Frazer, 'The French Derrideans: Politicizing Deconstruction or Deconstructing the Political', *New German Critique* 33 (1984), pp. 127–54, and Simon Critchley, 'Lacoue-Labarthe and Nancy: Re-tracing the Political' in his *The Ethics of Deconstruction: Derrida and Levinas* (Oxford: Blackwell, 1992), pp. 200–19.

2 Although the co-ordinates are well known, it is perhaps worth signposting some of the major moments of this extensive study. (Publication references will be found in the notes below.) On the one hand (Lacoue-Labarthe), the readings of Hegel and Nietzsche in *Le Sujet de la philosophie*, and of Heidegger in the brilliant 'Typographie', *La fiction du politique* and *L'imitation des modernes*. On the other (Nancy), the reading of Descartes in *Ego Sum*, of Kant in *Le discours de la syncope*, *L'impératif catégorique* and *L'expérience de la liberté*, of Hegel in *La remarque spéculative: Un bon mot de Hegel* and 'Le juridiction du monarque hégélien', and of Heidegger in *Le partage des voix*. Need one add here the remarkable readings of Lacan in *Le titre de la lettre* and German Romanticism in *L'absolu littéraire* which take place, as it were, on both hands?

As regards these proper names, 'Lacoue-Labarthe' 'and' 'Nancy', it is perhaps worth recalling Derrida's remarks made on the occasion of the English publication of a volume of Lacoue-Labarthe's essays (see 'Désistance' in Jacques Derrida, *Psyché: Inventions de l'autre* (Paris: Galilée, 1987), p. 602; translated by Christopher Fynsk as 'Desistance' in Philippe Lacoue-Labarthe, *Typography: Mimesis, Philosophy, Politics* (Cambridge, Massachusetts: Harvard University Press, 1989), pp. 6–7): 'I hasten immediately to reiterate that, despite such common paths and work done in common, . . . the *experience* of each [i.e. of 'Lacoue-Labarthe' and 'Nancy'] remains, in its singular proximity, absolutely different.'

3　See Martin Heidegger, *Sein und Zeit* (Tübingen: Max Niemeyer, 1987), pp. 385–86; translated by John Macquarrie and Edward Robinson as *Being and Time* (Oxford: Blackwell, 1992).

4　Philippe Lacoue-Labarthe, *La fiction du politique* (Paris: Bourgois, 1987), p. 18; translated by Chris Turner as *Heidegger, Art and Politics* (Oxford: Blackwell, 1990), p. 4. Lacoue-Labarthe continues: 'This pure contradiction defines an impossible situation; and in fact the limit here, as regards philosophy, is that of its possibility [*son possible*].'

5　Ibid., p. 19/ ibid., p. 5.

6　See 'Désistance', p. 603/ 'Desistance', p. 7.

7　'Opening Address', p. 110, below.

8　Ibid., p. 109, below.

9　Ibid.

10　Indeed, it is difficult to see how one could move from the 'wholly other politics' which is outlined in the texts below in terms of a critique of totalitarian immanence itself erected upon an effacement of transcendence (and that is to say of the originarily differential structure of being-in-common), to an actual or praxical politics. But perhaps this is precisely the point. And this is so even if – on a purely anecdotal and personal level – Lacoue-Labarthe and Nancy's own political position is not difficult to deduce from their writings. As they say in '*La panique politique*', 'if confrontation is necessary, we know where to put ourselves, and since it seems unavoidable today to be as specific as possible, let us say, on the left' (p. 2, below). However, as Nancy points out in the preface to the English translation of his *La communauté désoeuvrée* (see Jean-Luc Nancy, *The Inoperative Community* (Minneapolis: Minnesota University Press, 1991), p. xxxvi): 'the task that now befalls us is to elucidate, to review, indeed to revolutionise what the term "left" means.' See also Fynsk and Lacoue-Labarthe's remarks on the Marxist text in the 'Political Seminar' (ch. 4, below) and the footnote to the 'Opening Address' (ch. 6, n. 3, below).

11　The proceedings of which were published as Philippe Lacoue-Labarthe and Jean-Luc Nancy, eds, *Les fins de l'homme: À partir du travail de Jacques Derrida* (Paris: Galilée, 1981). Lacoue-Labarthe and Nancy's opening comments appear there as the 'Ouverture', pp. 9–18, and the 'Annexe', pp. 19–21.

12　See 'Les fins de l'homme', in Jacques Derrida, *Marges – de la philosophie* (Paris: Editions de Minuit, 1972), p. 134; translated by Alan Bass as 'The Ends of Man' in

Jacques Derrida, *Margins of Philosophy* (Chicago: University of Chicago Press, 1982), p. 114.

13 Ibid., p. 135/ ibid., p. 114.

14 Ibid., p. 131/ ibid., p. 111. Emphasis added.

15 Lacoue-Labarthe and Nancy, *Les fins de l'homme*, p. 21.

16 I am thinking here of the moment in *Being and Time* where Heidegger lists a series of questions of or approaches to human existence in order to differentiate them from fundamental ontology: philosophical psychology, anthropology, ethics, 'politics', poetry, biography. Only politics is suspended, mentioned without being mentioned, by quotation marks (see *Sein und Zeit*, p. 16).

17 See 'Opening Address', p. 110, below.

18 See Heidegger's Rectoral Address (*Die Selbstbehauptung der deutschen Universität* (Frankfurt a.M.: Klostermann, 1983), pp. 11–12; translated by William S. Lewis in Richard Wolin, ed., *The Heidegger Controversy* (Cambridge, Massachusetts: MIT Press, 1993; 2nd edn), p. 32), where, drawing on a framework already operative within the *Republic*, Heidegger will understand *theoria* as the 'supreme realisation [*Verwirklichung*] of genuine *praxis*'.

19 On the necessity of deconstructing the 'coherence between theory and practice', see the 'Annexe', p. 140, below.

20 See Jean-Luc Nancy, *Ego sum* (Paris: Flammarion, 1979), especially pp. 51–52.

21 Philippe Lacoue-Labarthe and Jean-Luc Nancy, 'Scène', *Nouvelle revue de psychanalyse*, 17 (1992), pp. 73–98.

22 *Poetics*, 1450a. Aristotle writes:

> Thus, tragedy as a whole must have six constituent parts, which give it its qualities: plot, character, diction, thought, spectacle and lyric poetry. Of these, [the first] two represent the media of the mimesis, one [the third: i.e. 'οψισ] its mode of enactment, and [the other] three the objects. Nothing else than these is required.

23 *Editor's note*: See Philippe Lacoue-Labarthe, 'Il faut', *Modern Language Notes* 107 (1992), pp. 421–40, in particular pp. 436ff.

24 Lacoue-Labarthe and Nancy, 'Scène', p. 74.

25 'Opening Address', pp. 109, 110, 111, below.

26 'La trancendance fini^e/$_t$ dans la politique', in Philippe Lacoue-Labarthe, *L'imitation des modernes* (Paris: Galilée, 1986), p. 173; translated by Peter Caws as 'Transcendence Ends in Politics', in *Typography*, p. 300.

27 Nancy writes: 'The epoch of representation is as old as the West'. See 'Naître à la présence', in Jean-Luc Nancy, *Le poids d'une pensée* (Quebec: Editions Le Griffon d'argile, 1991), p. 129; translated by Brian Holmes as 'The Birth to Presence', in Jean-Luc Nancy, *The Birth to Presence* (Stanford, California: Stanford University Press, 1993), p. 1.

28 'Opening Address', p. 110, below.

29 'The Spirit of National Socialism and its Destiny', p. 154, below.

30 Martin Heidegger, *Hölderlins Hymnen 'Germanien' und 'Der Rhein'*, *Gesamtausgabe* 39 (Frankfurt a.M.: Klostermann, 1980), p. 214.

31 'La trancendance fini^e/$_t$ dans la politique', p. 173/'Transcendence Ends in Politics', p. 300. On identification as the 'very problem of the political', see also chs 1 and 8 below.

32 'La mythe interrompu', in Jean-Luc Nancy, *La communauté désoeuvrée* (Paris: Bourgois, 1990; new edn), p. 133–34; translated by Peter Conner as 'Myth Interrupted', in *The Inoperative Community*, p. 53.

33 Jean-Luc Nancy, *Le sens du monde* (Paris: Galilée, 1993), p. 142.

34 Ibid.

35 'Le peuple juif ne rêve pas', in *La psychanalyse, est-elle une histoire juive?* (Paris: Seuil, 1981), p. 58; translated by Brian Holmes as 'The Jewish People do not Dream', *Stanford Literary Review* 6, 2 (1989), p. 193.

36 Nancy, *Le sens du monde*, pp. 14–15.

37 'Opening Address', p. 112, below.

38 Ibid., p. 111, below.

39 Ibid., p. 110, below.

40 'The "Retreat" of the Political', p. 131, below.

41 'The Spirit of National Socialism and its Destiny', p. 153, below.

42 The terms are those used by Thomas Mann in *The Theme of the Joseph Novels*: 'In this book, myth has been taken out of fascist hands and humanised down to the last recesses of its language' (See *The Theme of the Joseph Novels* (Washington: Library of Congress, 1942), p. 21.) See also the letter that Mann writes to Karl Kerenyi in 1941, where he outlines his programme: 'Myth must be wrested from intellectual fascism and its function diverted in a human direction' (cited by Nancy, in *La communauté désoeuvrée*, p. 116 note 37; *The Inoperative Community*, p. 160 n. 6).

43 'The "Retreat" of the Political', p. 131, below.

44 Ibid., p. 133, below.

45 'Annexe', p. 139, below.

46 See the citation from 'Scène', above, where Nancy understands their divergence over the figure in terms of 'the "interruption of myth" as an element or as a decisive event for a thinking of being-in-common today' on the one hand, and 'an effacement of the "figure" (you speak freely of "de-figuration" . . .)', on the other.

47 'Opening Address', p. 114, below.

48 Nancy, *The Inoperative Community*, p. xxxvi.

49 'Annexe', p. 140, below.

50 'Opening Address', p. 113, below.

51 *Les fins de l'homme*, p. 15.

I am indebted to Andrew Benjamin and Richard Stamp for their comments on an earlier version of this introduction.

[*Note*: all notes contained in square brackets are the work of either the individual translators or, when noted as such, the editor. Where possible, references are provided to both the original language edition and to the standard English translation, and always in that order. Translations have been modified throughout.]

Chapter 1: *La panique politique*

1 [The two essays 'La panique politique' and 'Le peuple juif ne rêve pas' appear together in the German journal *Frag-Mente: 'Religion – Mythos – Illusion, Die Visionen der Erlösung und der Entzug der Bilder'* (Kassel), 29–30 (März 1989) as 'Panik und Politik' and 'Das jüdische Volk träumt nicht', to which the translator is indebted.]

2 [*The Standard Edition of the Complete Psychological Works of Sigmund Freud*, translated and edited by J. Strachey (London: Hogarth, 1953–74; henceforth abbreviated as *SE*), vol. XVIII, p. 97.]

3 [*Kant's Political Writings*, edited with an introduction and notes by H. Reiss, translated by H. B. Nisbet (Cambridge: Cambridge University Press, 1991), p. 46.]

4 For example, P. Kaufmann, 'Pour une position historique du problème de la pulsion de mort', in *Matière et pulsion de mort* (Paris: Christian Bourgois, collectif 1975, 10/18); J. Florence, *L'identification dans la théorie freudienne* (Brussels: Publications des Facultés Universitaires Saint-Louis, 1978).

5 [*An Autobiographical Study*, Postscript, *SE* XX, p. 72.]

6 [See *The Interpretations of Dreams*, *SE* V, p. 568.]

7 [The continuity between *la scène plus large* and its situation off-stage (*hors-scène*) and *ob-scène* cannot be maintained if, according to existing English translations of Freud, *Schauplatz* is rendered by 'stage'.]

8 This does not disqualify this type of undertaking, especially when, instead of ascribing an identity to psychoanalysis, it loosens up its relation to itself. Thus, for example, M. Mannoni, *La théorie comme fiction* (Paris: Seuil, 1979).

9 [*Civilisation and its Discontents*, *SE* XXI, pp. 131–32. Henceforth *Civilisation*.]

10 [*Moses and Monotheism: Three Essays*, *SE* XXIII, p. 118. Henceforth *Moses*.]

11 [Ibid., p. 110.]

12 [*Civilisation*, p. 144.]

13 [*Moses*, p. 58.]

14 But it is no different for everything which concerns the death drive. Thanatos and culture share a similar and largely common destiny. We will let it appear here only in a veiled way.

15 [Dr S. Jankélévitch, the first French translator of *Massenpsychologie und Ich-Analyse*, rendered *Massenpsychologie* into *Psychologie collective (Psychologie collective et analyse du moi)* (Paris: Payot, [1924] 1950). In the two subsequent French versions of the essay, *Massenpsychologie* is translated into *Psychologie des foules* (in S. Freud, *Essais de psychanalyse*, translated by J. Altounian, A. and O. Bourguignon, P. Cotet and A. Rauzy (Paris: Payot, 1981)) and into *Psychologie des masses* (*Oeuvres complètes*, vol.

XVI: *1921–1923*, Directeurs de la publication A. Bourguignon, P. Cotet, Directeur scientifique Jean Laplanche (Paris: Presses Universitaires de France, 1991)). The translator's note (pp. 119–22) to the 1981 publication describes the problems which the translation of the words *Masse* and *Massenpsychologie* pose, given that Freud uses other terms belonging to the same semantic field as *Masse* (*Gruppe*, *Menge* and *kollectiv*) in the 1921 essay, and indeed throughout his work. The translators refer their choice of the word *foule* (at least in the title) partly to Gustave Le Bon's *Psychologie des foules* (Paris: Alcan, 1895), the commentary on which forms an important aspect of Freud's essay. With reference to the concerns of '*La panique politique*', it is interesting to note the fact that the translators rule out the rendering of *Massenpsychologie* into *Psychologie des masses*, and associate the latter with the French translation of W. Reich's *Massenpsychologie des Faschismus (Psychologie de masse du fascisme)* and consequently argue that the 'word *masse* [in French] has socio-political connotations which are absent in Freud' (p. 122).

The problem is taken up again in A. Bourguignon, P. Cotet, J. Laplanche, F. Robert, *Traduire Freud* (Paris: Presses Universitaires de France, 1989) pp. 112–13, this time with respect to the translation of *Massenpsychologie* into *Psychologie des masses*. There, in addition to attaching to the term *masse* the socio-political connotations which the translators excluded in the previous version, the question arises as one of retranslation or 'trilinguisme'. Indeed, in *Massenpsychologie und Ich-analyse*, Freud refers to the 2nd edition of Rudolf Eisler's translation of Le Bon's *Psychologie des foules* (*Psychologie der Massen*) ([1908] 1912), but also to William McDougall, *The Group Mind* (Cambridge: Cambridge University Press, according to the editors, 'from the outset, a hybrid of two erroneous translations' of *foule* and 'group'. As far as the English translation is concerned, the editor of the *Standard Edition* justifies the use of the term 'group' in the title and throughout Freud's essay, in terms of uniformity and as the best English equivalent to the 'more comprehensive German *Masse*', even if, according to the editor, the English equivalent of *foule* is *crowd*. (See the English translation of Le Bon's *Psychologie des foules*, *The Crowd: A Study of the Popular Mind* (London, 1920).)

When they are not using the German title of Freud's essay (as well as the German term *Masse*), the authors quote from the 1924 translation. Hence, one finds in the text 'psychologie collective' and 'psychanalyse collective' here turned into 'group psychology' following the translation of the *Standard Edition* ([1922] 1955) which we are employing (with rare modifications). Rather than attempting to systematise the various uses of the terms in question, let us emphasise the fact that problems around the notion of the *Masse*, including problems of translation, are precisely a crucial preoccupation of '*La panique politique*': 'the Freudian *mass*, as Adorno already said, is also that of fascism: such is basically the proposition, the analysis of which . . . should effectively emerge in these notes' (p. 8, above).]

16 [*Group Psychology and the Analysis of the Ego*, SE XVIII, p. 69. Henceforth *Group Psychology*.]

17 [Ibid.]

18 ['Jokes and their relations to the unconscious', *SE* VIII, p. 179. Translation modified. Henceforth Jokes.]

19 [Ibid., p. 179.]

20 See the beginning of chapter III. It is there, moreover, that Freud declares that, to the term *Narzissismus*, he prefers 'the name of "*Narziβmus*" which may not be as correct, but is shorter and less cacophonous' (*SE* XII, p. 60 n. 3). Let us dream a little and adopt for a moment the transcription which the French translators have chosen: narcism [*le narcisme*], an abridged narcissism, both contracted and amputated, a narcissism intact but audible: could it be the truth of narcissism, its social or sociable truth?

21 [S. Ferenczi, 'Freuds Massenpsychologie und Ich-analyse. Der individualpsychologische Fortschritt' (1922) in *Schriften*, vol. II, ed. M. Balint (Frankfurt a.M.: S. Fisher, 1971), pp. 122–26.]

22 [*Group Psychology*, p. 119.]

23 [Ibid., p. 103.]

24 [Ibid., p. 105. Translation modified in accordance with Lacoue-Labarthe and Nancy's text.]

25 [Ibid., p. 87.]

26 Need one be reminded of this, however? The 'sameness' is never simple. From fascism to socialism there is neither identity nor continuity – probably even when it is a question of a socialism with a personality cult. But the differential analysis can only derive from beyond this.

27 [*Group Psychology*, p. 121.]

28 [Ibid.]

29 [Ibid., p. 121.]

30 [Ibid., p. 110.]

31 [Ibid., p. 116.]

32 P.-L. Assoun's book, *Freud, la philosophie et les philosophes* (Paris: Presses Universitaires de France, 1976) contains a valuable exposition of Freud's relations to philosophy.

33 But Lipps is also and first of all the psychologist who started to thematise *the unconscious* and who, on this account, Freud salutes from the *Traumdeutung* through to the *Short Account*. See letters 94 and 95 to Fliess, and this passage among others: 'I found the substance of my insights stated quite clearly in Lipps, perhaps rather more than I would like' [Letter of 31 August 1898 in *The Complete letters of S. Freud to Wilhem Fliess 1887–1904*, edited and translated by J. M. Masson (Cambridge, Massachusetts: Belknap Press, 1985).] (This text has been pointed out to us by Mikkel Borch-Jakobsen.)

34 He uses the notion on a few other occasions, notably concerning the attitude of the analyst (*On the Beginning of the Treatment*, for example, or in 'Little Hans'); in *Totem* the difficulty of the *sich einfühlen* in the primitive mind is an obstacle to the analysis of the totem (a passage pointed out to us by Yves Mougins). Let us here note a supplementary question which we will take up again elsewhere: behind *Einfühlung*,

it would be necessary to examine the entire nature and structure of the Freudian *Gefühl* (feeling). Which is not, if one looks at the text, a simple matter. In psychoanalysis, feeling might not lend itself to being scrutinised any more than in philosophy.

35 [*Group Psychology*, p. 131.]

36 But on condition that it be itself related back to the rest of this analysis. A necessary precaution with regard to a certain fashion which seems to have begun to seize *Moses* in order to discover in it, quite staggeringly, Freud's religious testament. One should consult, on the other hand, Jean-Joseph Goux, 'Freud et la structure religieuse du nazisme', in *Les iconoclastes* (Paris: Seuil, 1978) for its reading of *Moses*.

37 At least as a point of departure, see Marthe Robert, *D'Oedipe à Moïse: Freud et la conscience juive* (Calmann-Lévy, 1974). [Translated as *From Oedipus to Moses: Freud's Jewish Identity* (London: Routledge, 1971).]

38 See J. Trilling, 'Freud, Abraham et le Pharaon', *Etudes freudiennes*, 1–2 (1970), and certain notes by Michel de Certeau in 'La fiction de l'histoire' and 'L'écriture de 'Moïse et le monothéisme', in *L'écriture de l'histoire* (Paris: Gallimard, 1975). [Translated by Tom Conley as *The Writing of History* (New York: Columbia University Press, 1988).] One must point out, moreover, that the break with Jung was occasioned by a disagreement concerning the interpretation of the monotheism of Ikhnaton. Jung was opposed to reducing it, as Freud did, to a conflict with the father. (See J.-B. Fagès, *Histoire de la psychanalyse après Freud* (Privat, 1976). This suggestion was given to us by Renée Bouveresse). In 1936, Freud no longer agrees with his thesis of 1912.

39 In addition, however, one should – this really exceeds these notes – examine the prolongations and the modifications brought about by Reik – as if in response to Freud – in *Mythe et culpabilité* (particularly chs XXIX and XXX). See the translation by J. Goldberg and G. Petit (Paris: Presses Universitaires de France, 1979). [Translated as *Myth and Guilt: The Crime and Punishment of Mankind* (London: Hutchinson, 1958).]

40 On that subject, see the indications of Marie Moscovici in 'Mise en pièces du père dans la pensée freudienne', *Confrontation*, 1 (1979).

41 Thus neither a Father, and no more an invisible Father than any other, and nor a Father-which-does-not-exist: all the theologisations, whether they be ancient or all new with false ingenuousness, here collapse.

42 But as regards the meal (manducation, digestion, assimilation and even excretion), suffice it to reread the text to see that it is the process of the indefinite exchange of the literal and the metaphorical, of the real and the imaginary, of the without-figure and of the figure – the place of trans-substantiation.

43 [See *Moses*, p. 79: 'He *clung* to his mother herself more and more anxiously (*An die Mutter selbst* klammerte *er sich immer ängstlicher an*)'.]

44 It would here be necessary to make more than one reference to the concept of '*cramponnement*' in Imre Herman and its developments in the 'Anasémies' of N.

Abraham and M. Torok would be here necessary. See *Le verbier de l'homme aux loups et l'écorce et le noyau* (Paris: Aubier-Flammarion, 1978).

45 This word alone here refers to the entire analysis which it entitles in Levinas which, in turn, needs to be taken up again in the problematic of an infinite alteration of the face.

46 [*Economic and Philosophic Manuscripts of 1944*, Third Manuscript: 'Private Property and Communism' in Karl Marx and Fredrich Engels, *Collected Works, Marx and Engels: 1843–44* (London: Lawrence & Wishart, 1975), p. 301.]

47 [*Group Psychology*, p. 136.]

48 See on this subject A. Green, 'Psychanalyse, langage: l'ancien et le nouveau', *Critique*, no. 381 (Febuary 1979).

Chapter 2: The Free Voice of Man

1 [Henry Birault, *Heidegger et l'expérience de la pensée* (Paris: Gallimard, 1978).]

2 [Throughout this essay, Nancy maintains a distinction between the two forms of the imperative in French: *il faut* and *on doit*. Whereas the latter (which, in its nominal form, *le devoir*, has been translated here as 'duty') can be rendered as 'one must' or 'one should' with some degree of consistency, the impersonality of the former means that its translation is much more dependent upon context. This impersonal necessity of the imperative *il faut* (usually followed by an infinitive) has, wherever possible, been translated as 'it is necessary to . . .'. Such impersonality, however, also mitigates against the unwieldy nature of the English phrase, as on this occasion. The problem of satisfactorily translating *il faut* is rendered still more problematic by Nancy's continual employment of *il faut* as, in itself, a nominal form, here rendered as either 'the "one must"' or 'the "it is necessary"', again depending on context.]

3 ['Violence et métaphysique: Essai sur la pensée d'Emmanuel Levinas', in Derrida, *L'écriture et la différence* (Paris: Seuil, 1967), p. 119; translated by Alan Bass as 'Violence and Metaphysics', in Derrida, *Writing and Difference* (London: Routledge, 1978), p. 80.]

4 [*Editor's note*: '*sans autre forme de procès*'. The French *le procès* has, outside of this particular idiomatic context, the meaning of legal proceedings or court action played upon by Nancy in the parenthetical remark which follows.]

5 ['Signature, événement, contexte', in Derrida, *Marges – de la philosophie* (Paris: Editions de Minuit, 1972), p. 392; translated by Alan Bass as 'Signature, Event, Context', in Derrida, *Margins of Philosophy* (Chicago: University of Chicago Press, 1982), p. 329. Translation modified.]

6 ['Tympan', in *Marges*, p. iv/*Margins*, p. xiii.]

7 [Ibid., p. xviii/ibid., p. xxii. Translation modified.]

8 [Derrida, *La voix et la phénomène* (Paris: Presses Universitaires de France, 1967),

p. 115; translated by David B. Allison as *Speech and Phenomena* (Evanston, Illinois: Northwestern University Press, 1973), pp. 102–03.]

9 ['Violence et la métaphysique', pp. 117–18/'Violence and Metaphysics', p. 79. Translation modified.]

10 [Ibid., pp. 117–18/ibid., pp. 79–80. Translation modified.]

11 [Ibid., p. 119/ibid., p. 80. Translation modified.]

12 [Ibid./ibid..]

13 [Martin Heidegger, *Kant und das Problem der Metaphysik* (Vittorio Klostermann: Frankfurt a.M., 1973), p. 210; translated by Richard Taft as *Kant and the Problem of Metaphysics* (Bloomington: Indiana University Press, 1990), p. 147. Translation modified.]

14 ['Violence et la métaphysique', pp. 179–80/'Violence and Metaphysics', p. 122.]

15 [In what follows, this translation has been co-ordinated with, on the one hand, the established translations of Husserl (most notably the *Logical Investigations*, translated by J. N. Findlay [New York: Humanities Press, 1970]); and on the other, Derrida's translations presented in *Speech and Phenomena*. Husserl's German terms have occasionally been added by the editor in order to clarify certain points.]

16 [It should be noted that the French term *la conscience* means both 'consciousness' and 'conscience'.]

17 [*La voix et la phénomène*, p. 79/*Speech and Phenomena*, p. 71.]

18 ['La forme et le vouloir dire', in *Marges*, p. 203/'Form and Meaning', in *Margins*, p. 170.]

19 [Ibid/ibid.]

20 [*La voix et la phénomène*, p. 78/*Speech and Phenomena*, p. 70.]

21 [Ibid., p. 77/ibid., p. 69. Translation modified.]

22 [Ibid., p. 80/ibid., p. 72.]

23 [Ibid., p. 95/ibid., p. 85.]

24 [*Editor's note*: in the context of *L'impératif catégorique* (Paris: Flammarion, 1983), the book in which Nancy will later include 'The Free Voice of Man', one needs to hear in the word *mal* both the sense of 'wrong', 'incorrect' or 'bad' behaviour proper to this discussion of Husserl and Derrida vis-à-vis the former's example in the *Logical Investigations*, but also the sense of 'evil' carried in the French. In his introductory remarks to *L'impératif catégorique*, Nancy will interrogate the Kantian imperative in terms of an ontology of 'being-obliged'. The question of evil (*mal*) is there 'present on the horizon of interpretation'. Indeed, as he suggests, the whole analysis of the categorical imperative would be itself preparatory to a more 'necessary' (*faut*) discussion of the problematic of evil (p. 13). See on this, Nancy's, *L'expérience de la liberté* (Paris: Galilée, 1988), ch. 12; translated by Bridget McDonald as *The Experience of Freedom* (California: Stanford University Press, 1993).]

25 ['*Ousia et grammé*', in *Marges*, p. 76/'*Ousia* and Gramme' in *Margins*, p. 65.]

26 [Immanuel Kant, *Critique of Practical Reason* (New York: Macmillan, *LLA* edn, 1993), p. 3.]

27 [*Editor's note*: On the possibility of 'repeating' the Kantian institution or foundation – and on Heidegger's own repetition of this same – see Nancy's early text on Kant, *Le discours de la syncope: I. Logodaedalus* (Paris: Galilée, 1976), p. 9. Nancy writes:

> the history of interpretations of Kant is different from every other: if one excepts the doctrinaire transpositions – of 'neo-Kantianism', to go very quickly – it is the history of a series of questions, opened, reopened, gaping or hanging, before which one must stumble, turn aside, sublimate, or lose oneself. It is a matter of repeating the repetition of this Kantian aporia.]

28 [*La voix et la phénomène*, p. 114/*Speech and Phenomena*, p. 102.]

29 ['Davos Dispute between Ernst Cassirer and Martin Heidegger', in Heidegger, *Kant und das Problem der Metaphysik*, p. 251/*Kant and the Problem of Metaphysics*, pp. 174– 75. Translation modified.]

30 Immanuel Kant, *Handschriftliche Nachlass*, in *Kants gesammelte Schriften* (Akademie Ausgabe) (Berlin, 1902–1912), Band 18, R5440.

31 [*Editor's note*: The term areality has formed part of Nancy's vocabulary since 1977 and 'Lapsus judicii' (with the current paper, collected in *L'impératif catégorique*). In relation to what is being said here, one should consult Nancy's work on Descartes, *Ego Sum* (Paris: Aubier–Flammarion, 1979) and, in particular, the final paper of that work, '*Unum quid*'. There, apropos the question of enunciation, he notes (p. 163) that 'man is that which spaces himself, and who perhaps only ever dwells in this spacing, in the *areality* of his mouth'. His most explicit words on areality, however, are to be found in the later *Corpus* (Paris: Métailié, 1992), where he writes (p. 39): '"Areality" is an archaic word meaning the nature or the property of an *area*. Accidentally, the word also lends itself to suggesting a lack of reality, or else a slender, light or suspended reality: that of the break which localises a body'.]

32 [Immanuel Kant, *Critique of Judgement* (New York: Hafner Press, 1951), §87, p. 299.]

33 [Ibid., §87, pp. 299–300 n. 14.]

34 ['Ellipse', in *L'écriture et la différence*, p. 429/'Ellipsis', in *Writing and Difference*, p. 294. Translation modified.]

35 [*Kant und das Problem der Metaphysik*, p. 252/*Kant and the Problem of Metaphysics*, p. 175. Translation modified.]

36 [On the *tutoiement*, see Philippe Lacoue-Labarthe, 'In the Name of . . .', ch. 3, below.]

37 [See 'En ce moment même dans cet ouvrage me voici', in Derrida, *Psyché: Inventions de l'autre* (Paris: Galilée, 1987), pp. 159–202: p. 159; translated by Ruben Berezdivin as 'At This Very Moment in this Work Here I Am', in Robert Bernasconi and Simon Critchley, eds, *Re-Reading Levinas* (Bloomington: Indiana University Press, 1991), pp. 11–48: p. 11.]

Chapter 3: In the Name of . . .

1 [Throughout this essay Philippe Lacoue-Labarthe addresses Jacques Derrida by the familiar *tu* form (or *tutoiement*), as opposed to the more formal *vous*. This is worth noting insofar as Lacoue-Labarthe goes on to write that 'what matters, both to my question and – I think – in general, is the second person utterance.']

2 [See 'Force et signification', in *Critique* 19, 3–4 (1963), pp. 483–99, 619–36. Reprinted in Derrida, *L'écriture et la différence* (Paris: Seuil, 1967), pp. 9–49; translated by Alan Bass as 'Force and Signification', in Derrida, *Writing and Difference* (London: Routledge, 1978), pp. 3–30.]

3 [See 'Envois', in Derrida, *La carte postale: De Socrate à Freud et au-delà* (Paris: Aubier–Flammarion, 1980), pp. 7–273; translated by Alan Bass as 'Envois', in Derrida, *The Post Card: From Socrates to Freud and Beyond* (Chicago: University of Chicago Press, 1987), pp. 3–256.]

4 ['Les fins de l'homme', in Derrida, *Marges – de la philosophie* (Paris: Editions de Minuit, 1972), p. 135; translated by Alan Bass as 'The Ends of Man', in Derrida, *Margins of Philosophy* (Chicago: University of Chicago Press, 1982), p. 114. Translation modified.]

5 [Ibid., p. 131/ibid., p. 111. Translation modified.]

6 [Ibid., p. 147/ibid., p. 123. Translation modified.]

7 [See 'Le retrait de la métaphore', in *Poésie* 7 (1978), pp. 103–26; reprinted in Derrida, *Psyché: Inventions de l'autre* (Paris: Galilée, 1987), pp. 63–93; translated by Frieda Gasdner, Biodun Iginla, Richard Madden and William West as 'The *Retrait* of Metaphor', *Enclitic* 2, 2 (1978), pp. 5–33.]

8 ['Les fins de l'homme', p. 148/'The Ends of Man', p. 123–24. Translation modified.]

9 [Ibid., p. 153/ibid., p. 128.]

10 [Ibid., p. 148/ibid., p. 124.]

11 [Ibid., p. 153/ibid., p. 128. Translation modified.]

12 [See Heidegger's inaugural lecture of 1929 to the Freiburg University faculties, 'Was ist Metaphysik?', in Heidegger, *Wegmarken*, *Gesamtausgabe* 9 (Frankfurt a.M.: Klostermann, 1976), pp. 103–22; translated by David Farrell Krell as 'What is Metaphysics?', in Heidegger, *Basic Writings*, ed. Krell (London: Routledge, 1993; 2nd edn), pp. 93–110.]

13 [*une première 'mise au point'* sur son attitude politique: Lacoue-Labarthe deliberately leaves open the ambiguity of such a *'mise au point'*, which bears the sense of adjustment ('fine-tuning' or 'de-bugging'), as much as it does one of clarification. The sense, then, that not only does the 'Letter on Humanism' give Heidegger the chance to present his viewpoint or 'set the record straight' on his political involvement, but that it also provides him with his first (strategic) opportunity to set an agenda or 'get his story straight' on those events.]

14 [See *Der Spiegel* of 31 May 1976, 'Nur ein Gott kann uns noch retten'; translated by

174

Maria P. Alter and Thomas D. Caputo as 'Only a God Can Save Us', in *Philosophy Today*, 20, 4 (1976): pp. 267–85.]

15 [See 'Heimkunft' and 'Andenken' in Heidegger, *Erläuterungen zu Hölderlins Dichtung*, *Gesamtausgabe* 4 (Frankfurt a.M.: Klostermann, 1982).]

16 ['Was ist Metaphysik?', p. 104/'What is Metaphysics?', p. 94.]

17 [Ibid., pp. 104–05/ibid., p. 95.]

18 [Ibid./ibid..]

19 [See Heidegger, *Die Selbstbehauptung der deutschen Universität* (Frankfurt a.M.: Klostermann, 1983); translated by William S. Lewis as 'The Self-Assertion of the German University', in Richard Wolin, ed., *The Heidegger Controversy* (London: MIT Press, 1993; 2nd edn), pp. 29–39.]

20 ['Was ist Metaphysik?', pp. 111–12/'What is Metaphysics?', p. 101. Translation modified.]

21 [See Heidegger, *Sein und Zeit* (Tübingen: Niemeyer, 1972), p. 38; translated by John Macquarrie and Edward Robinson as *Being and Time* (Oxford: Blackwell, 1992).]

22 [See 'Brief über den Humanismus', in *Wegmarken*, p. 356/'Letter on Humanism', in *Basic Writings*, p. 258.]

23 ['Was ist Metaphysik?', p. 118/'What is Metaphysics?', p. 106. Translation modified.]

24 [Ibid., p. 117/ibid..]

25 [See Heidegger, 'Hölderlin und das Wesen der Dichtung', in *Erläuterungen zu Hölderlins Dichtung*, pp. 33–48.]

26 [*Einführung in die Metaphysik* (Tübingen: Niemeyer, 1987), pp. 109–10; translated by Ralph Manheim as *Introduction to Metaphysics* (New Haven: Yale University Press, 1959), pp. 143–44. Translation modified in accordance with both the German and Lacoue-Labarthe's own translation.]

27 [See Lacoue-Labarthe, 'La transcendance fini$^e/_t$ dans la politique', in Lacoue-Labarthe, *L'imitation des modernes* (Paris: Galilée, 1986), pp. 135–73; translated by Peter Caws in Lacoue-Labarthe, *Typography: Mimesis, Politics, Philosophy* (Cambridge, Massachusetts: Harvard University Press, 1989), pp. 267–300.]

28 [*Einführung in die Metaphysik*, p. 29/*Introduction to Metaphysics*, p. 38.]

29 [Ibid., p. 117/ibid., p. 192. Translation modified.]

30 [Editor's note: 'Der Ursprung des Kunstwerkes', in Heidegger, *Holzwege*, *Gesamtausgabe* 5 (Frankfurt a.M.: Klostermann, 1977), p. 66; translated by Albert Hofstadter as 'The Origin of the Work of Art' in *Basic Writings*, p. 203. (The first rendering of this line is Hofstadter's.) Wolfgang Brockmeier's French version, 'L'origine de l'oeuvre d'art', the last word of which Lacoue-Labarthe each time modifies (respectively, '*à faire face*' and '*à soutenir*'), gives 'le poète de l'oeuvre dont il reste encore aux Allemands à s'acquitter' (see Heidegger, *Chemins qui ne mènent nulle part* (Paris: Gallimard, 1962; collection Tel), p. 89).]

31 [See *Einführung in die Metaphysik*, pp. 114ff/*Introduction to Metaphysics*, pp. 149ff.]

32 ['Anmerkungen zur Ödipus', in Friedrich Hölderlin, *Sämtliche Werke*, Grosse

Stuttgarter Ausgabe (Stuttgart: Kohlhammer, 1985), Band 5, p. 201; translated by Thomas Pfau as 'Remarks on "Oedipus"', in Pfau, ed., *Friedrich Hölderlin: Essays and Letters on Theory* (New York: SUNY Press, 1988), p. 107. Translation modified.]

33 [*Einführung in die Metaphysik*, p. 114/*Introduction to Metaphysics*, p. 149. Translation modified.]

34 [Ibid., p. 115/ibid., p. 151. Translation modified.]

35 [Ibid., p. 116/ibid. Translation modified.]

36 [Ibid./ibid..]

37 [Ibid., p. 122/ibid., p. 159. Translation modified.]

38 [Hölderlin, *Werke*, Band 4, p. 246. Cited by Heidegger in 'Hölderlin und das Wesen der Dichtung', p. 38.]

39 [See the concluding section of 'Der Ursprung des Kunstwerkes'/'The Origin of the Work of Art']

40 [See 'Restitutions de la vérité en pointure', in Derrida, *La Vérité en peinture* (Paris: Aubier–Flammarion, 1978), pp. 291–436, especially pp. 392ff; translated by Geoff Bennington and Ian McLeod as 'Restitutions of the Truth in Pointing', in Derrida, *The Truth in Painting* (Chicago: University of Chicago Press, 1987), pp. 255–382, especially pp. 343ff.]

41 ['Les fins de l'homme', p. 163/'The Ends of Man', p. 136.]

42 [Ibid., pp. 163–64/ibid.. Translation modified.]

43 [See Heidegger, *Der Feldweg* (Frankfurt a.M.: Klostermann, 1953), and *Hebel der Hausfreund* (Pfullingen: Neske, 1957).]

44 [Like Lacoue-Labarthe, Derrida will throughout employ *tutoiement*.]

45 [See Derrida's response to Nancy's 'The Free Voice of Man', pp. 52–54, above.]

46 [Heidegger, *Die Frage nach dem Ding* (Tübingen: Niemeyer, 1962); translated by W. B. Barton and Vera Deutsch as *What is a Thing?* (Chicago: Regnery, 1967).]

Chapter 4: Political Seminar

Contribution I: Christopher Fynsk

1 [*Editor's note*: The entire seminar was conducted across three days of the colloquium and was made up of five different papers. (See Lacoue-Labarthe and Nancy, eds, *Les fins de l'homme: A partir du travail de Jacques Derrida* (Paris: Galilée, 1981), pp. 487–529.) Apart from the two contributions translated here, the other papers were given by Rodolphe Burger ('Intervention', pp. 500–5), Gayatri Spivak ('Il faut s'y prendre en s'en prenant à elles', pp. 505–16), and Jacob Rogozinski ('Déconstruire – la révolution', pp. 516–29).]

2 [See 'Ouverture', in *Les fins de l'homme*, pp. 9–18.]

3 [*Positions* (Paris: Editions de Minuit, 1972), p. 85; translated by Alan Bass as *Positions* (London: Athlone Press, 1987), pp. 62–63.]

4 [See *Positions*, p. 85/*Positions*, p. 63.]

5 ['*Ja*, ou le faux-bond II', *Diagraphe* 11 (Mar 1977), p. 86; translated by Peggy Kampf as '*Ja*, or the *faux-bond* II', in *Points . . .: Interviews, 1974–1994* (Stanford, Calif: Stanford University Press, 1995), p. 32.]

6 ['Les fins de l'homme', in *Marges – de la philosophie* (Paris: Editions de Minuit, 1972), p. 131; translated by Alan Bass as 'The Ends of Man', in *Margins of Philosophy* (Chicago: University of Chicago Press, 1982), p. 111. Translation modified.]

7 ['*Ja*, ou le faux-bond II', p. 115/'*Ja*, or the *faux-bond* II', pp. 69–70.]

8 ['Ouverture', in *Les fins de l'homme*, pp. 11–12.]

9 ['Violence et la métaphysique', in *L'écriture et la différence* (Paris: Seuil, 1972), pp. 117–18; translated by Alan Bass as 'Violence and Metaphysics', in *Writing and Difference* (London: Routledge, 1990), pp. 79–80.]

10 On this, see Derrida's article 'Philosophie des Etats Généraux', in *Etats Généraux de la Philosophie (16 et 17 juin 1979)* (Paris: Flammarion, 1979), p. 29. This essay might be articulated with a series of other texts which are concerned with the crisis in the university, and where the affirmation to which I have referred makes itself heard. See in particular two articles by Jean-Luc Nancy: 'La détermination philosophique', in *Esprit* (Feb 1981) and the uncollected 'Note sur la formation et la philosophie'; and by Gérard Granel: 'Appel à ceux qui ont affaire avec l'université en vue d'en preparer une autre', in *Les temps modernes* (May 1979) and 'Et tu, qui es?', in *Critique* (Feb 1978).

11 ['Violence et la métaphysique', p. 119/'Violence and Metaphysics', p. 80. Translation modified.]

12 [See Heidegger, 'Brief über den Humanismus', in *Wegmarken*, *Gesamtausgabe* 4 (Frankfurt a.M.: Klostermann, 1976), pp. 313–64, especially p. 318; translated by Frank A. Capuzzi and J. Glenn Gray as 'Letter on Humanism', in Martin Heidegger, *Basic Writings*, ed. David Farrell Krell (London: Routledge, 1993; expanded edn), pp. 217–65, especially pp. 222–23.]

13 [*De la grammatologie* (Paris: Editions de Minuit, 1967), p. 142; translated by Gayatri Spivak as *Of Grammatology* (Baltimore: Johns Hopkins University Press, 1976), p. 93. Translation modified.]

14 [Granel, 'Et tu, qui es?', p. 180.]

15 [*De la grammatologie*, p. 193/*Of Grammatology*, p. 132.]

16 [See *Sein und Zeit* (Tübingen: Niemeyer, 1972), §§26–27 and §58; translated by John Macquarrie and Edward Robinson as *Being and Time* (Oxford: Blackwell, 1992).

17 ['Brief über den Humanismus', pp. 341–42/'Letter on Humanism', pp. 244–45.

Contribution II: Philippe Lacoue-Labarthe

18 [*Editor's note*: '*une* hantise *commun pour le* politique'. Although in this context the word '*hantise*' implies an obsessive fear, Lacoue-Labarthe's use of the word also retains the sense of a haunting or of a being-haunted. On the relation between the

political and the matter of '*hantise*', see in particular Nancy's suggestive remarks in 'Le *katègorein* de l'excès', in *L'impératif catégorique* (Paris: Flammarion, 1983), especially pp. 10–13, and Lacoue-Labarthe's comments in 'The Spirit of National Socialism and its Destiny', pp. 151–52, below.]

19 [See '*Ja*, ou le faux-bond II', p. 86/'*Ja*, or the *faux-bond* II', p. 32; 'Les fins de l'homme', p. 153/'The Ends of Man', p. 111; '*Ja*, ou le faux-bond II', p. 115/'*Ja*, or the *faux-bond* II', pp. 69–70].

20 [See *Sein und Zeit*, in particular §40.]

21 [See 'An Interview with Jacques Derrida', in *Literary Review* 14 (April–May 1980), pp. 21–22.]

Chapter 5: Foreword to The Centre for the Philosophical Study of the Political

1 The sessions took place each third Monday of the month at 5 o'clock.

2 With the exception of Paul Thibaud's talk (16 Mar 1981) whose text did not reach us in time. [*Editor's note*: As well as Lacoue-Labarthe and Nancy's opening address, ch. 6 of the present volume, *Rejouer le politique* (Paris: Galilée, 1981) contained the following texts:

1 Luc Ferry, 'De la critique de l'historicisme à la question du droit (sur la querelle des Anciens et des Modernes)', pp. 29–50;

2 Jean-Luc Nancy, 'La juridiction du monarque hégélien', pp. 51–90; translated by Mary Ann and Peter Caws as 'The Jurisdiction of the Hegelian Monarch', in Jean-Luc Nancy, *The Birth to Presence* (Stanford, California: Stanford University Press, 1993), pp. 110–42;

3 Jean-François Lyotard, 'Introduction à une étude du politique selon Kant', pp. 91–134; a substantially revised version of this text translated by Geoff Bennington as 'The Sign of History', in Derek Attridge, Geoff Bennington and Robert Young, eds., *Post-Structuralism and the Question of History* (Cambridge: Cambridge University Press, 1987), pp. 162–80;

4 Etienne Balibar, 'Marx, le joker ou le tiers inclus', pp. 135–69';

5 Philippe Lacoue-Labarthe, 'La transcendance fini^e/t dans la politique', pp. 171–214; translated by Peter Caws as 'Transcendence Ends in Politics', in Lacoue-Labarthe, *Typography: Mimesis, Philosophy, Politics* (Cambridge, Massachusetts: Harvard University Press, 1989), pp. 267–300.

The ellipses in the text mark my excision of Lacoue-Labarthe and Nancy's brief discussion of these texts from this translation.]

Chapter 6: Opening Address to the Centre for Philosophical Research on the Political

1 [*Editor's note*: This text was delivered as the inaugural address to the *Centre for Philosophical Research on the Political* on 8 Dec 1980.]

2 The clearest text in this regard is doubtless 'Überwinding der Metaphysik', in *Vorträge und Aufsätze* (Pfullingen: Neske, 1954) [translated by Joan Stambaugh as 'Overcoming Metaphysics', in Richard Wolin, ed., *The Heidegger Controversy* (Cambridge, Massachusetts: MIT Press; 1993; 2nd edn), pp. 67–90]. See in particular theses XIX–XXVIII.

3 Since we have been asked – and to be mysterious about this would be frivolous – the itinerary of one of us (J.-L.N.) runs through *Esprit* and the CFDT, whilst the other (Ph.L.-L.) for a long time found himself in accord with the positions of *Socialisme ou Barbarie* and, for a while, of *The Situationist International*.

4 [Lacoue-Labarthe and Nancy use the term '*l'État séparé*' (literally, 'the separated State': I have followed the author's capitalisation of 'State'), here rendered as 'the *purely formal* or *abstract* State', to designate the particular existence of the state in democracy. For the reference, see Karl Marx, 'Critique of Hegel's Doctrine of the State', in *Karl Marx: The Early Writings*, ed. Lucio Colletti (Harmondsworth: Penguin, 1974), pp. 88–89:

> Property, contractual agreements, marriage, civil society appear in [the monarchy or in the republic, for example] as *particular* modes of existence alongside the *political* aspects of the state . . . Such phenomena appear as the content within the framework of the political state which functions as the organised *form*, as the mere understanding devoid of any content which defines and limits, now affirming, now negating. If in a democracy, *the political state exists separately* [my emphasis – Editor] from this content and is distinguished from it, it nevertheless exists itself only as a *particular* content, as a particular *form of existence* of the people . . . In all forms of the state other than democracy, the *state*, the *law*, the *constitution* is dominant, but without really dominating, i.e., without materially penetrating the content of all the non-political spheres.]

5 [See Marx, 'Critique of the Gotha Programme', in Karl Marx, *The First International and After*, ed. David Fernbach (Harmondsworth: Penguin, 1974), p. 355. The translation collected in this volume renders this line as follows: 'the future public affairs of communist society'.]

6 [On Heidegger's compromise of 1933 see, amongst others, Lacoue-Labarthe, 'The Spirit of National Socialism and its Destiny', ch. 8, pp. 148–56, below. For Bataille's *éloge* of the Marshall Plan, see *La part maudite*, I. *La consumption*, in Georges Bataille, *Oeuvres complètes* VII (Paris: Gallimard, 1976), pp. 159–79; translated by Robert Hurley as *The Accursed Share*, vol. I, *Consumption* (New York: Zone Books, 1991), pp. 169–90.]

7 See '*La panique politique*', ch. 1 above, and 'Le peuple juive ne rêve pas', in *La*

psychanalyse, est-elle une histoire juive? (Paris: Seuil, 1981), pp. 57–92. [This latter is translated by Brian Holmes as 'The Jewish People do not Dream', in *Stanford Literary Review* 6, 2 (1989), pp. 191–209, and 8, 1–2 (1991), pp. 39–55. The two essays appear as a single work in German translation in the journal *Frag-Mente: 'Religion – Mythos – Illusion, Die Visionen der Erlösung und der Entzug der Bilder'* (Kassel), 29–30 (März, 1989).]

8 [On 'originary sociality' and its relation to the problematic of identification, see Lacoue-Labarthe and Nancy, 'Le peuple juive ne rêve pas'.]

9 [Lacoue-Labarthe and Nancy's comments here on the problematic of the non-figure of the mother draw upon the detailed analyses presented in 'Le peuple juive ne rêve pas' where it is a matter of turning from the identity principle of the Father towards 'a more obscure maternal instance' (ibid., p. 62/ibid., p. 196). There, the mother is understood as the disruption of the figure of identity (the Father as the founding instance of figurality), as the non-figural figure which withdraws identity. As they write (ibid., p. 68/ibid., p. 203. Translation modified):

> In originary sociality, it would be, therefore, a matter of an identification not with the mother [this would be, properly speaking, impossible, insofar as the mother is identified with the retreat of (unitary) identity], but with what could be called the beyond-mother [*l'outre-mère*]. That is to say, in accordance with an inaudible, untenable formula, which we must risk nonetheless, an identification with the retreat of identity.

On the political force of the beyond-mother, see also '*La panique politique*', p. 28, above and 'The 'Retreat' of the Political', pp. 133–34, below.]

10 [See Lacoue-Labarthe, 'Poétique et politique', in *L'imitation des modernes: Typographies II* (Paris: Galilée, 1986), pp. 175–200.]

11 [See the texts collected in Nancy, *L'impératif catégorique* (Paris: Flammarion, 1983).]

Chapter 7: The 'Retreat' of the Political

1 [*Editor's note*: This address was delivered to the Centre on 21 June 1982 at the close of its second year. As Lacoue-Labarthe and Nancy point out in their foreword to the volume in which it is published, *Le retrait du politique* (Paris: Galilée, 1982), 'the Centre's work had been placed under the following regulative statement':

> *Taken as a philosophical question, and from the point of view of what we have for the time being called the essence of the political, the question of the political evokes the necessity of dwelling on what makes the social relation possible as such; and that is also to say on what does not constitute it as a simple relation (which is never given), but which implies a 'disconnection' or a 'dissociation' at the origin of the political event itself.*

As well as Lacoue-Labarthe and Nancy's closing address, the volume also contained the following texts:

1 Jacob Rogozinski, 'A double tour (introduction à l'ontologique de Marx)', pp. 11–69;

2 Claude Lefort, 'La question de la démocratie', pp. 71–88; translated by David Macey as 'The Question of Democracy', in Lefort, *Democracy and Political Theory* (Oxford: Polity Press, 1988), pp. 9–20;

3 Jacques Rancière, 'La representation de l'ouvrier ou la classe introuvable', pp. 89–111;

4 Denis Kambouchner, 'De la condition la plus générale de la philosophie politique', pp. 113–58;

5 Philippe Soulez, 'La mère est-elle hors-jeu de l'essence du politique?', pp. 159–82.

Throughout this text Lacoue-Labarthe and Nancy will refer to these analyses (as well as to those collected in *Rejouer le politique* (Paris: Galilée, 1981): see the 'Foreword', ch. 5 n. 2, above). Except for those instances where some sort of reference – citation, summary, etc. – seems necessary in order to understand Lacoue-Labarthe and Nancy's argument, I have followed the authors in not providing references.]

2 See the 'Foreword' and the 'Opening Address', pp. 105ff, above.

3 [Lacoue-Labarthe and Nancy's reference is to the opening lines of Derrida's text, 'Les fins de l'homme', in *Marges – de la philosophie* (Paris: Éditions de Minuit, 1972), p. 131; translated by Alan Bass as 'The Ends of Man', in *Margins of Philosophy* (Chicago: University of Chicago Press, 1982), p. 111.]

4 'Opening Address', pp. 109–10, above.

5 Ibid., p. 110.

6 Work on totalitarianism has obviously come a long way since then, but Arendt's analyses remain the first major study of the phenomena. Doubtless there has, until now, been no thematic use of this author in the Centre; the implicit reference has, however, been constant, and if, today, we are once more adopting certain motifs from her descriptions, this in no way signifies a pure and simple support on our part to the whole of her thinking.

7 [See the 'Opening Address', p. 111, above.]

8 [See, for example, Arendt, *The Origins of Totalitarianism* (New York: Harcourt Brace, 1966), 'Total Domination', pp. 437–59.]

9 [The working through of this paradox is, in fact, the general trajectory followed by Arendt in *Between Past and Future* (New York: Penguin, 1968) and in *The Human Condition* (Chicago: University of Chicago Press, 1958).]

10 And that is to say, as the logic of an idea through which 'the movement of history is explained as one consistent process' (Arendt, *The Origins of Totalitarianism*, p. 469).

11 [The reference is to Lefort's text presented earlier in the 1981–82 session of the

Centre. There, apropos the monarchical system of the Ancien Régime, Lefort writes:

> Embodied in the prince, power gives body to society. And, precisely because of this, there was a latent but effective knowledge of what one meant for the other across the whole breadth of the social. This model marks out the revolutionary and unprecedented trait of democracy. The place of power becomes an *empty place* . . . Empty and unoccupiable – such that no individual or group can be consubstantial with it – the place of power turns out to be unfigurable. All that is visible are the mechanisms for the exercise of power exercise, or else the men, mere mortals, who hold political authority.

(See Lefort, 'La question de la démocratie', p. 82/'The Question of Democracy', p. 17. Translation modified.)

12 [Jean-François Lyotard, *La condition postmoderne* (Paris: Editions de Minuit, 1979), pp. 102 and 102–03. [Translated by Geoff Bennington and Brian Massumi as *The Postmodern Condition* (Manchester: Manchester University Press, 1984), pp. 63 and 63–64. Translation modified.]

13 [See Arendt, *The Human Condition*, pp. 320–25.] It would be necessary to relate this motif to Jünger's analysis in *Der Arbeiter* and, especially, to its 'critical resumption' by Heidegger in *Zur Seinsfrage*, and that is to say to the de-limitation of the Figure (*Gestalt*) of the Worker, or of the Worker as the Figure of modern man. [See Jünger, *Der Arbeiter* (Stuttgart: Ernst Klett, 1981), and Heidegger, *Zur Seinsfrage*, translated by William Kluback and Jean T. Wilde as *The Question of Being* (bilingual edition; New York: Twayne, 1958).]

14 See 'What is Authority?', in Arendt, *Between Past and Future*, pp. 91–141.

15 [See 'Critique of Hegel's Doctrine of the State', in *Karl Marx: The Early Writings*, ed. Lucio Colletti (Harmondsworth: Penguin, 1974), p. 89, where Marx describes democracy in terms of its 'really dominating', and that is to say its 'materially penetrating the content of all the non-political spheres.']

16 [Lacoue-Labarthe and Nancy draw their terms from Bataille's analyses in 'La structure psychologique du fascisme', in Georges Bataille, *Oeuvres complètes* I (Paris: Gallimard, 1970), pp. 339–71, especially §§I–V; translated by Alan Stoekl with Carl R. Lovitt and Donald M, Leslie, Jr, as 'The Psychological Structure of Fascism', in Bataille, *Visions of Excess: Selected Writings 1927–1939* (Minnesota: Minnesota University Press, 1985), pp. 137–60. On the heterogeneity of fascist action, see especially §§VI ff.]

17 [Arendt, *The Human Condition*, p. 56.]

18 We refer here to the resources of the re-treat exploited by Jacques Derrida in 'Le retrait de la métaphore', in *Poésie* 7 (1978), pp. 103–26; reprinted in *Psyché: Inventions de l'autre* (Paris: Galilée, 1987), pp. 63–93. [Translated by Frieda Gasdner, Biodun Iginla, Richard Madden and William West as 'The *Retrait* of Metaphor', *Enclitic* 2, 2 (1978), pp. 5–33.]

19 [See Georges Bataille, *La souveraineté*, *Oeuvres complètes* VIII, p. 291ff; translated by

Robert Hurley as *Sovereignty* in *The Accursed Share* (New York: Zone Books, 1993), p. 247ff.]

20 [See Jean-Luc Nancy, 'La juridiction du monarque hégélien', in *Rejouer le politique* (Paris: Galilée, 1981), pp. 51–90; translated by Mary Ann and Peter Caws as 'The Jurisdiction of the Hegelian Monarch', in Jean-Luc Nancy, *The Birth to Presence* (Stanford, California: Stanford University Press, 1993), pp. 110–42.]

21 Jean-François Lyotard, 'Introduction à une étude du politique selon Kant', in *Rejouer le politique*, pp. 131–32.

22 Etienne Balibar, 'Marx, le joker ou le tiers inclus', ibid., p. 161.

23 [See the discussion which followed Lefort's address to the Centre, *Le retrait du politique*, p. 87. In underlining the problem of the phenomenological presuppositions of Lefort's analyses, Lyotard addressed the difficulty attendant upon Lefort's 'preservation, in the opposition to "integrated" society and a "substantial subject", of the presupposition of an "*us*" . . . [H]ow, then, to think an intuition of the social which would not be the fact of a subject?']

24 [See Michel Henry, *Marx*, vol. I: *Une philosophie de la réalité* (Paris: Gallimard, 1976), *passim*; translated by Kathleen McLoughlin as *A Philosophy of Human Reality* (Bloomington: Indiana University Press, 1983).]

25 [Sigmund Freud, *Group Psychology and the Analysis of the Ego*, in *The Standard Edition of the Complete Psychological Works of Sigmund Freud*, translated and edited by J. Strachey (London: Hogarth, 1953–74), vol. XVIII, p. 105. Translation modified in accordance with Lacoue-Labarthe and Nancy's text. (I am indebted to Nicola Bailey for this reference.) For Lacoue-Labarthe and Nancy's most sustained examination of the question of identification, see '*La panique politique*', chapter 1 above, and 'Le peuple juive ne rêve pas', in *La psychanalyse, est-elle une histoire juive?* (Paris: Seuil, 1981), pp. 57–92; translated by Brian Holmes as 'The Jewish People do not Dream', *Stanford Literary Review* 6, 2 (1989), pp. 191–209, and 8, 1–2 (1991), pp. 39–55, where it is a matter of 'another identification' (58; 193) '*beyond the identity principle*' (60; 195), in terms of 'the failure, or at least the suspension of the analysis of identity in Freud' (61; 196), itself read in terms of the identificatory affection at the heart of what they locate as 'a retreat of identity' (66; 201).]

26 [The reference is to thesis III of the 'Über den Begriff der Geschichte', where Benjamin writes: 'A chronicler who recites events without distinguishing between major and minor ones acts in accordance with the following truth: nothing that has ever happened is to be given up as lost for history.' See 'Über den Begriff der Geschichte', in Walter Benjamin, *Gesammelte Schriften*, vol. I.2 (Frankfurt: Suhrkamp, 1974), p. 694; translated by Harry Zohn as 'Theses on the Philosophy of History', in Benjamin, *Illuminations* (New York: Schocken Books, 1969), p. 254. Translation modified.]

Chapter 8: Annexe

1 During the discussion following Claude Lefort's paper, 'La question de la démocratie', on 18 January 1982, Derrida intervened to recall the conditions of his incarceration by the Czechoslovak authorities. He had, amongst other things, insisted upon the difficulty in making an ethico-political gesture (supporting the resistance of philosophers in Prague, a resistance inspired by respect for human rights, and articulated on a philosophy of the subject, the person, individual freedom, etc.) coincide with a philosophical work governed by the necessity to deconstruct such philosophemes. [On Derrida's arrest (while in Prague for a clandestine philosophy seminar) on the charge of 'production and trafficking of drugs', a spurious and politically motivated charge which was later lifted after a signature campaign and intervention by François Mitterand, see his interview with Catherine David in *Le nouvel observateur* ('Derrida l'insoumis'), 9–15 September 1983; translated by David Allison et al., in David Wood and Robert Bernasconi, eds, *Derrida and Différance* (Evansten, Illinois: Northwestern University Press, 1988), pp. 71–82.]

2 [See 'Die Zeit des Weltbildes', in Heidegger, *Holzwege*, *Gesamtausgabe* 5 (Frankfurt a.M.: Klostermann, 1977), p. 70; translated by William J. Lovitt as 'The Age of the World Picture', in Heidegger, *The Question Concerning Technology and Other Essays* (New York: Harper Torchbooks, 1977), p. 116.]

Chapter 9: *Chers Amis*: A Letter on the Closure of the Political

1 [*Editor's note*: In fact, this volume was never published. Moreover, Jean-Luc Nancy informs me that neither he nor Philippe Lacoue-Labarthe have any recollection of its projected contents. *Après coup*, one has – perhaps – a single text added to the corpus of the Centre's work: Derrida's *Politiques de l'amitié* (Paris: Galilée, 1994). Derrida suggests that his text 'would be, as a sign of recognition, a modest and belated contribution to this research which has been so important to me' (p. 152).]

Chapter 10: The Spirit of National Socialism and its Destiny

1 [See the version of the 1935 lecture course, published by Heidegger in 1953 as *Einführung in die Metaphysik* (Tübingen: Niemeyer, 1987), p. 152; translated by Ralph Manheim as *Introduction to Metaphysics* (London: Yale University Press, 1987), p. 199. Here, Lacoue-Labarthe cites Otto Pöggeler's detailed reconstruction of Heidegger's actual remarks delivered in 1935, leaving until later Heidegger's own 'rectifications of imprecisions' (as they are called in the Prefatory Note to the published edition of the *Einführung*). For this reconstruction, see the postscript to Otto Pöggeler, *Der Denkweg Martin Heideggers* (Pfullingen: Neske, 1983; 9th edn), pp. 340ff. See also n. 6, below.]

2 [*Editor's note*: Although *dénégation* is more usually translated as 'denial' (which would, moreover, fit more comfortably with the specific sense of *le retrait* (*du politique*) Lacoue-Labarthe is evoking here), it has been rendered as 'negation' in order to maintain a continuity with the German *Verneinung* which it normally translates, and hence with the 'translation' of Freud announced in '*La panique politique*' ch. 1, above.]

3 [See Heidegger, 'Brief über Humanismus' in *Wegmarken*, *Gesamtausgabe* 4 (Frankfurt a.M.: Klostermann, 1976), pp. 313–64; translated by Frank A. Capuzzi as 'Letter on Humanism' in Heidegger, *Basic Writings*, ed. David Farrell Krell (London: Routledge, 1993; 2nd edn), pp. 217–65.]

4 [See *Einführung in die Metaphysik*, p. 117/*Introduction to Metaphysics*, p. 152.]

5 [See Heidegger, 'Der Ursprung des Kunstwerkes' in *Holzwege*, *Gesamtausgabe* 5 (Frankfurt a.M.: Klostermann, 1977), p. 49–50; translated by Albert Hofstadter as 'The Origin of the Work of Art' in *Basic Writings*, ed. Krell, pp. 186–87.]

6 [For the emendation to the earlier citation and the subsequent – and parenthetical – clarification, see *Einführung in die Metaphysik*, p. 152/*Introduction to Metaphysics*, p. 119. For a full account of Heidegger's retrospective 'clarification', see Dominique Janicaud's excellent 'La lettre volée' in his *L'ombre de cette pensée: Heidegger et la question politique* (Grenoble: Jérôme Millon, 1990), pp. 77–96.]

7 [See Heidegger, *Nietzsche*, vol. 1: *Der Wille zur Macht als Kunst* (Pfullingen: Neske, 1961), especially p. 92ff; translated by David Farrell Krell as *Nietzsche*, vol. 1: *The Will to Power as Art* (New York: Harper & Row, 1979), especially p. 77ff.]

8 [See Lacoue-Labarthe, *La fiction du politique* (Paris: Bourgois, 1987), especially ch. 6; translated by Chris Turner as *Heidegger, Art and Politics* (Oxford: Blackwell, 1990).]

9 [See Jacques Derrida, 'La main de Heidegger (*Geschlecht* II)' in *Psyche: Inventions de l'autre* (Paris: Galilée, 1987), pp. 415–51; translated by John P. Leavey, Jr as '*Geschlecht* II: Heidegger's Hand', in John Sallis, ed., *Deconstruction and Philosophy: The Texts of Jacques Derrida* (Chicago: University of Chicago Press, 1987), pp. 161–96.]

10 [*Editor's note*: '*La hantise fasciste est, de fait, la hantise de la figuration, de la Gestaltung.*' Whilst *hantise* is here translated as 'haunting', it should be borne in mind that the French more usually contains the sense of an obsessive fear. Thus, this sentence could also be rendered as follows: 'The fascist phobia is, in fact, the phobia of figuration, of *Gestaltung.*' The English 'haunting' has been preferred insofar as it contains also, in however residual a manner, the sense of fear more explicitly present in the French. On *hantise*, see also ch. 4 n. 17, above.]

11 [See Heidegger, *Sein und Zeit* (Tübingen: Niemeyer, 1972), §74; translated by John Macquarrie and Edward Robinson as *Being and Time* (Oxford: Blackwell, 1992).]

12 [See Heidegger, *Die Selbstbehauptung der deutschen Universität* (Frankfurt a.M.: Klostermann, 1983), especially p. 12; translated by William S. Lewis as 'The Self-Assertion of the German University' in Richard Wolin, ed., *The Heidegger Controversy* (London: MIT Press, 1993; 2nd edn), pp. 29–39, especially p. 33.]

13 [See Heidegger, *Hölderlins Hymnen 'Germanien' und 'Der Rhein'*, *Gesamtausgabe* 39 (Frankfurt a.M.: Klostermann, 1980), p. 214.]

14 [*Editor's note*: See Wilhelm Furtwängler's letter to Goebbels of 12 April 1933 and Goebbels' response of the same date in P. Meier-Benneckenstein, ed., *Dokumente der Deutschen Politik*, vol. 1 (Berlin, 1939/40), pp. 296ff; translated by J. Noakes and G. Pridham in *Nazism 1919–1945: A Documentary Reader*, vol. 2: *State, Economy and Society 1933–1939* (Exeter: University of Exeter Press, 1994), pp. 407ff. Lacoue-Labarthe cites and comments on this exchange in *La fiction du politique*, ch. 7. See also Goebbels' diary entry of 11 April 1933 [*sic*] where, apropos this exchange, he writes:

> Have a correspondence with the Director-General of Music, Dr. Furtwängler, on the principles of German style, the publication of which causes quite a stir . . . In my answer to Furtwängler *I attempt to explain the essence of a national art.*'
> (Joseph Goebbels, *My Part in Germany's Fight*, translated by Kurt Fiedler (London: Pasternoster, 1938), pp. 244–45. Emphasis added).]

15 [See Johan Joachim Winckelmann, 'Gedanken über die Nachahmung der griechischen Werke in der Malerei und Bildhauerkunst', in *Winckelmanns Werke (in Einem Band)* (Berlin: Aufbau, 1969), p. 2.]

16 Cited by Arno Münster, *Nietzsche et le nazisme* (Paris, 1995).

17 Cited by Botho Strauss, *Anschwellender Bockgesang*.

18 ['*la parole testamentaire*': a reference to Heidegger's 'posthumous' interview with *Der Spiegel* of 31 May 1976, 'Nur ein Gott kann uns noch retten'; translated by Maria P. Alter and Thomas D. Caputo as 'Only a God Can Save Us', in *Philosophy Today*, 20, 4 (1976), pp. 267–85.]

Index

References to texts by Lacoue-Labarthe and Nancy included in this volume or to remarks from the debate participants are indicated in **bold** type.